Praise for
This Is Your Brain on Sports

"Wertheim and Sommers wield serious research to diagnose the myriad symptoms of the human brain on sports, and what they find is, by turns, hilarious, slightly frightening, and always illuminating."

—David Epstein, author of *The Sports Gene: Inside the Science of Extraordinary Athletic Performance*

"Smart, funny, and brimming with insights."

—Daniel Gilbert, Edgar Pierce Professor of Psychology, Harvard University, and author of *Stumbling on Happiness*

"Eye-opening, captivating, and hilarious, *This Is Your Brain on Sports* shines a fascinating and scientific spotlight on human nature. Wertheim and Sommers offer expert lessons for athletes and sports fans, sure, but also for business leaders, managers, entrepreneurs, parents, youth sports coaches, and more."

—Amy Cuddy, Harvard Business School professor and author of *Presence*

"A rollicking read that offers dozens of sparkling insights into social psychology, cognitive science, and behavioral economics. Wertheim and Sommers are the perfect writing duo—one part Watson and Crick, another part Brady and Gronkowski."

—Daniel H. Pink, author of *Drive* and *To Sell Is Human*

"Wertheim and Sommers have achieved the Holy Grail: a book that's as fun as it is informative."

—Adam Alter, associate professor of marketing and psychology, Stern School of Business, and *New York Times* bestselling author of *Drunk Tank Pink*

"Not just an entertaining read, but a book filled with wisdom that will help fans, athletes, coaches, and executives understand sports a little differently and a little better."

—Ivan Gazidis, chief executive, Arsenal Football Club

This Is Your Brain on Sports

THE SCIENCE OF UNDERDOGS,
THE VALUE OF RIVALRY,
AND WHAT WE CAN LEARN
FROM THE T-SHIRT CANNON

L. Jon Wertheim and Sam Sommers

THREE RIVERS PRESS
NEW YORK

For A, B, & E, the brains of the operation.

—LJW

For M, A, & S, the cornerstones of the franchise.

—SS

CONTENTS

Your Brain on Sports

Name a memorable sports commercial or ad campaign from the last quarter century, and odds are good that it's the handiwork of Wieden+Kennedy. Based in Portland, Oregon, the firm made its bones as the creative agency for Nike. It was Dan Wieden, one of the two founders, who coined *Just Do It*. The agency conceived of everything from the campaign featuring Michael Jordan and his hyperactive fanboy, Mars Blackmon—played, of course, by Spike Lee—to Tiger Woods's *Hello, World* to Charles Barkley's *I Am Not a Role Model* to Bo Jackson's *Bo Knows* to Lance Armstrong's Livestrong bracelets to the ode to Title IX, *If You Let Me Play*.

Wieden+Kennedy also counts ESPN among its clients. A few years ago, the agency came up with a gem of a campaign for the network: *It's Not Crazy, It's Sports*. Featured among these spots: a fan who lost a sports bet and had to eat a bagel topped with a healthy sprinkling of his friend's chest hair; a schlub proposing marriage to his girlfriend not on a Caribbean beach, as she had hoped, but on the Jumbotron of Detroit's Comerica Park; an army of Alabama football fans intoning "Roll Tide" while doing everything from making wedding toasts to issuing speeding tickets.

And it wasn't just fans who were spoofed. Maybe the funniest of the commercials featured clips of college basketball coaches such as Mike Krzyzewski and Jim Boeheim—otherwise dignified men dressed in tailored suits and silk ties—contorting on the sidelines during games while disco music played. Another spot depicted the evolution of the touchdown dance. By 2015 the commercials had morphed into a cinematic effort, too, as ESPN rolled out a series of documentary shorts directed by Oscar winner Errol Morris. A renowned chronicler of the human condition, Morris explained his interest in the project as follows: "Sports, as we all know, touches on everything."

The *It's Not Crazy, It's Sports* campaign connected with both of us immediately. One of us (Jon) works in sports media and has a passion for behavioral science. The other (Sam) is a behavioral scientist with a passion for sports. We instantly recognized what these ads and film shorts were trying to convey.

In a dry press release that was wildly at odds with its typically edgy work, Wieden+Kennedy claimed, "The *It's Not Crazy, It's Sports* campaign celebrates what makes sports inspiring, entertaining and dramatic." Translation: It highlights all the batshit craziness that courses through the sports ecosystem.

We see examples of this lunacy all the time, right? Athletes lose all poise in the heat of competition and even during postgame interviews. They "choke," betraying years of training, allowing their minds and bodies to desert them when the stakes are highest. They find the damnedest ways to rationalize cheating. They insist on feeling "disrespected" even when there's little or no indication that anyone is slighting them.

Coaches routinely make decisions that don't maximize their chances of winning. Owners who have accumulated vast fortunes with their business acumen buy a team and immediately make basic financial and personnel mistakes.

Some fans wear threadbare but "lucky" T-shirts when the Indiana Hoosiers play important games, convinced that failure to do so will inevitably trigger defeat (that would be Jon). They jeer athletes they find reprehensible—unless those athletes play for their team. They reflexively side with the underdog—the team that, by definition, has the lower probability of winning.

Other fans think the perfect present for a friend's 40th birthday is paying for Ickey Woods to record a personalized video greeting (that one was Sam). They hurl themselves over railings to catch a free T-shirt propelled by an air cannon—a T-shirt they wouldn't spend a dime to buy. They riot after their team *wins*. They root for the New York Jets.

This behavior that, on its face, makes no sense? These acts that, viewed objectively, are absurd? We embrace them. They reinforce the organizing principles of sports: It is diversion, escapism, almost an altered state. In the Universe of Sports, the usual rules of behavior and social convention don't apply.

Or do they? Because so often the appearance of lunacy in sports isn't lunacy at all. As outlandish as sports conduct might seem, it is rooted in basic human psychology, neuroscience, and cognitive tendency. All that *crazy* we associate with sports? We're going to explain why it's not so crazy after all. And then we'll explore what lessons and principles sports offer for better navigating our daily lives as managers, business owners, consumers, parents, and more. As Errol Morris said, sports touches on everything.

In the chapters that follow, we'll show you what running on a treadmill teaches us about running a company. How rooting for lovable losers relates to IKEA's successful business model. What you have in common with Floyd Mayweather Jr., Brett Favre, and Serena Williams—and what you don't with Tom Brady (besides his paycheck, Super Bowl rings, famous hair, and equally famous spouse).

Writing this book has been educational as well as entertaining. Chapter after chapter, we found that the quirkiness of sports taught us something deeper about who we are, what we care about, and the forces that shape our behavior. We hope reading it offers you a similar experience. We're confident that by the end, you'll come to see sports—and human nature—a little differently.

How confident? We'll bet you a chest-hair sandwich.

Why the T-Shirt Cannon Has Something to Teach Us About Human Nature

If sports fans were conferred military-style awards for valor, we would be inclined to nominate season ticket holders for the 2014–15 New York Knicks. In particular Dennis Doyle, for demonstrating heretofore unsurpassed levels of courage and fortitude. A thirty-something recovering lawyer, Doyle left his job, withdrew $25,000 from his savings, and devoted the next year to attending every New York Knicks game. Not every home game. *Every game.* That meant venturing as far as London to watch his team.

The Knicks fell in that overseas contest to the Milwaukee Bucks, 95–79. Which was in keeping with a season in which it sometimes felt as if the franchise had signed a non-compete pact with the rest of the league. The Knicks weren't merely bad. They were putrid, wretched, miserable. So much so that they flirted with the 9-73 record of the 1972–73 Philadelphia 76ers, the benchmark for NBA futility (the Knicks limped to a 17-65 finish, worst in the conference). So much so that by midseason the New York roster was gutted of players such as J. R. Smith, Iman Shumpert, and Amar'e Stoudemire, all either traded or waived. So much so that the venerable *New York Times* mercifully released the writer assigned to the team and offered him a new beat mockingly titled "Not the Knicks."

Doyle endured it all. The blowouts and the blown leads. The thousands of shots that clanged off the rim. The missed defensive switches. The failure to grasp the Triangle Offense. He dutifully watched every moment of every game. And he even kept a sense of humor, blogging about the experience at theoakmancometh.com. Sample post: "Asking a friend to a Knicks game at the Garden this season is a little like asking someone to a funeral—you shouldn't have to do it, but you can always count on the close ones to appear among the bereaved."

But this chapter is not about Dennis Doyle. Rather, our focus is on yet another amazing occurrence that took place game after game at Madison Square Garden that season. Night in and night out, no matter how dismally the team was playing, at least once per contest the fans stood and emitted full-throated yells and cheers as an unmistakable energy swelled in the arena. A spirited Knicks comeback? No. A flashy play by a fan favorite? Also, no.

This surge in vitality was triggered by something having absolutely nothing to do with basketball: The 7th Avenue Squad was about to shoot T-shirts into the crowd.

You don't need to have Dennis Doyle's attendance record to know that this has become a sports-event ritual as sacrosanct as the seventh-inning stretch or the singing of the National Anthem. A cohort of muscular and unnaturally peppy twentysomethings, their demeanor and high energy often totally at odds with the tenor of the game, emerge from the tunnel and, after making the obligatory *I-can't-heeeeear-you* hand gestures, start catapulting rolled-up shirts in the general direction of fans. Most of the squads are equipped with air cannons. Others go old-school and use slingshots made of surgical tubing. The Phillie Phanatic, never one to be outdone, shoots off free hot dogs using a four-foot pneumatic gun.

Reliably, the crowd goes wild. Fans fall over themselves trying to snag a prize—as David Babusiak of St. John, Indiana, can attest. In 2007 Babusiak attended a White Sox game at Chicago's U.S. Cellular Field. Between innings, the Chevrolet Pride Team fired a shirt into the section where Babusiak was sitting. He made his move for the shirt. So did a gaggle of his fellow fans. In the scrum, Babusiak later claimed, he was shoved to the ground and suffered a permanent back injury. He filed a civil suit against U.S. Cellular Field and the Pride Team, seeking more than $75,000 in damages. The defendants, he alleged, were liable because they were "engaging in an abnormally dangerous activity, namely, shooting free T-shirts as projectiles into an unsupervised crowd of spectators, some of whom may not have been sober." (Records from the U.S. District Court in Northern Indiana indicate that "claims between the Parties have been amicably resolved.")

From the perspective of the teams, it's easy to understand the T-shirt-cannon phenomenon. It's a cheap and easy way to keep your fans happy, sometimes in the midst of a dreary Knicksian season. Give them something to look forward to, even during another blowout or uninspired performance, and they might stick around longer and spend more money on concessions—not to mention keep coming back for more games, perhaps against their better judgment.

But from the fans' perspective, the phenomenon seems mystifying: Why *do* spectators all over the world go to such lengths, risking even paralysis, for an inexpensive prize? These shirts, after all, aren't particularly special or high-quality. They're of arbitrary size and often emblazoned with the logo of a team sponsor. (A Knicks shirt is arguably cool; much less so when it says "Modell's Sporting Goods" on the back.) So what's the big deal?

That the product is scarce adds some appeal: Not everyone gets a shirt, so those who do feel special. It's the same reason a sales promotion is billed as a limited-time offer, or a collectible is called "special-edition" and has its own serial number. That the "lucky" fan has to catch a flying polyester projectile also adds a certain cachet that wouldn't exist if the shirt were simply handed out at the turnstiles (see *IKEA Desk,* page 144).

But the real appeal seems to be simply this: The shirts are *free.*

You've no doubt heard the expression "If it's free, it's for me." That's not just a throwaway line. *Free* is catnip for humans, an enticement so strong that it sometimes causes us to behave ridiculously—or at least in ways at odds with common sense and our best interests.

One famous series of studies—repeated, modified, and critiqued in equal measure—has been dubbed "the Hershey's Kiss experiments." Dan Ariely, a professor at Duke's Fuqua School of Business and a nimble behavioral economist, gave subjects a choice of two chocolates. They could buy premium Lindt truffles (which usually cost around 50 cents apiece) for 26 cents each, or they could buy the beloved but mundane Hershey's Kiss for a penny. In the outcome of this study, participants were equally split between the two chocolates. Fair enough.

Then Ariely reduced the price of each chocolate by one cent. The Lindt was now 25 cents; the Hershey's Kiss was free. What happened? Tastes changed dramatically. A full 90 percent of respondents opted for the Hershey's. At first blush this makes no sense. The price differential was the same—still 25 cents more for the Lindt. Why would demand change so drastically? As Ariely later put it: "The power [that] *zero* exercises over people's choice in chocolate nicely demonstrates the irrational draw of free things."

Not that it's only free chocolate that causes us to act questionably. Ariely is quick to include himself among those seduced by the power of "free." Several years ago he was in the market for a practical minivan. Instead he drove home a sleek Audi. Why? One big reason was that the Audi came with the promise of free oil changes for three years. "In fact, those services were worth only about $200, but the promise of 'free' anything was very appealing," Ariely explains. "They could have offered me a $2,000 discount on the minivan, and I still would have bought the wrong car because the free oil-change offer was so tempting in the heat of the moment."

Who among us can't relate? We have zero interest in taking part in your telephone survey, but promise us free movie passes and we'll stay on the line for half an hour answering tedious questions about how many times a week we use soap powder. We opt for "free" credit cards with exorbitant interest rates over cards with a modest annual fee but much lower interest, even though we know we're going to carry a balance each month. And how many of us go to Trader Joe's or Costco with no interest in buying, say, jalapeño kale chips but gladly stand in line and have a bite when we can try them for free? (Empirical analysis of in-store sampling promotions shows that they work: Shoppers spend more money at a store after getting a free sample, as if they feel obligated to return the favor. As Ariely has noted, "Reciprocity is a very, very strong instinct. If somebody does something for you, you really feel a rather surprisingly strong obligation to do something back for them.")

We'll even make *long-lasting* bad decisions due to the allure of "free." Ariely writes about a Dutch movie theater that offered patrons, in conjunction with the release of *The Girl with the Dragon Tattoo*, the opportunity to see unlimited free movies for an entire year if they simply got a tattoo of the theater's logo: a doglike creature flying under a film reel. More than a dozen moviegoers were up for it.

Irrationality like this can accelerate when consumers have already paid an exorbitant sum for something. Spending hundreds of dollars on floor seats to watch a crappy basketball team (not to mention $50 for parking and $12 per beer) leaves us feeling entitled to something in return. "Entitled consumers often believe that their every whim should be catered to," explains Mike Norton, Ariely's collaborator and a co-author of *Happy Money*, a book on the science of spending. "Sports fans in this state of mind likely do more than experience the allure of giveaways," he told us. "They can more or less demand them, as though the $500 they shelled out for a ticket gives them a God-given right to one of those flying T-shirts."

Fans aren't the only ones swayed by the power of free stuff. For years, teams' radio broadcasters struggled to cajole players and coaches to appear on postgame shows. Then they got smart and started offering guests free watches or steakhouse gift certificates in exchange for their time. Rationally this shouldn't have affected the players' behavior. For the most part, these are multimillionaire athletes, often making thousands of dollars per hour. Yet the siren song of a free Timex or Morton's voucher was too seductive to resist.

Or consider a story recounted by a former tennis star in her autobiography. At the height of her popularity, tournaments offered her large appearance fees simply to show up. Despite her initial misgivings, she committed to one such tournament in Japan. "It was just too far from home, and I was tired from the travel grind," she writes. "They kept offering me more and more money for an appearance fee—well over a hundred thousand dollars—but I said no.

Finally, they offered to fly my whole family over [for free]. That did it. We went, and I won easily."

In his review of the book, the writer David Foster Wallace was struck by this anecdote and by the player's "odd financial sense." Writes Wallace: "She won't come for $100,000+, but will come if they add a couple thousand in airfare?" But such is the powerful inducement of "free." Had she (or, more likely, her agent) negotiated a bump in fee from, say, $100K to $105K, it would not have changed her mind. But, by accident or design, when the tournament promoter dangled the prospect of something "free," it got the job done.

One more example: In the early 2000s, the Portland Trail Blazers hired a crew of workers to wash and wax players' vehicles during practices. Rationally speaking, this was silly: These millionaire athletes were singularly well suited to pay for their own buffing and polishing. Cynical journalists held this out as another example of athletes being pampered and cosseted. But perhaps a shrewd member of the Portland brass realized that the value would outstrip the cost—that in exchange for the free services, the athletes might do things they ordinarily wouldn't. Such as play defense. Or hustle for loose balls. Or respect the U.S. penal code (this was, after all, the height of the Jail Blazers era). It was the NBA version of Google providing its employees on "campus" with free gourmet food and dry cleaning, all in the effort to boost worker morale and performance.

All of which is to say: When we get something for nothing, we feel as if we're putting one over on the world. Except that often it's just the opposite.

Why Tom Brady and All Those Other Quarterbacks Are So Damned Good-Looking (or Are They?)

Rugby had plenty to recommend it: the importance of leverage and incremental gains; the teammates of different sizes, shapes, and functions working in unison; the advancement of a ball past a designated marker on the field for a score; the garnishing of that score with a kick of the oblong ball through the goalposts.

Yet to Ivy Leaguers of the late nineteenth century, this imported British sport also felt too plodding and inelegant, clogged as it was with 30 players on the field at once. So they made gradual adjustments and improvements.

On October 12, 1880, representatives of Harvard, Princeton, and Yale met at the Massasoit House, in downtown Springfield, Massachusetts, and held what they called an "intercollegiate football convention." Predating agents, shoe-company reps, and executives from sports networks, it was just a dozen or so student-athletes intent on improving the American rugby cognate that was slowly coming into vogue.

One of the Yale delegates, Walter Camp, pushed through a measure designed to address overcrowding, whereby only 11 members of each side would be permitted on the field at a time. Then came an even bolder stroke for opening up the game. Instead of starting each possession with one of those untidy rugby scrums, what if one side had clear, undisturbed possession? That way the offensive side could strategize while the defensive side tried to impede progress. Camp proposed the following rule change:

A scrimmage takes place when the holder of the ball puts it on the ground before him and puts it in play while on-side either by kicking the ball or by snapping it back with his foot. The man who first receives the ball from the snap-back shall be called the quarter-back and shall not rush forward with the ball under penalty of foul.

It was a brilliant idea. This new position, quarter-back, would infuse the game with both elegance (no scrum to put the ball in play) and practicality (one centralized leadership position). The establishment of this quarter-back—this pilot who would devise and impart tactics and touch the ball on every offensive play—was a marked departure from rugby. To quote from a history published by the Professional Football Researchers Association, "When [Camp's] proposition was accepted unanimously, American football began."

Camp then added this little-known proviso:

Aforementioned quarter-back must be the most physically attractive member of the team, if not the entire school community. He shall possess a square jaw, piercing eyes, flawless and flowing hair—be a dreamboat, if you will. He shall be sufficient eye candy to grace the cover of a gentlemen's quarterly. He shall be the type of man so confident in his looks as to leave an actress girlfriend in order to squire a Brazilian supermodel.

We joke, of course. But it's been a long-standing article of faith in football: We like our signal-callers handsome. The quarterback may not have existed before Camp and his contemporaries descended upon the Massasoit House 135 years ago, but his brainchild has since evolved into the most glamorous position in all of sports (North American jurisdiction, at least).

The storied lineage spans from Broadway Joe Namath to Joe Montana and Dan Marino to Brett Favre to Tom Brady, Aaron

Rodgers, and Russell Wilson. The polarizing, short-lived cult of Tim Tebow? Even his biggest detractors must concede: not the worst-looking guy. As we write this, the attractiveness of Texas Tech coach Kliff Kingsbury is an Internet meme. (*Hot Kliff Kingsbury Flirts with Moms of Recruits*.) Naturally, Hot Kliff Kingsbury is a former college quarterback.[1]

Pop culture has cemented this image. Name a leading man (Burt Reynolds, Kurt Russell, Warren Beatty, Keanu Reeves, Dennis Quaid, Jamie Foxx) and odds are good he has played the role of a quarterback. There are examples of the reverse, too. Before he was Special Agent Leroy Jethro Gibbs on *NCIS*, Mark Harmon was a quarterback at UCLA.

In fact, the allure of being an alluring QB can be enough to motivate a position change. Brad Grayson—father of Garrett Grayson, a Saints rookie as we write this—described his son's decision several years ago to switch from running back to quarterback as a calculated one. "Gotta consider the ladies," explained the elder Grayson with a smile.

The inevitable question, then: *Why are quarterbacks so damned good-looking?*

As he tends to do, radio host Colin Cowherd offers a theory that is based less on specific research studies and more on the effort to play provocateur. Cowherd reckons that quarterbacks are good-looking because of natural selection. As he once put it, "When boys growing up are picking teams and positions, they always pick a good-looking kid to be quarterback. They never pick an ugly kid. That . . . sets up the pattern." In other words, the best-looking kids in the schoolyard are selected for the glamour position. They are put on a "quarterback track," and by the time they begin playing organized football, they are experienced at the position. It's akin to a self-fulfilling prophecy.

---

1. Trivia: Kingsbury was selected in the sixth round of the 2003 NFL draft by the New England Patriots—the same team and same round as Tom Brady, picked three years before.

It actually makes sense—until we pose this hypothesis to Tom Brady, perhaps the fairest quarterback in the land. A sandlot Casanova, he was conferred the quarterback position at an early age, and the rest was history, right? Um, not so much. Here's what Brady had to say: "I played football for the first time in high school. They didn't have much Pop Warner where I grew up. From the first day I put pads on, I loved it. I actually was a much better baseball player. By junior year, I started to grow into my body. I always could throw the ball really [well]. We tried to improve my athleticism. We did a lot of six a.m. workouts. Rope courses. Dot drills. I was always the slowest kid in high school. I was the slowest kid in college. Now I'm still [slow], and I'm playing with the best athletes."

There's a corollary to Cowherd's theory that goes like this: The best-looking kids gravitate to quarterbacking because they sense it is the most glamorous position. When we posed this to another line-of-scrimmage Lothario, we had to cover our ears to mute the deep, familiar laughter on the other end of the line. "I never considered myself good-looking," said Joe Namath, a man once described by *Playboy* as a figure *transmogrified from grid superstar into cult hero . . . a kind of Belmondo with a jockstrap*. "My hair, my teeth. Don't get me started! Trust me, kids want to play quarterback, but it has nothing to do with their looks." (Namath then ticked off the names of a few quarterbacks from his era whom he considered homely—and promptly asked us to keep the list off the record.)

How *did* Namath become a quarterback, anyway? "I was always one of the smaller kids, but could always throw fairly well," he said. "I played some football but was more into basketball. My freshman year, the first-string quarterback was a kid named Jake Lotz, and he broke his arm. So in I went. But in tenth grade, I was fifth or sixth on the depth chart and didn't even get invited to go to camp with the rest of the team. When they got back, I told the coach I wanted to quit: 'I'm gonna play baseball.' He asked me to stay. Fine.

"I spent a season carrying tackling dummies. And then between my sophomore and junior years, I hit a growth spurt and probably got to six feet. I started four games, but I had fumbles and missed receivers and got replaced by Rich Niedbala, who went on to play at the University of Miami. It wasn't until senior year that I really got to be the quarterback. So, long story short: *None* of this had to do with looks."

Namath was still cackling genially when he added: "Let me tell you one more thing about quarterbacks: They don't look nearly as good when they're losing."

When we asked NFL players at other positions to address the alleged pulchritude of the passer, we found limited support for the idea. "I can see that being kind of true," said Greg Olsen, the Carolina Panthers tight end. "People are drawn to good-looking people. Maybe they would be more likely to follow or rally around a good-looking person." But far more non-QBs were skeptical. "Want me to really tell you what's going on?" said London Fletcher, a Pro Bowl linebacker who played in the NFL from 1998 to 2013. "The television camera is trained to focus on the quarterback, so that's who fans see. Trust me, [players] at other positions, we're just as good-looking."

Larry Fitzgerald, maybe the best NFL wide receiver over the last decade, took similar umbrage. "I'm not sure quarterbacks *are* better-looking," he told us. "For every good-looking one, I can think of one who's not so good-looking at all."

These varied responses got us thinking: Before explaining *why* quarterbacks are so damned good-looking, maybe we should test the very premise. *Are* quarterbacks so damned good-looking?

FIRST we set out to answer the fundamental question: Just how good-looking are QBs, anyway? We learned that there's more than one way for researchers to measure attractiveness. Consider a study conducted by a team of U.S. and British economists a few years ago. They were interested in how a quarterback's physical appearance related to his salary. So they assessed the attractiveness of 138 active and former NFL QBs using computer software that calculated the facial symmetry of each player's official media photo. (The premise: Facial symmetry usually predicts perceptions of attractiveness. The evolutionary explanation is that symmetry tends to indicate health and reproductive fitness, marking someone as a desirable mate with "good genes." High symmetry? Think George Clooney. Low symmetry? Try Googling Lyle Lovett.)

By this measure, the economists reported, Matt Ryan of the Atlanta Falcons came out on top of all active quarterbacks. More interesting, the researchers found that the more symmetrical a QB's face was, the more money he made. These findings are consistent with results in domains outside of sports. Attractive employees tend to earn more than their less attractive colleagues in a variety of professions.

Jennifer Van Gilder, one of the study's authors, told *the Wall Street Journal*, "Socially, we've been trained to think that the quarterback is the most beautiful person on the team." According to Van Gilder, "When we evaluate other people, a lot of the ways we evaluate them have nothing to do with performance. . . . We are taught to look for and respect beautiful things."

But this study didn't test whether QBs are actually more attractive than other football players; that wasn't its objective. The economists did find that QBs scored higher in attractiveness than the average person, but the idea that physically fit professional athletes would be deemed better-looking than Joe Twelve-Pack is hardly surprising.

We wanted to document whether quarterbacks *are* more attractive than their fellow players. Intrigued as we were by the computer-based measure of facial symmetry, we decided to go old-school in defining attractiveness. Like researchers before us, we compiled official media photos of NFL quarterbacks, but then we simply asked respondents to rate the attractiveness of each face. In a time-honored tradition that started, in our experience at least, with junior high school yearbooks, we used a rating scale of 1–10 (10, of course, being the quintessence of beauty).

For our first survey, we used photos of all 32 NFL quarterbacks who opened the 2014 season as their team's starting QB.[2] Each

---

2.   In almost all cases, this was the Week 1 starter; for the Carolina Panthers we went with Cam Newton, who topped the depth chart even though he missed the opening week recovering from injury.

photo was cropped at the neck so no team uniform was visible: We wanted our raters to be unaware that they were looking at NFL players, much less NFL quarterbacks.

Next, we needed other position groups for comparison. After some deliberation we settled on wide receivers and defensive backs, ruling out other positions because of body type. Linemen are too bulky; kickers and punters, too scrawny.

We also factored in ethnicity. About three-fourths of the NFL's starting QBs over the past decade have been white, so we held this demographic rate constant across all our positions. To do this, we randomly selected one white and one nonwhite wide receiver and defensive back from as many teams as possible. (Some teams didn't have, for example, a white WR.) Then we randomly selected players from that pool until we had a comparison group of wide receivers that was 75 percent white and 25 percent nonwhite, and defensive backs at that same racial split. We cropped their photos the same way.

Next, we recruited 100 people online to rate, using the 1–10 scale, players whose photos we presented in random order. Again, we didn't tell the raters that these were football players. Then we ran the study a second time, recruiting a new group of 100 raters (and swapping in linebackers for defensive backs).

Who was the fairest of them all, according to our superficial ratings? Feel free to satisfy your curiosity by consulting the following data table, based on all 200 raters.

2014 QB1 Attractiveness Ratings (1–10 scale)

Name	2014 Team	Attractiveness Rating
Alex Smith	Kansas City Chiefs	6.54
Tom Brady	New England Patriots	6.21
Ryan Tannehill	Miami Dolphins	5.80
E. J. Manuel	Buffalo Bills	5.58

Matt Cassel	Minnesota Vikings	5.51
Nick Foles	Philadelphia Eagles	5.41
Aaron Rodgers	Green Bay Packers	5.39
Jay Cutler	Chicago Bears	5.26
Derek Carr	Oakland Raiders	5.14
Carson Palmer	Arizona Cardinals	5.06
Philip Rivers	San Diego Chargers	4.97
Eli Manning	New York Giants	4.88
Tony Romo	Dallas Cowboys	4.86
Russell Wilson	Seattle Seahawks	4.81
Colin Kaepernick	San Francisco 49ers	4.69
Andrew Luck	Indianapolis Colts	4.67
Matt Ryan	Atlanta Falcons	4.61
Joe Flacco	Baltimore Ravens	4.56
Cam Newton	Carolina Panthers	4.39
Josh McCown	Tampa Bay Buccaneers	4.32
Ben Roethlisberger	Pittsburgh Steelers	4.21
Chad Henne	Jacksonville Jaguars	4.20
Matthew Stafford	Detroit Lions	4.19
Brian Hoyer	Cleveland Browns	4.16
Geno Smith	New York Jets	3.97
Jake Locker	Tennessee Titans	3.96
Andy Dalton	Cincinnati Bengals	3.94
Drew Brees	New Orleans Saints	3.90
Peyton Manning	Denver Broncos	3.85
Robert Griffin III	Washington Redskins	3.65
Ryan Fitzpatrick	Houston Texans	3.65
Sam Bradford	St. Louis Rams	3.28

Some highlights: The Chiefs' quarterback Alex Smith took the top spot, followed by Brady and then Ryan Tannehill of the Dolphins. To repeat—and, we hope, preempt angry correspondence from the Sam Bradford Fan Club or RG1 and RG2—these ratings were based on nothing more than strangers' impressions of solitary head shots, enabling any QB near the bottom of the list to chalk up his poor rating to a bad hair day or an awkward smile in his media photo.[3]

What about the positional comparison? Just how much more attractive were QBs than other players? The answer in our first sample of 100 respondents? *Not a bit.* In fact, quarterbacks received the *lowest* ratings of the three positions. Of course, they weren't identified as QBs when the raters saw them. But that's the point: When presented as just a series of unknown dudes, quarterbacks scored an average attractiveness rating of 4.5. For wide receivers it was 4.7. For defensive backs, 5.0.

When we ran the study a second time, with a fresh set of 100 raters? Same finding. Quarterbacks came in last, behind both the wide receivers and the linebackers. London Fletcher and Larry Fitzgerald would be proud, not to mention vindicated.

Wait—what? you ask. Quarterbacks are actually *less* attractive

---

3.   Again, we wanted ratings of sheer attractiveness, nothing more, nothing less. We didn't want raters giving, say, a low score to Ben Roethlisberger just because they were Ravens fans and hated the Steelers; if Big Ben was going to get a low rating, we wanted him to earn it, damnit. So we also asked respondents whether they recognized the person in each photo, and anytime they said "yes," we excluded that rating from our analysis. This means that the numbers you see listed in the table, as well as all the other analyses we describe in this chapter, were compiled using only ratings of unfamiliar faces. But then we re-ran these analyses using all ratings from all participants. The results remained the same. In short, familiarity isn't the driver here: The results remain remarkably consistent whether or not respondents recognized each face that they were rating.

It's worth noting that our sample was not composed of hard-core football fans: The raters were all Americans, but each was asked to assess how big an NFL fan he or she was, and the average rating was 3.5 out of 10. The gender split was 64 percent female/36 percent male. Among the QBs, the most recognized faces were the Mannings (Peyton, 48%; Eli, 30%), Brady (33%), Drew Brees (22%), Aaron Rodgers (20%), and Tony Romo (20%). No non-QB was recognized by more than 10 percent of raters. Consistent with the details reported above, the most recognized QBs are spread throughout the attractiveness rankings; some familiar QBs were seen as attractive but some much less so.

than wide receivers and defensive players? This wasn't what we expected either. So we collected yet more data. To account for the possibility that there was something unusual about the NFL QB1 Class of 2014, we shifted to college football. We picked 20 Division I schools at random, and for each one located a starting quarterback, wide receiver, and defensive back, again holding constant the racial demographics of 75 percent white and 25 percent nonwhite. Then we ran the same study with their photos. Guess what? The results were the same: College quarterbacks were rated third out of the three positions in terms of attractiveness.

In no study that we ran did we find any evidence that quarterbacks are more attractive than players at other positions, no matter how we sliced the data: not among male raters and not among female raters; not among big NFL fans and not among those who know Aaron Rodgers only as the Discount Double-Check Guy in insurance commercials. In fact, the quarterbacks came in dead last *every time*, with every sample demographic.

So back to our original question: Why are quarterbacks so damned good-looking? Apparently they're not. We just *assume* they are.

VAN GILDER, the economist, nailed it when she said, "Socially, we've been trained to think that the quarterback is the most beautiful person on the team." Why is this? In large part it's because when we form impressions of people, our global assessments alter the ways in which we perceive their more specific characteristics, as demonstrated in a study conducted several years ago by Dick Nisbett and Tim Wilson.

The two psychologists told students at the University of Michigan that they would be watching a video interview with a professor and then answering a series of questions about the man. But there were actually two versions of the video. In the first, the professor came across as warm and personable, and he expressed enthusiasm for teaching college students. In the second version, the same professor was scripted to come across as much colder; he was abrupt and standoffish, and he said he had little use for classroom discussion because he knew a hell of a lot more than the students did.

Not surprisingly, the students who saw the warmer professor rated him as more likable than those who saw the cold fish. Who wouldn't? But this global impression of the man shaped the way the students rated him on other dimensions as well. Students who saw the warmer professor rated his nonverbal mannerisms as more appealing. Same for his noticeable French accent: Those who saw the first video thought it was charming; those who saw the second found the accent irritating.

And same for—you guessed it—physical attractiveness. The friendly professor was rated as significantly better-looking than the unfriendly professor. Even though they were *the same guy*.

This tendency is known as the *halo effect*. The formation of positive overall impressions of people projects a perceptual halo around them, casting their other characteristics in a similarly positive light. And the effect applies even to perceptions of attractiveness.

When you stop to consider it, this isn't how we usually think attractiveness works. Sure, we're all familiar with the stereotype, *What is beautiful is good*. We expect the hero of an action movie to be good-looking; it's a quick and easy shorthand for identifying whom to root for. You're probably not surprised to learn of research indicating that attractive people are more socially popular, that attractive applicants get more job offers, and even that attractive defendants are judged less harshly at trial (with one interesting exception: Try to capitalize on your good looks while committing a crime, like the handsome swindler, and the jury will throw the book at you).

What the halo effect proposes, however, is that this link works in reverse as well. If you think highly about someone's character, you'll do the same about his looks. See someone as charming or witty or of good disposition, and you'll also perceive her as more attractive.[4]

---

4.   This may be one reason why computer assessments of facial symmetry seem unsatisfying or incomplete as a measure of attractiveness: They don't capture the subjectivity of beauty, the ways in which even our most superficial judgments are colored by expectation and context. After all, Lyle Lovett did land Julia Roberts—at least briefly.

So why *are* quarterbacks so damned good-looking? They're not, by objective standards, at least no more so than any other NFL players; that's all in your head. But why are they *perceived* to be so damned good-looking? We propose that it's the halo effect in action—because the quarterback is (choose your archetype here) the Big Man on Campus, the gunslinger, the field general, the face of the franchise.

More than any other player in any other sport today, the quarterback has the power to determine single-handedly whether a team succeeds or fails. We talk vaguely in sports about "team leaders," but in football, following Walter Camp's proposal, the quarterback actually leads every play. And along with all his responsibilities come other great expectations. Namely, as Van Gilder suggested, the assumption that Camp's on-the-field leader will also be a leading man off the field.

WHILE we found no evidence that quarterbacks are more attractive than their teammates, this didn't mark the end of our inquiry. When designing our study, we concluded that if we were going to go to all the trouble of finding, cropping, and presenting photos to raters, why not ask more than one question? So we added another rating to the mix, a line-of-scrimmage audible that wound up going for a big gain.

After rating the attractiveness of each player, respondents were also asked to rate the strength of his leadership skills, using the same scale of 1–10. Granted, the raters didn't have much to go on. All they had in front of them was a photo of a stranger on a computer screen. But what we found was pretty remarkable.

In our original sample of 100 respondents, the QBs came out on top in terms of leadership. Even though no one knew the faces belonged to NFL quarterbacks, they were still rated as the strongest leaders. We got the same result from our second set of 100 raters. The differences weren't huge, but they were consistent across samples: Quarterbacks averaged 5.5, defensive players 5.3, wide receivers 5.2.

For further confirmation we ran yet another study, with yet another sample of 100 people. This time we bypassed any mention of physical attractiveness. We asked the leadership-skills question again, but we also asked about four other attributes: intelligence, confidence, poise, and social skill. Again, all the respondents had to go on was a photo; all they were asked for were knee-jerk ratings of smiling strangers.

On four of the five ratings (all except confidence), the quarterbacks came out on top. And when we combined the five ratings into an overall score of perceived leadership quality, the quarterbacks' superiority was again statistically significant.

How could this be? How could a simple head shot convey enough information for raters effectively to differentiate players by position—to attribute greater leadership skills to the actual on-field leaders?

We posed this question to Nick Rule, a psychologist at the University of Toronto who specializes in nonverbal behavior and appearance-related cues. We described our basic research design and asked whether he'd be surprised to hear that we found that quarterbacks weren't judged to be more attractive than other players, but that they elicited superior ratings for other, supposedly internal characteristics, based on only a photo. Surprising, huh? "No, not at all," Rule responded. He said he sees things like this all the time in his research.

"All of this has to do with our ability to perceive meaningful information from the social environment," Rule explained. "As we walk around in the world, we're constantly trying to evaluate whether something is going to be good or bad for us. And so out of that has been born this ability to be really sensitive to all these little cues about how someone might behave toward us or how we should behave toward them."

Rule suggested that these perceptual tendencies grow out of natural instincts related to survival: "You can really boil it down to evolutionary pressures: Is this someone I can mate with or is this someone that's going to kill me? And from that starting point, we start drawing other inferences about people."

Take, for example, sexual orientation. In a series of studies, Rule and colleagues explored the scientific basis of what's known colloquially as "gaydar." They found that people are pretty good at guessing sexual orientation from photos of faces. Gaydar isn't flawless—the average hit rate from photos is about 65 percent, but that's still a lot better than chance. In one set of studies that appears to support Rule's evolutionary survival theory, women more accurately inferred sexual orientation from photos of males (but not of females) the closer they themselves were to ovulation. In other words, gaydar is more important during times of peak fertility.

Okay, we asked Rule, what other attributes are similarly perceptible? *Dominance*, he replied: the tendency to behave in ways that are assertive, self-assured, and forceful. People are really good at judging how socially dominant a person is based solely on physical appearance.

There's also consensus about trustworthiness, according to Rule. People agree with each other about who looks trustworthy and who doesn't. Of course, these ratings don't always reflect the individual's actual behavior. From an evolutionary standpoint, there's a big advantage to being able to spot liars. But there's an equally big advantage to being able to lie and get away with it, and the two forces seem to cancel each other out.

Leadership, too, "is pretty legible [on the face]," said Rule. "At about the same level as sexual orientation, in fact."

Turns out, there's a lot of research documenting our ability to infer leadership skills from physical appearance. Researchers at Princeton presented participants with pairs of photos of political opponents running for the U.S. Congress. Each pair appeared on a computer screen for just one second, and respondents were asked to decide which candidate appeared "more competent."

Across more than 600 races over three election cycles (2000, 2002, 2004), the researchers found that the candidate rated as more competent—based only on a photo, shown for sub-Snapchat duration—won the election the majority of the time. For House races, the perception of superior competence predicted the winner 67 percent of the time. For the Senate, the rate was 72 percent.

Ratings of candidates' attractiveness, on the other hand, did not predict election outcomes.

Rule also described for us his work focusing on corporate leaders, in which he has observed similar processes at play in perceptions of CEOs and law-firm managing partners. "We get pretty consistent results," he told us. "In the business world, the selection of a leader is predicted [by] facial appearance." And, as in the Princeton study of politicians, it's not physical attractiveness that drives these results, but rather perceptions of competence and leadership.

Then Rule piqued our curiosity further. "Facial appearance also predicts how *successful* a leader is," he said. "What we've seen is that people who lead companies that are more successful actually *look* like they're better leaders. These perceptions scale with the amount of profit that the company makes, the gold standard of assessing success in business." In other words, the more respondents think a CEO's photo conveys an aura of leadership, the more successful that CEO's company turns out to be—and vice versa.

Would this work for our quarterbacks as well? We went back to our data.

We figured a QB's success should be quantified at both the team and individual levels. So we checked how our five-trait average of perceived leadership qualities in quarterbacks—the combined ratings for leadership, intelligence, confidence, poise, and social skill—correlated with two NFL outcome measures: (1) wins minus losses as a starter, and (2) QB rating (the regular kind that contributes to your fantasy team, not the attractiveness kind). Indeed, our respondents' ratings of a QB's leadership qualities correlated positively—and statistically significantly—with both outcome variables.[5] In other words, the more a QB looks like a leader, the more successful his actual track record tends to be.

The prediction also passed the less rigorous eyeball test with our QB dataset. Our Top Five quarterbacks in terms of photo-based

---

5. rs = .25 and .27, respectively, for those of you scoring at home.

perceived leadership were led by a dark-horse candidate but otherwise included players with relatively successful track records:

1. E. J. Manuel
2. Matt Ryan
3. Alex Smith
4. Tom Brady
5. Carson Palmer

Others near the top included Philip Rivers, Aaron Rodgers, Russell Wilson, and Drew Brees.

The Bottom Five? A less distinguished quintet of Sam Bradford, Matthew Stafford, Ryan Fitzpatrick, Jay Cutler, and, finally, Jake Locker.

There seem to be at least two viable explanations for what's going on in these studies, including ours. One: We humans are surprisingly good at picking up the subtle facial and nonverbal cues that tell us something meaningful about other people's social skills (or various genetic predispositions). Two: We are surprisingly consistent in how we jump to conclusions about other people based on such cues, and then we treat them in a way that brings out the tendencies we expect.[6]

According to Rule, both processes may operate simultaneously. "There's something about someone's appearance that honestly advertises their skills," he told us, "and, then because they look a certain way throughout their entire life, they're also getting groomed by other people to take on that position."

Could the same thing be happening with quarterbacks? "Absolutely," replied Rule. "You've got a bunch of eight-year-olds out on a football field, and at first you're pretty arbitrarily picking who's

---

6. Indeed, on this latter count, recall our earlier discussion of stereotypes about the attractive? They have a way of becoming self-fulfilling. Physically attractive people *are* often more popular, socially skilled, and sexually experienced than less attractive people, in large part because they get more opportunities to interact with engaged, interested conversation partners.

going to play where—mostly, it's by body size. But for the ones who don't clearly look like linemen, you're going to pick the kid who *seems* like he's the right one [to be quarterback]. Whether or not he does well at first, he gets plenty of practice being the quarterback. By high school he *is* a quarterback. And it goes on from there."

An interesting hypothesis, though one that would be tough to test directly (*you* try getting permission from a youth football league to show photos of eight-year-olds to their coaches and ask for ratings). But this idea that a premium is placed on the general perception of "quarterbackishness" is certainly consistent with our experience. As hard as it was to get NFL players to go on record about a QB's looks, they often gushed about his leadership skills.

Here's Matt Cassel on Tom Brady, the player he spent years backing up for the New England Patriots: "I think that he's just been born with the leadership quality. Some guys just talk the talk, to be a voice. But he really is thoughtful about what he says. He doesn't speak just to speak. He says stuff for a purpose. That's why he's such a great leader. He's also one of the great leaders I've been around in knowing what type of people he's dealing with. Certain guys, he could yell at. With other guys it was better to have a one-on-one conversation."

Remember the withering critique Joe Namath made of his own looks? Well, when we asked him about his leadership qualities, he was less self-deprecating. "I seemed to have a knack for that," he said. "Not in a rah-rah way, but I got the idea of leading by example. I think two things helped. I had older brothers, so I was learning from them but I couldn't pound my chest at home; I just had to prove myself. And my dad loved football. He and I would watch games, and he would call the plays before the ball was snapped. By the time I started playing, I was living football in my brain."

Which is to say that Colin Cowherd, in his off-the-cuff way, hit it (almost) on the head. Quarterbacks *are* likely groomed for the job. Except this isn't based on the perceptions of their attractiveness; it's based on perceptions of *leadership*. When we, collectively, talk about how good-looking QBs are, we are probably, thanks in no small part to the halo effect, conflating looks with leadership.

• • •

WE began with a simple question: Why do quarterbacks seem so good-looking? In trying to answer it, the data took us in unexpected directions, through explanations both ridiculous and scientific. As we bring this chapter to a close, let's take up the scientific first; it's always fun to end with the ridiculous.

Across a variety of samples and studies, we focused on quarterbacks. But what we learned wasn't confined to football or even sports. We uncovered something more far-reaching about how we view our leaders, in arenas ranging from politics to law to Fortune 500 companies. With QBs as with CEOs, much of what constitutes "leadership" appears to be all in our heads. Or, perhaps more aptly, written on our faces: Politicians who look more competent are more likely to win elections; people with faces conveying power are more likely to become corporate leaders.

This is fascinating. And more than a little disconcerting. Because even when the stakes are highest, our impressions of others are colored by considerations that most of us would dismiss as trivial and shallow—the type of superficial cues we associate with Tinder swipes, not federal elections. No voter cites a candidate's jawline when answering exit-poll questions. No board of directors mentions facial maturity when ranking candidates for CEO. Instead, they talk about track record, emotional intelligence, "leadership qualities," and intangibles, a certain *je ne sais quoi*. But that *quoi* is often little more than the physical traits captured by a head shot (or media day photo).

There's a temptation to react with, *so what?* Or to tout this relationship between physical appearance and actual performance as evidence of the unconscious wisdom of first impressions. Indeed, in our studies, quarterbacks with a more leaderlike appearance also exhibited superior on-field performance. But bear in mind: The expectations that others have for us shape the people we get the opportunity to become. How many great potential QBs have fans and coaches missed out on because these players were steered to other positions or other sports? Perhaps their physiques didn't fit the prototype. Perhaps they just didn't convey the mojo of a field general by the right age, or to the right scout.

Also relevant here is an important issue we glossed over earlier: What of the racial split among QB1s? Football has come a long way since Doug Williams became the first African American quarterback to win a Super Bowl, in 1988. But what do we make of the fact that in a league in which close to 70 percent of players are African American, more than three-quarters of QBs are white? Or that across sports, front-office and owner's-box demographics are even less representative? Research suggests that such disparities do not require overt bias or the endorsement of stereotypes. Unconscious expectations and varying degrees of opportunity can be enough to do the trick.

But to be honest, we never sought to solve the world's social ills in this chapter. We just wanted to better understand how people view the most glamorous of today's glamour positions. And all of this talk about quarterbacks is thrown into sharp relief by a story that has long echoed through the halls of Time Inc. (Jon, a longtime Time Inc. employee, assumes that the details can be shared now that the 15-year statute of limitations has expired.) In 1998, the editors of *People* magazine selected its "12 Sexy Men" for the year. In a meeting, editors decided that the sports choice would be (no surprise) an NFL quarterback: Rich Gannon of the Kansas City Chiefs. He'd join the likes of Usher, Carson Daly, and Mark McGrath.

The lore goes like this: A photographer was dispatched to the Chiefs' facility to inform Gannon of this honor and conduct a brief interview. Alas, the photographer was no sports fan and simply asked one of the team operatives to point to the starting quarterback's stall. There was only one problem: The Chiefs platooned at quarterback. The previous season, Gannon had won five consecutive starts down the stretch, but the quarterback for the first nine weeks—not to mention the regular-season finale and the playoff opener—was Elvis Grbac. The two men continued to split snaps during the 1998 season, and on the day that *People* visited, Grbac was actually the starting quarterback. So the photographer was directed to *his* locker. Elvis Grbac may be a man of many talents,[7] but you'd be hard-pressed to use superlatives in describing his sex appeal. A statistically insignificant sample of Jon's colleagues agreed that Grbac most resembled the actor Michael Rapaport.

But Grbac was the quarterback, and, perhaps blinded by the halo effect, the photographer did not second-guess the editors' apparent choice. He asked Grbac, resplendent in a plain gray T-shirt, blue jeans, and bare feet, to assume a series of come-hither poses.

When the editors gathered around the light table in New York and saw the images, they realized that the wrong quarterback had been selected. Owing to a combination of social awkwardness and concern over deadlines, the choice stood. Rich Gannon, the intended quarterback, was denied an honor that was rightfully his. A reporter, who recounted the story to us between guffaws, was assigned to write the accompanying text.

Thus did Elvis Grbac appear in the November 16, 1998, issue of *People*, seated casually in the locker room, his legs crossed and a grin on his face. The text block quoted a clearly befuddled former coach as saying, "I never pictured him as a ladies' man," and ended with that eternally damning bit of faint praise, "His personality makes him sexy."

Were this a player at any position other than quarterback, you can't help but think it would have invited more skepticism.

---

7. Though ESPN reporter John Clayton once noted that Grbac was "not much of a leader." Exhibit A: After one Chiefs defeat, Grbac groused, "I can't catch the ball and throw it, too." Lovers of irony will note that Tom Brady's supermodel wife, Gisele Bündchen, made a similar observation—"My husband cannot fucking throw the ball and catch the ball at the same time"—after the Patriots' defeat in Super Bowl XLVI.

Why We Channel Our Inner Mayweather and Secretly Crave Disrespect

Floyd Mayweather Jr.'s training facility in Las Vegas is nestled in a mini-mall, a few miles off the Strip. It's a sweatbox of a joint, hemmed in by dry cleaners and all-you-can-eat Chinese buffets. The temptation is to call it *nondescript* or *inconspicuous*, but the signifiers of wealth and celebrity and sybaritic living appear out in the open. There's a fleet of Rolls-Royces, Lamborghinis, and black SUVs in the parking lot. Abnormally large men in sweat suits, with thick tubes of gold around their thick necks—Mayweather's security team—stand sentry at the entryway.

Inside the gym on a Tuesday afternoon in 2013, Mayweather was preparing for his upcoming fight, a WBC welterweight title bout against Robert (The Ghost) Guerrero. Mayweather was working over a pitiable sparring partner imported from Brooklyn before moving on to smack around a series of leather punching bags and jump rope for 15 minutes straight at blinding speed.

As the session wrapped up, the gallery—a clot of about 50 publicists, managers, trainers, and nutritionists, as well as garden-variety entourage members—applauded and whistled and yelled encouragement, the word *champ* in especially heavy rotation. Most of the entourage followed Mayweather into the locker room for a prearranged one-on-one interview with Jon that suddenly resembled a 40-on-one.

Ostensibly, Jon and Mayweather were there to discuss the fighter's vast wealth—his status as the world's highest-earning athlete. But, as is often the case with Mayweather, the man was overcome by a certain conversational wanderlust, and no bobbing and weaving could get him on point. On this day it was not money but another topic he wanted to discuss, an elusive opponent: respect.

In particular, why he was accorded so little of it. And the more Mayweather spoke, the more incensed he grew. Veins bulged in his neck, as if attempting a jailbreak from his skin, and small reservoirs of spittle formed in the corners of his mouth.

"I'm just sick of this shit," he said. "I live to prove the critics wrong. But it's like, what do I have to do before Floyd Mayweather gets his due, you know?"

It was hard to trace the source of all this. True, Guerrero's father/trainer had recently mocked Mayweather in a memorable rant, declaring, "We're gonna beat up that woman beater . . . he's gonna get it from a real man." But that was less a show of disrespect than a bit of predictable theater in the absurdist exercise that is the prefight boxing press conference.

Disrespect? Mayweather is uniformly regarded as the best pound-for-pound boxer in the world. His name figures prominently when discussions turn to the best fighters of all time. This upcoming fight against Guerrero marked Mayweather's first time in the ring in nearly a year and the first since he served a prison sentence for domestic battery and harassment. Still, the boxing public had little doubt he would win. Depending where and when you put down a bet, Mayweather was a 7- or 8-to-1 favorite. No one gave Guerrero more than, well, a puncher's chance.

When athletes talk of the straw man that is "disrespect," it often pertains to their salary and a belief that inferior players are being paid more. But in the case of Mayweather—whose boxing nickname is Money—the marketplace conveys nothing but admiration. For this fight Guerrero was being paid $3 million; Mayweather was guaranteed $32 million, tying the all-time mark for the highest purse in boxing. The man whose record he equaled? That would be . . . Floyd Mayweather, who was paid $32 million for a fight the previous year against Miguel Cotto. (In the spring of 2015, May-weather would shatter that, with a haul approaching $200 million for his fight against Manny Pacquiao.)

Mayweather, who had recently left HBO for Showtime/Via-com, would earn more than that guarantee in pay-per-view buys—collected from an adoring public that sure wasn't coughing up 50 bucks to watch Robert Guerrero. Mayweather was on pace to earn close to $100 million in 2013 alone, far more than any other athlete in any other sport and more than LeBron James and Tiger Woods *combined*.

When Jon gently pointed this out, Mayweather had a terse response. "None of that means shit. No respect. So many people want me to do bad."

Who? Who are these critics?

"Everyone, man."

It wasn't as though we had caught Mayweather on a bad day. He's expressed these feelings time and again over the years. One example among many: a 2011 interview with the website fighthype .com. "Most people should be talking about how Floyd Mayweather is a great undefeated future Hall of Famer that's his own promoter and that works extremely hard to get to where he's at," Mayweather said. "Instead, all you hear is hate and jealous remarks from critics who criticize me."

A few weeks after this lament, Mayweather beat Guerrero decisively, betraying no trace of ring rust or advancing age. It was not a dazzling performance, but Mayweather was never in anything resembling trouble and was the better fighter on every dimension, winning handily on the scorecards of all three judges. With the win, he moved to 44-0. Reverence for Mayweather's skill was such that fans and the boxing media were demanding that, for his next fight, he pick an opponent capable of mounting more resistance. But Mayweather took this, too, as a personal affront. After the fight, he declared: "I'm tired of getting disrespected."

He's in good company.

Name a star athlete, no matter how revered or prodigiously compensated, and there is a good chance he or she feels like a human

repository for disrespect. They have all been overlooked, underestimated, discounted, taken for granted. And they find motivation in
discrediting the army of doubters, critics, cynics, and—to use the
voguish term—haters.

A quick scan of the headlines on the day we started writing this
chapter revealed that aggrieved athletes were legion. The Boston
Bruins felt disrespected by the Montreal Canadiens, their opponents in the 2014 Stanley Cup playoffs. The Canadiens felt disrespected by the world. "Nothing has come easy for us all year," said
Montreal defenseman P. K. Subban. "We've worked hard for everything we've gotten." (This disrespected group, which finished
fourth in the Eastern Conference, was picked by many to upset the
Bruins, which it did.) Meanwhile Ray Allen, the future Hall of Fame
NBA sharpshooter—and, usually, a man known for his measured
disposition—was reiterating that disrespect from the Boston Celt-
ics in 2012 was what prompted him to sign with the Miami Heat.
David Ortiz, the Red Sox slugger, felt disrespected by the baseball
fans who had stopped believing in him. Keep in mind: This was all
in *one day's* news cycle. And just in Boston.

The doubters, apparently, were also raising a skeptical brow in
the direction of Chris Johnson, the former Tennessee Titans running back who had signed with the New York Jets. "I know a lot of
people are doubting me," said Johnson. "I want to prove everybody
wrong who has doubts in me." Player after player selected in the
NFL draft reported feeling disrespected, more than one also pro-
fessing to have "a chip on my shoulder." (Which makes one wonder
about the disrespect felt by the many players that weekend who
weren't drafted at all.)

Coaches, of course, have long used allegations of disrespect to
motivate their minions. For instance, when the brackets for the 2014
NCAA tournament were announced, the undefeated Wichita State
Shockers were placed in the Midwest regional—alongside Kentucky,
Duke, Michigan, and defending champ Louisville. Never mind that
Wichita State was the top seed; the team's coach, Greg Marshall,
rallied his team with this: "No one believes in us; but we believe
in ourselves." (Actually, plenty of people believed in Wichita State.

More fans filling out online brackets picked the Shockers to advance to the Final Four than any other team in the region.) Then again, in this case the doubters were correct: Marshall's team lost to Kentucky in the second round.

Often, when athletes and teams accorded little respect *do* succeed, they aren't content to have simply proved the critics wrong. They need to have *shocked the world*. Muhammad Ali, perhaps, should be credited with first using this trope. Ali, then named Cassius Clay, beat Sonny Liston in 1964 and promptly shouted repeatedly, "I shook up the world!"

Watch the grainy black-and-white footage and you sense that Ali was being playfully ironic. But since then the phrase has hardened into cliché, and the irony has vanished. *Shock jocks*, as a colleague calls them, include everyone from victorious UFC fighters to successful bowlers. When the UConn men's basketball team beat Duke in the final of the 1999 NCAA Tournament, the Huskies' portly, impossible-to-dislike guard, Khalid El-Amin, declared, "We shocked the world." (UConn was a No. 1 seed, a team flush with future NBA players that had lost only two games all season.)

According to their irrepressible coach, Pete Carroll, the Seattle Seahawks "shocked everyone" when they won Super Bowl XLVIII—never mind that Seattle was a popular preseason pick and well regarded throughout the season. And as the Seahawks entered the 2014 season favored to repeat as champions, Richard Sherman, their voluble cornerback, remarked that the team was still getting only stinting respect. "We're fueled by the same thing," he said. "We're a bunch of underdogs, a bunch of guys nobody wanted, who didn't fit schemes."

An athlete's need to find disrespect can even take a vulgar (albeit entertaining) turn. Matt Barnes, the NBA journeyman, is actually grateful for your disrespect. So much so, in fact, that he knows just the way to convey his appreciation. As he told *Sports Illustrated*'s Chris Ballard in 2015, "If I ever win a ring, I'm going to get it sized for my middle finger. To thank all the people who doubted me, because you guys are what drove me to my ultimate goal." In her 2015 memoir, *My Fight/Your Fight*, Ronda Rousey, the incomparable UFC fighter, makes repeated mention of doubters and skeptics. In the final line of the acknowledgments section, she saves her last thanks "for every asshole who motivates me to succeed out of spite."[1]

What underlies this need for well-compensated (and celebrated) athletes to see themselves as underappreciated or undervalued? How are they able to convince themselves of this in the face of staggering evidence to the contrary? And what is it about this exercise in self-delusion that turns success—even when predicted and wagered on by many—into something earth-shattering?

It feels natural to dismiss such claims of disrespect as yet another example of professional athletes being divorced from reality. But in this respect, the psychology of the Hall of Famer isn't so different from that of Joe Public. We humans—even those of us without an entourage or a cut of the pay-per-view take—make regular use of false narratives, whether to motivate ourselves, boost our reputations, or bounce back from frustration and failure. That Floyd Mayweather views Rodney Dangerfield as a kindred spirit is consistent with a grand human tradition.

Psychologist Tony Greenwald, in his seminal paper on the topic titled "The Totalitarian Ego," suggests that the way we view our performances and think about our abilities has much in common with how Kim Jong-un runs North Korea (minus the Dennis Rodman play dates, we assume). It's not as outlandish as it seems. Greenwald isn't referring to totalitarian characteristics such as suppressive terror and public violence. What he proposes is that our typical self-views "correspond disturbingly to thought control and propaganda devices that are considered to be defining characteristics of a totalitarian political system." Specifically, Greenwald suggests that our personal histories—the autobiographical stories we tell ourselves about past performance and how we've gotten to where we are today—are replete with revision, fabrication, and an

---

1. Rousey, ironically, is one figure who truly *did* disrespect Mayweather. While receiving an ESPY award for Best Fighter in the summer of 2015, Rousey mentioned Mayweather and wondered how he felt getting "beat by a woman for once." This was, of course, a stiff jab at Mayweather's history of domestic violence.

unrealistically egocentric perspective. We twist the past (and the present) into narratives that make us look better to others and feel better about ourselves.

Much as the totalitarian leader does. Legend (that is, official governmental record) has it that Kim Jong-un's father, Kim Jong-il, learned to walk at three weeks old, wrote 1,500 books and six full operas over a span of two years, and shot a 38-under-par with 11 holes-in-one the only time he played a round of golf. Joseph Stalin was notorious for airbrushing out of photographs those who later became his enemies (or mortal victims). The rest of us? Our egocentrism and fabrications are less outrageous but still pervasive. Here are but two examples:

1. **We always think we're the center of attention**. We're convinced that every slight variation in our appearance or performance is immediately noted by everyone around us. Researchers have dubbed this the *spotlight effect*, and it's the reason many of us spent junior high convinced that that cafeteria table full of kids breaking up in laughter was doing so at our expense— that they must have noticed that giant pimple on our nose, our latest bad hair day, or the ridiculous new pants Mom made us wear. Even when, in fact, no one was actually paying us much attention at all.

In one clever study, researchers at Cornell put participating students in the unenviable position of reexperiencing those adolescent insecurities. Each subject was forced to march into a group of peers wearing something embarrassing: in this case a T-shirt with a gaudy Barry Manilow photo (as if there were any other kind) splashed across the front. The student then had to sit and complete a written survey while surrounded by conventionally clad peers. Afterward, the Manilow wearers were asked how many people around them had noticed what they had on. They wildly overestimated how noticeable and memorable the embarrassing shirt had been.

As the researchers concluded, "People tend to believe that the

social spotlight shines more brightly on them than it really does."
Welterweight boxers and tyrannical rulers aren't the only ones
who think the world revolves around them. Most of us do—it's
a consequence of spending much of our day engaged in internal
conversation but lacking insight into the monologues everyone
else is producing.

2. We think we're more powerful than we are. We regularly
succumb to the *illusion of control*, overconfident in the role we
play in outcomes around us. And not just in a tongue-in-cheek,
if-I-wear-my-lucky-socks-and-watch-the-game-sitting-on-Uncle-
Ted's-left-we'll-win kind of way. No, we genuinely overvalue our
control over events, even financial ones.

In another study, employees at two Long Island firms were
approached by researchers and offered a chance to buy into an
informal company lottery. The Super Bowl was a week away, so
instead of standard tickets with pre-printed numbers, they used
NFL trading cards as entries. For $1, workers could buy a player,
and his card would be placed into the drawing. The only catch
was that half of the entrants were allowed to choose their own
player and the other half were given a card at random. That was
enough to kick-start egocentric thinking: People who were able to
choose a trading card lulled themselves into inflating their odds of
winning, as if picking their own football player made them more
likely to win a game of chance.

How do we know this? Because the morning of the drawing,
a researcher approached each respondent and explained that
someone else at the office wanted to get into the lottery, but since
there weren't any tickets left, the new entrant would like to buy
theirs. How much would it take for them to let it go?

Keep in mind, this was a $1 ticket and a $50 pot. The average
asking price among those who had been assigned an NFL player
was $1.96, a slight mark-up. But people who got to pick their
own trading cards set an average value of $8.67—price-gouging
that would make a stadium beer concessionaire proud. Except

this wasn't simple greed. It was overvaluation born of an inflated sense that anything in which we have a personal hand must have a larger chance of success.

These two illusions reflect the totalitarian characteristics Greenwald described: egocentrism, fabrication, the creative revision of reality. We can't help but see ourselves as the center of attention and as masters of our own fates, despite rational evidence to the contrary. These and a variety of other egocentric biases help us stay optimistic even when the going gets tough. In fact, some psychologists argue that illusions like these are *essential* components of mental health—that looking at life *without* such ego-friendly lenses is a recipe for despondency.

In much the same way, the athlete's belief that "no one respects me" plays an adaptive psychological role. That's why it persists: A false narrative must serve a function in order to perpetuate itself. In Floyd Mayweather's case, by the time we finished this book, his record was up to 48-0; what's left to motivate him? More belts? History? More money? (Perhaps, though it would seem as if the latter pursuit has grown stale. Mayweather's increasingly exorbitant and well-publicized wagers suggest that net worth has taken a backseat to the thrill of the bet.) But proving wrong the naysayers? Now, *there's* a motivator—even if it takes some revisionist thinking, because there aren't too many out there who actually say nay to Floyd.

We work harder when we have something to prove. That's why every good training montage needs some form of personal motivation at its core. Why was Rocky Balboa running through freezing rivers, sawing wood, and wearing an ox's yoke in the Russian countryside? Because he had to avenge Apollo Creed's death (plus, he heard *Hearts on Fire* pumping on the soundtrack in the background). Ivan Drago's clinical training methods never stood a chance.

Luckily, in real life, we don't need the death of a rival-cum-sparring partner to find that motivation. Trailing at intermission, for example, is enough to boost competitive effort in the second half. That's the finding of researchers who have analyzed the outcomes of tens of thousands of college and professional basketball games.

Being slightly behind at halftime predicts a small but reliable in-crease in a team's chance of winning (a 2 percent increase for NCAA games, controlling for other relevant factors; a 6 percent increase in the NBA).

But regardless of the actual scoreboard, athletes looking for a reason to stay sharp can almost always find it through a quick totali-tarian infusion of perceived underappreciation. Maybe from oppo-nents or the media; perhaps from fans or team management—really, there's no shortage of sources of bulletin-board material. Whether or not athletes are aware of it, this pursuit of inspiration keeps send-ing them back to the mindset of deluded disrespect. Can we be far away from the day when an agent or a team hires a blogger to plant negative stories about their own players for motivational purposes?

NOT that this is the only false narrative athletes tell themselves.

Rafael Nadal is a terribly overrated tennis player, a poseur for-tunate to win a club championship, let alone more than a dozen Grand Slam singles titles. Just ask . . . Rafael Nadal. Reflexively, he characterizes his wins as "lucky." Ritually, he denigrates his play and lavishes praise on the most unremarkable opponents. At the 2013 French Open—an event Nadal had won every year but one since 2005—he defeated his first-round opponent in four sets and remarked, "I was a few points from losing." In the next round he faced Martin Klizan, a Slovakian journeyman who had never won a professional title. "If I don't play my best," Nadal predicted, "I will lose."

He went on to win the title yet again. A year later he repeated once more, creeping ever closer to Roger Federer's all-time record for major titles. Not that it helped inflate his confidence. "You drop your guard when you stop having doubts about yourself," he told a reporter from the *Financial Times*. "I've always had doubts. I've never believed that I am very good, nor do I believe it now."

That was at the beginning of 2014, when Nadal was ranked No. 1 in the world. Sensing false modesty, the reporter pushed Nadal: *Not very good? You can't be serious.* Nadal replied: "It's evident that my numbers say I am good, sure—I know I am number one because the numbers say I am. But I don't see myself that way."

This, too, is a refrain familiar to sports fans. Pep Guardiola, the Spanish soccer coach who has won multiple national and European club championships, has a habit of referring to his team's opponents with phrases such as "one of the best teams in the world," even when he himself is helming a Champions League juggernaut such as Barcelona or Bayern Munich.

Or on the other side of the pond, Lou Holtz, the former Notre Dame football coach, was as renowned for downplaying his team's chances as he was for recruiting and play-calling. "We're not a good enough football team to play the people we have to play," he said in 1993. At the time his team was 5-0 and ranked fourth in the country. This led a Seattle columnist to write snarkily in 2007: "Ex–Notre Dame coaching greats Ara Parseghian and Lou Holtz have been named head coaches for the Irish's annual Blue-Gold spring game on April 21. Holtz . . . immediately called a news conference to declare 'we're just not a very good football team right now' and proclaimed Parseghian's squad 'the best team we'll play all spring.'"

This type of sandbagging—*I'm not as good as people say I am; our opponents are much better than you think they are*—is another false narrative that serves a clear psychological function. Several functions, in fact. For one, it's a close cousin of "nobody respects us" as a motivational ploy that competitors use to keep themselves sharp and that coaches employ to maintain their players' focus. As Nadal explained, it's a way to make sure you don't drop your guard. Consider this headline in *The Onion*, which, as usual, is only a slight exaggeration: "All 32 NFL Teams Announce They Are Underdogs Headed into Season."

The ploy can also be used to alleviate pressure. As with this quote from Tim Belcher, the Dodgers' starting pitcher, on the eve of the 1988 World Series against the Oakland A's: "I don't think anyone is going to fall over in their seat if Oakland beats us. But if we beat them, whether it takes seven games or seven years, people will be very, very surprised. So where's the pressure there?" (Actually, it took only five games for Los Angeles to pull off the upset.) Belcher was right, though: The Dodgers really were underdogs.

But favorites, too, try to reduce pressure through a Holtzian lowering of expectations. The classic sandbaggers are the favorites who rebrand themselves as underdogs, at least in their own eyes. Sometimes teams even fight over Cinderella status, arguing over which of them should be viewed as the worse bet. Before Game 7 of their 2014 NHL playoff series, Darryl Sutter (L.A. Kings) and Bruce Boudreau (Anaheim Ducks) squared off in the media, each vociferously claiming that his was the inferior team. Boudreau ultimately won . . . in the sense that his team lost.

Sandbagging is a game of managing expectations—others' as well as your own. Being the favorite isn't always fun: Winning is expected, so it produces a *meh* reaction; losing is unexpected and, thus, attention-grabbing. So athletes often look for a way out of the dilemma—sometimes by jockeying for underdog status (not least because everyone loves an underdog; see page 43) or, after defeat, by blaming the officials or injuries.

That's the moral of a recent analysis of college and pro tennis matches. Researchers at the Wharton School of Business interviewed varsity collegiate players and statistically analyzed professional men's singles matches. They found that among first-set losers, it was the favorite who was significantly more likely to quit and cite injury; underdogs were more willing to tough it out. Why? Because of the pressure of being the favorite (and the distress of failing to live up to that status). As one college player explained, "[Retiring] is kind of a way out. . . . It's not 'I lost because the girl was better than me,' it's 'I lost because I'm hurt.'"

But again, athletes are not the sole practitioners of these distortions and egocentric revisions. Politicians sandbag before debates, setting expectations for their own performances so low—and for their opponents' performances so high—that the mere ability to stand upright at a podium for 90 minutes passes as raging success. Customer-service industries are notorious for gaming expectations in similar fashion, artificially inflating wait times on automated phone lines and at crowded restaurants so that when the delay is shorter, we're pleasantly surprised.

And let not we who live in glass houses throw too many stones, because most of us live in glass houses. Who among us hasn't self-handicapped to turn an endeavor into a no-lose proposition? Take the student who thinks, *Instead of studying for that big exam tomorrow, I'll go out with my friends tonight.* If she gets a poor grade, well, like the collegiate tennis player with the curiously touch-and-go knee, she's got a built-in excuse. But if she does well on the exam in spite of the late-night carousing? Just think how much more impressive her feat becomes, having limped Willis Reed–like to an improbable success.

THE false narrative told well is an invaluable tool for motivation and ego protection. It can help us ward off complacency as well as pressure. It can preempt disappointment and magnify success. The trick is figuring out for each scenario the right combination of psychological ingredients to produce the desired outcome.

Most of us merely dabble in this realm. But there exist gurus who have learned to harness these powers to inspire themselves and their charges to greatness. Some of them become wealthy motivational speakers and authors. Others lead innovative companies with global impact. Still others wear fish ties to work and then retire to a life of playing poker in a beach house with Willie Nelson.

That would be Don Nelson, who had the whole thing figured out. Among other magic tricks, he coached the eighth-seeded Golden State Warriors past the top-seeded Dallas Mavericks in the first round of the 2007 NBA playoffs. How did Nellie get his team ready to pull off the epic upset? As he told *Sports Illustrated*, "The first thing you gotta do if you're the worst and playing the best is you gotta convince your team they can win. You tell them, *We're gonna beat those fuckers.*"

He paused. "Then you go say the opposite to the press."

Why We Are All Dog Lovers at Heart (but Not Deep in Our Hearts)

> I'm a poor underdog
> But tonight I will bark
> —Robert Frost, "Canis Major," 1928

The word *underdog* seems, fittingly, to have competing origins. According to most references, the term derives from dogfighting. The superior competitor, the top dog, was in the advantageous position. It was up to the losing fighter, the under dog, to reverse its predicament.

Other linguists trace the origins of the word to the shipbuilding industry. Logs were placed over a pit, secured by saddle blocks nicknamed *dogs*, to be cut into planks using a two-handled saw. One relatively lucky shipbuilder, a senior sawyer, would stand over the pit, cutting from above and guiding the saw; his less fortunate junior colleague would stand in the pit and saw upward, becoming blanketed in sawdust. The man sawing from above was the *overdog*, and the poor guy sawing from below was the *underdog*.

Today we most closely associate *underdog* with sports, of course. Throughout history, the underdog has been a stock character, one of the essentials in sports. It's the 1980 U.S. Olympic hockey team, composed mostly of college kids, beating the more skilled, experienced Soviets—the Miracle on Ice—on their way to winning the gold medal. It's the tiny Hawaiian school of Chaminade knocking off Ralph Sampson and mighty Virginia in basketball. It's Buster Douglas knocking out the seemingly indestructible Mike Tyson. It's the 1968 New York Jets and the 1969 New York Mets. From *Rudy* to

Rocky to *Hoosiers* to *The Mighty Ducks* to the Cutters in the criminally underrated *Breaking Away*, the underdog is the central conceit of virtually every sports movie ever made.

Rooting for the team that is more likely to lose might defy rationality and logic, but to those of us who watch sports it seems utterly normal, even instinctual. Even the giants themselves acknowledge this. It was Wilt Chamberlain who, memorably, rued that "everybody pulls for David; nobody roots for Goliath."

The underdog breed is on particularly vivid display during the NCAA basketball tournament each March. The selections are made, the brackets take shape, and—as surely as the CBS theme music lodges in our brains—we start to root against the favorites and for the little guys. We might not be able to name a single player on the floor for Creighton or Butler or Virginia Commonwealth; we might not have known that the mascot of Campbell University is Gaylord the Camel; we might not know the location of such schools as Mercer and Wofford[1]—but damned if we don't pull like hell for those teams to beat Kentucky and Arizona and Duke.

The March Madness underdog might be best embodied by the University of Richmond. As we write this, the school has made the Big Dance nine times since 1984, never arriving seeded higher than No. 7. Nevertheless, the Spiders are consistent giant killers. With players who went unrecruited by bigger schools, Richmond reliably comes into the NCAA tournament punching above its weight.

In 1984 Richmond beat Auburn, a team led by Charles Barkley and Chuck Person. In 1988 the Spiders reached the Sweet 16 by beating Indiana, then the defending NCAA champs, as well as Georgia Tech. Three years after that, Richmond became the first No. 15 seed to beat a No. 2 seed when the Spiders took down Syracuse. In so doing the program achieved the distinction of winning NCAA tournament games as a No. 12, 13, 14, and 15 seed. And most of us were cheering for Richmond all the way.

---

1. Georgia and South Carolina, respectively.

Against this backdrop, it's not hard to see why a seminal study on the psychology underlying our fondness for the underdog was performed by researchers at none other than the University of Richmond. The data confirmed what we suspected: Our love of the underdog is no myth. It can be quantified.

The study was called "Perceptions of Shapes." In campus recruitment flyers, students were offered $5 to participate. This was easy money: Each research session entailed simply sitting at a computer monitor and watching a series of video clips of moving geometric shapes. Four clips, to be precise, each lasting about 15 seconds—just the right duration to keep the attention of the participants, most of whom presumably hadn't spent time watching animated dancing shapes for a good decade or so. (Then again, these were college students, so who knows?)

Each of the four clips, created by JongHan Kim, Scott Allison, and their fellow researchers, depicted one or two shapes moving across the screen from left to right. The clips were all variations on the same theme: circles rolling up and then down a hill. But each clip was slightly different from the others, and the order in which participants saw them was random.

- **Clip A:** A solitary circle makes its way horizontally before going up and down a hill (*see below*). The speed never wavers, even on the uphill portion of the course. The researchers called this version the *single non-struggling entity*.

Adapted from Kim, 2008.

- **Clip B:** Again, just one circle and one hill. But this time our circular protagonist slows as the incline begins, recalling an experience familiar to anyone who exercises at inconsistent elevation. Ergo, a *single struggling entity*.

- **Clip C:** One circle proceeds from left to right, again losing speed
  as it goes uphill. But at the onset of the slowdown, a second circle
  emerges from the left. This circle moves much faster than the
  first. And unlike the first circle, it flies right through the course,
  including up and over the hill. In short: two entities, one struggling
  but accompanied by another that is *benign and non-struggling*.

- **Clip D:** Just like Clip C—except forget any notion of *benign*. The
  second, faster circle again shows no sign of struggle as it powers
  up the hill, but it also gives no indication of mercy. Shortly after
  overtaking the first circle, the second circle reverses direction
  and knocks its geometrical contemporary back down the hill
  before speeding off to the end of the course. *Asshole.* Or in the
  researchers' more refined parlance: two entities, one struggling
  and the other *malicious and non-struggling*.

Four clips about rolling circles, presented in random order. After
watching each one, the participants answered a few questions about
what they'd just seen.

So, how much did they root for each circle on a scale of 1–7?
Results indicated more rooting for a struggler than a non-struggler.
For example, respondents rooted more for the solitary circle in Clip
B than for the one in Clip A. In Clip C, the sight of another entity
flying effortlessly up the hill seemed to deepen the protagonist's
plight; students responded by rooting for the first circle even more.
And our poor hero of Clip D? It received the highest ratings of all, as
respondents watched its seemingly valiant struggle against a malicious rival that appeared to gloat over its superiority.

The study's results went beyond rooting. When asked to rate
their feelings of *sympathy* toward the circles, the participants' responses varied by clip: Sympathy was lowest for the circle in Clip A,
higher for the one in Clip B, and highest for the strugglers in Clips C
and D, which had to contend with the non-struggling competitors.

This same pattern emerged in the degree to which participants
personally identified with each circle. Yes, that's right: feelings of
personal identification with an *animated circle*. In the words of the re-

searchers, the study demonstrates the degree to which "an entity's struggle, by itself, is enough to engender emotional support." Apparently, not only can we bring ourselves to root for anything that moves, but we'll also do so with gusto and emotional investment.

"Perhaps the most notable aspect of this study is that participants [completed] the questionnaires," the researchers noted. "They had no hesitation about doing so. They did not think it odd or difficult to be asked how much they were rooting for rolling circles."

If we're this emotional about the underdog when it's a rolling circle, you can imagine how moved we are by human beings in actual competition.

IF you want a good example of an underdog sports figure, you could do worse than David Blatt. Once a member of the Princeton basketball team—another famous tournament giant-slayer—Blatt couldn't kick his basketball jones after graduation. So while his classmates and teammates made their fortunes in finance, law, and medicine, Blatt played and coached all over the world, though mostly in Israel.

It took three decades, but word of his talents finally penetrated the pro basketball mainstream. Despite his lack of NBA coaching experience (let alone playing experience), Blatt was chosen in June 2014 to be the coach of the Cleveland Cavaliers. The following month a certain ex-Cavalier immeasurably re-raised the profile of the franchise by deciding to take his talents back to Lake Erie. Suddenly, at age 55, Blatt was a prominent figure in basketball: the unlikely new coach of LeBron James.

But in May 2014, weeks before the NBA beckoned, Blatt was on the bench for Maccabi Tel Aviv as it faced CSKA Moscow in the first semifinal of the Euroleague Basketball Final Four. The game was loaded with intrigue, in part because of Blatt's backstory: Before coaching Maccabi, he had helmed the Russian national team; he had coached six of the CSKA players against whom his Maccabi charges would compete for a league title.

Beyond Blatt's divided loyalties, the matchup was noteworthy in that it featured two of the most storied franchises in international club basketball. Maccabi entered the game with five previous Euroleague championships and nine second-place finishes. CSKA checked in with six titles and six other trips to the final. In this latest game between the two pedigreed franchises, Blatt and his Maccabi team won in dramatic fashion, 68–67.[2]

This clash of two Euroleague titans pierced the consciousness of few American sports fans, however. In fact the teams' illustrious pasts—not to mention their legacy of head-to-head matchups, noteworthy for their geopolitical as well as athletic implications—are unknown to all but the most ardent fans on this side of the Atlantic.

Which is why, when Joe Vandello and his colleagues at the University of South Florida sought to investigate the psychology of sports rooting, they showed their U.S. participants a 15-minute clip from an unremarkable Maccabi-CSKA game held 10 years earlier. Vandello wanted a blank canvas on which to work. While average Americans might feel strongly about Israel and Russia from an international-relations standpoint, they know nothing about the countries' top basketball clubs.

Blissfully ignorant, then, the participants were at the mercy of whatever the researchers told them about the matchup they were about to watch. Half were told that Maccabi had little hope of winning. They were told that CSKA had won all 15 of the teams' previous playoff matchups (not true) and that oddsmakers had made the Russians 9–1 favorites for this game (another fabrication).

These expectations had a dramatic effect on how participants felt as they watched. The Americans' baseline tendency to cheer for Israelis over Russians became even more exaggerated. Much like the Richmond study participants who pulled for the circle struggling on the hill, the South Florida viewers rooted for the long shot.

How powerful is the allure of the underdog? Enough to bridge the geopolitical divide between Americans and Russians. Because

---

2. Two days later, in Blatt's last overseas game before decamping for the NBA, Maccabi would capture its sixth Euroleague championship, drawing even with CSKA for the second-most all-time, behind Real Madrid (eight titles).

the other half of the participants in this study were given the mirror-opposite expectation. They were told that *Maccabi* had won all 15 of the previous playoff tilts. That the *Israelis* were the nine-to-one favorites. Accordingly their rooting interests flipped, with American fans showing (ever so slight) signs of pulling for the underdog Russians.

But the spectators in Vandello's study did more than just root differently depending on which team they believed to be the favorite heading into the game. They also interpreted what they saw in drastically divergent ways. Regardless of which team supposedly faced the longer odds, respondents viewed the underdogs as hustling more, showing more heart, having a greater desire to win.

In short, ballgames are like Rorschach tests: Much as one person's inkblot butterfly is another person's pair of witches, one sports fan sees a group of gritty, blue-collar scrappers while another sees the same team as a bunch of cheap-shot artists. In the South Florida study, the notion of the underdog provided a lens through which the rest of the action was interpreted. And this was colored most by perceptions of effort.

That's the appeal of being the long shot. Not only do people root for you, but they also frame your performance favorably. Success becomes the legacy of hard work, industriousness, and hustle. For competitors as well as fans, it makes for a more dramatic and ego-rewarding story line than one based solely on natural ability. Thus the tendency for even defending champions and title favorites to bend over backward to stake dubious claims to underdog status (see *Inner Mayweather*, page 30).

And fans, too, go to great lengths to root for the underdog, fickle though it might make them seem. In 1991 researchers at Bowling Green—yet another school that could furnish a March Madness Cinderella story—offered a sociological analysis of the allure of the underdog, complete with a survey of students on campus. The researchers described two generic teams, Team A and Team B, playing in a best-of-seven series. Team A, the subjects were told, was "highly favored" to win. Which team would they support? Armed with no additional knowledge—not even the sport was specified—81 percent went with the underdog.

Then the researchers changed the facts. Despite being the underdog, Team B inexplicably jumped to a 3–0 lead in the series and was a game from an improbable sweep of the favorite. Now which team would the students support? Curiously, a full half of the participants who had initially sided with Team B switched to support Team A, the original favorite now supposedly fighting for its life.

How many of us have had a similar change of heart even *during* a game? We want, say, the underdog Colts to upset the Denver Broncos in the NFL playoffs because, well, why not? Upsets are fun. But in the fourth quarter, when the Colts are winning and Peyton Manning is struggling to complete the simplest of passes, we take our lead from one of those commercials in which everyone at the bar pulls for overtime just so they can stay and eat more wings. Suddenly we switch allegiances and root for Denver to mount a comeback. We're not ashamed for even a moment about our spineless waffling.

BACKING the underdog feels natural to many of us. But when you stop to consider it, there are basic psychological reasons why this tendency should be surprising. In various ways, this soft spot for the likely loser seems counterintuitive. Take, for instance, the well-documented notion that the groups with which we affiliate are sources of personal self-esteem. Examples:

- We're quick to tout our connections to famous or otherwise successful others, even when those ties are tenuous and we played absolutely no role in the others' success. (In fact, we'll even pay for the privilege; see *Gronk BBQ*, page 177.)

- We describe the victories of teams we root for using first-person terms (*we won*), but we use language to distance ourselves from defeats (*they lost*), thus protecting our egos from failure.

- Sure, when the team we're pulling for wins, we experience a quick uptick in mood. But rooting for a winner also boosts our self-esteem. We even become more confident in our mental aptitude and social skills—to the point that those who root for a team that wins are subsequently more convinced of their ability to seduce people they find attractive.

Being in bed with the winning team (figuratively, of course) feels good and looks good. So underdogs shouldn't be so appealing—yet they clearly are, and not just in sports. Underdogs matter, for instance, in international relations. In the same paper in which they described the Maccabi/CSKA research, Vandello and colleagues also reported a study on attitudes regarding the Middle East. College students read a primer on the Israeli-Palestinian conflict. This Cliffs-Notes distillation of millennia of strife was accompanied by a map. Half of the students received an Israel-centric map, in which Israel looks large next to the smaller Palestinian territories. The other half saw a map of the entire Middle East, in which Israel, in off-white, is surrounded not only by the Palestinian territories but also by Egypt, Jordan, Syria, et al., each shaded in the same darker color.

Participants were asked toward which side of the conflict they felt more supportive. Those who saw the Israel-centric map were split 53 percent to 47 percent, giving slightly more of their support to the Palestinians. But those who saw the map of the entire region—in which Israel was, visually at least, an "underdog" in a sea of Arab countries—supported the Israelis 77 percent to 23 percent.

Underdogs matter in domestic politics, too. For example, in a study run at the University of South Florida one week before the 2004 U.S. presidential election, researchers found that John Kerry voters were more likely than George W. Bush voters to see Kerry as the underdog. Meanwhile, Bush voters were more likely than Kerry supporters to see Bush as the underdog, despite his incumbent status. In other words, partisans on both sides wanted to perceive their candidate as the contender who overcame the odds—not the favorite who simply fulfilled expectations.

Or consider another study in the months leading up to the 2008 election. As in the Israel/Palestine study, respondents' expectations were manipulated by how the contest was framed. Half were informed that then-candidate Barack Obama was considered the front-runner for the Democratic nomination, based on polling numbers and campaign fund-raising. The other half were told that he was a clear underdog to Hillary Clinton based on the same criteria. Participants rated underdog Obama as warmer and slightly more competent than they did front-runner Obama. And, among registered Democrats, labeling Obama an underdog produced a small increase in the reported likelihood of voting for him.

Not that Hillary Clinton needs to be reminded of the value of being the underdog. Despite her impressive pedigree (including a Yale law degree), she often positions herself, like so many politicians before her, as an outsider whose rise to prominence was thoroughly unexpected. In much the same way, her husband was quicker to trumpet his modest upbringing and his Arkansas roots than his Rhodes Scholarship. As Bill Clinton once eloquently put it, "Every politician wants every voter to believe that he was born in a log cabin he built himself."

Underdogs matter for businesses' bottom line, too. Consumer researchers talk about the value of an underdog brand biography (UBB). *We started Nantucket Nectars with only a blender and a dream*, the drink label tells us. *We're the little company that could*, explains the chief marketing executive at Subaru. *Our company started in a garage*, according to Apple. And Microsoft. Not to mention Amazon, Disney, Google, and Hewlett-Packard.

A good UBB humanizes a company. It's effective "because consumers can relate these stories to their own lives," writes Neeru Paharia, now at Georgetown's McDonough School of Business. "The positive effect of underdog brand biographies is driven by identity mechanisms," she explains. After all, if we can identify with circles as they roll up a hill, we can identify with a company trying to make its way in a cutthroat consumer marketplace.

We can assume that Don Draper knew this; certainly his creator did. Matthew Weiner, the brains behind *Mad Men*, was recently asked in an interview why he made Draper's backstory one of transformation from neglect and poverty. Weiner's response: "Everyone loves the Horatio Alger version of life."

There are clear lessons in the allure of the underdog, even for those of us who don't seek elected office or the shareholders' vote of confidence. Simply put: Too often, we overlook the value of imperfection. For example, in one study conducted years ago at the University of Minnesota, researchers set out to learn more about the factors that make people seem more likable. Specifically, they asked respondents to form an impression of a fellow student trying out for a television quiz show in which he'd be representing their university against other schools. In some versions of the study, the guy was depicted as an impressive high-achiever. Honor student. Yearbook editor. Varsity track team. Quick on his figurative feet, too: In the audition he got 92 percent of the difficult quiz questions right. In other versions the candidate was more pedestrian. Average grades. Lowly yearbook proofreader. Cut from the track team. This guy managed to get only 30 percent of the audition questions right.

Not surprisingly, Mr. Hot Shot was rated as more likable than Mr. No Shot. Competence breeds attractiveness, after all. But you know who was even more likable? Mr. Hot Shot when he blundered a bit. In some of the study sessions, the candidate tripped and spilled a cup of coffee on his spiffy new suit. When it was the mediocre candidate who stumbled, study participants saw him as even less likable, even more mediocre. But the pratfall had the opposite effect on perceptions of the impressive candidate. Now he became more likable than ever.

It's a gambit familiar to many a manager, public speaker, and salesperson. Want to win people over? Show them you're human. Tell a self-deprecating joke. Share the story of a previous failure. Give yourself an underdog narrative, no matter how successful and proficient you are. If HP, Google, and Microsoft can do it, how hard can it be? Of course, as in the coffee-spill study, you have to begin by demonstrating some baseline competence. A slipup offers little help to the already unimpressive (much as, in sports, fans become more invested in the lower seed only after it proves it has at least some shot of winning). Highly competent but charmingly flawed is a tough combination to beat, on or off the court.

As Malcolm Gladwell has noted, being an underdog can also be about more than just public perception. His book *David and Goliath* extols the virtues of underdog status when it comes to actual performance outcomes such as perseverance and innovation. He describes the software engineer coaching youth basketball who has so little background in the sport that he doesn't know any better than to teach his undersized squad of girls to full-court press all game long—right into an unexpected title run. (This engineer and erstwhile novice coach is now co-owner of the NBA's Sacramento Kings.) And the high-powered trial attorney whose dyslexia hasn't proved to be a disadvantage in a reading-heavy profession; rather, it prompted him to develop an extraordinary memory that has made him an elite cross-examiner.

In Gladwell's words: "The fact of being an underdog can *change* people in ways that we often fail to appreciate: it can open doors and create opportunities and educate and enlighten and make possible what might otherwise have seemed unthinkable."

BUT let's return our focus to sports—the realm in which the lore of the underdog is most prominent. How are we to make sense of this central contradiction: that we support the side more inclined to lose? Explanations abound. Some are more economic in nature, such as the notion of greater potential return on the emotional investment in an underdog. When the favorite you're rooting for wins, the payoff can be tepid. A minimal spike in mood, perhaps merely a sense of relief. Throwing in with the underdog, on the other hand, is a riskier proposition, but when you hit on the long shot, the bet pays much more. Backing a favorite can't match the exhilaration of winning with an underdog.

Research points to equity concerns as well. Perhaps it's not that people pull for the underdog so much as they root for a close game. Recall our Colts-Broncos example? When one team is leading, we often root for the other to come back. And who's likely to be trailing? The dog that came out on the bottom the last time.

Of course, a strict equity argument would posit that people are equal-opportunity underdog fans. Experience and common sense say they're not. As we write this, millions are relishing the current struggles of the Lakers and the Knicks rather than pulling for comebacks; and it's hard to ever see the Yankees, Patriots, Duke basketball, or Manchester United in the Cinderella role, regardless of what the scoreboard or the standings say.[3]

---

3. Disclaimer: digression ahead—one that we found an interesting case study in who does (and doesn't) benefit from underdog status. But you won't offend us if a lengthy footnote isn't your cup of tea and you prefer an immediate return to the regularly scheduled programming above.

In 2009, Jon spent a few days on the road with the Harlem Globetrotters. The idea was to chronicle the world's most famous basketball team as it attempted to update a classic brand and stay relevant in an age in which anyone with a wi-fi connection has access to crazy dunks, trick shots, and abracadabra dribbling exhibitions.

Quickly, Jon became just as interested in the Globetrotters' foils, the Washington Generals. Though the two teams were inextricably linked throughout their uniquely symbiotic relationship from 1952 until its recent dissolution in 2015, a firewall of sorts always divided them. While the Globetrotters traveled in a tricked-out tour bus, the Generals motored to games in a generic van. The Globetrotters stayed at the Sheraton; the Generals, down the road at the Comfort Inn, sleeping two to a room. During games, of course, the Generals were the butts of the jokes, scampering to avoid the bucket of confetti, falling for the ball-on-a-string gag, getting unceremoniously divorced from their shorts.

If this were simply choreography in the manner of pro wrestling, it would be one thing. But the Generals players were cryptic about whether the outcomes were arranged in advance. "We know our role, let's put it that way," said Ammer Johnson, a longtime Generals player, once a starter at Idaho State. Others were adamant that they were trying their best; the Globetrotters were simply taller, faster, and more talented.

The Generals played hard. They weren't unskilled. But they didn't just lose; they were mocked in the process (one might call their celebrated opponents a human version of the *malicious and non-struggling* rolling circle). This tableau should have made them the quintessential underdogs. Except that the Generals were not at all perceived that way. They never benefited in the slightest from the allure of the underdog. When the Globetrotters beat the Generals in Holmdel, New Jersey, in the final game of Jon's assignment, they extended their winning streak to 12,873 games. As we started writing this, the streak verged on 15,000. No matter: At every game Jon attended, the fans cheered exclusively for the Globetrotters.

And it was always this way.

Little-known fact: the Generals did beat the Globetrotters one night. That was on January 5, 1971, inside a bandbox of a gym in Martin, Tennessee. The Generals, playing that night under their alter-ego name Jersey Reds, had lost each of their 2,495 previous games against the Globetrotters. On this night, though, they could scarcely miss, and the Globetrotters were decidedly off their game, clanging shots off the rim and throwing the ball out of bounds.

Trailing 99–98 with a few seconds left, Red Klotz, the Generals' 5'7" owner/coach/ bus driver/accountant/sharpshooter, caught the ball. Though Klotz was in his 50s at the time, he could still shoot. His 20-foot set shot flitted through the net. When Meadow-

Surely there's a cultural component in the mix, too, as the narrative of the underdog seems tailor-made for certain societies. The image of the lone hero battling the odds and ultimately prevailing plays right into the American ethos of rugged individualism and the Protestant work ethic. But it's worth noting that the underdog's appeal is cross-cultural. In the product research detailed earlier, a good corporate UBB went over exceptionally well with U.S. consumers. But its effect was also significant, if somewhat smaller, among Singaporean respondents, who likewise expressed greater purchasing intent when a brand boasted an underdog biography.

Mostly, though, at least from the perspective of sports fans, the appeal of the underdog label seems to be all about effort and heart—characteristics we like to see in ourselves and display for others. Optimism, too. When people hear about an underdog, they hold out hope. In one study, participants read about individuals or groups that were struggling and were asked to rate their likelihood

lark Lemon missed a hook shot at the buzzer, the Generals were suddenly on the left side of the ledger for the first (and only) time.

This was the equivalent of a No. 16 seed beating a top seed, Harry Truman beating Thomas Dewey, and 300 Spartans staving off the entire Persian army at Thermopylae, all rolled into one. Yet no one outside of the Generals' locker room celebrated that night. (With no champagne on hand, players doused Klotz with orange soda.) The crowd of 3,000 booed lustily and, by some accounts, threw objects on the court. One author of a book on the Globetrotters called this game a blow to America's confidence, an event on a par with the My Lai massacre and the release of the Pentagon Papers. Klotz's famous line from the time: "It was like we had killed Santa Claus."

The plight of the Generals illustrates that the allure of the underdog is finite. This lack of empathy for the Generals has been a source of curiosity for years. But then we happened upon an essay written by New York Times journalist Sam Dolnick. In a smart and sweet obituary of Klotz in 2014, Dolnick wrote about the Generals' lone win and the fans' hostile reaction that night in Tennessee. "The Harlem Globetrotters were permanent underdogs, a team of extraordinary athletes, long forced to compete outside white mainstream leagues. Cheering for their loss would have been like cheering for Jackie Robinson to strike out."

Dolnick seems to have been onto something. Decades of fans didn't overlook the Washington Generals or somehow discount their status because the games were more entertainment than sport. Rather, the theme of the underdog figures deeply in the Globetrotter experience. Fans come to games having undertaken their own "underdog analysis" and concluded that, on balance, the Globetrotters are more deserving of their support.

Pity the poor Generals. Now defunct, they were sports history's most perpetual on-court underdogs, and still they could never win for losing.

of ultimate success. Across domains—whether sports, politics, or business—when the entity was described as *disadvantaged*, the average rating of its probability of success was 38 percent. When the same entity was referred to as an *underdog*, that number climbed to 44 percent. A reliable but small effect.[4]

And, in the end, that's a fair assessment of the allure of the underdog: a reliable but small effect. Because as much as people love a good underdog, this love comes with qualifications and has an expiration date. As we just noted, fans will root for the long shot as long as it's not one of certain teams that seem unlikable to them under any circumstances. We'll pull for the team that's behind, but not if its loss would help our favorite team. Yes, we claim to give our hearts to the underdog, but our wallets (and hats and pennants and replica jerseys) belong to our personal favorites—disproportionately those same Lakers/Yankees/Patriots/Blue and Red Devils we called out earlier.

Indeed, as is so often the case, we can probe the depth of people's commitment to the cause by asking if they'll put their money where their mouths are. With underdogs, they won't. Take betting on the NFL. According to one analysis, over a 20-year window, home underdogs in the NFL have covered the point spread almost 54 percent of the time, yet they've drawn only 40 percent of the betting money. In fact, in another study, even when points were added to the spread to tilt the playing field toward underdog bets, the bias toward wagering on the favorite persisted.

And so it goes among consumers as well. For all our good intentions to support local businesses and pull for mom-and-pop stores, how many of us ultimately go with the big-box chain retailer or the point-and-click online purchase? We often talk a good game about shopping locally and voting with our wallets, but even a strong underdog brand biography can get shouted down by simple convenience and price point.

---

4. In other words, when sports fans hear *underdog*, they turn into Jim Carrey's Lloyd Christmas from *Dumb and Dumber*: "So you're telling me there's a chance!"

So, yes, we love us some underdog. But it's often an exhilarating one-night fling. Or, in the more erudite assessment of the University of Richmond researchers with whom we began this chapter, "although rooting for the underdog is pervasive, the effect is a mile wide and an inch deep." Not ideal dimensions for a swimming pool, but certainly worth considering for the next *office* pool.

Why Hockey Goons Would Rather Fight at Home

There are those who use their mastery of data and probability to find inefficiencies in capital markets and make a fortune for themselves or their clients. There are others who use those skills to beat the point spread or win at poker or achieve supremacy in their fantasy football league.

Then there's a set of, well, more altruistic quants who use advanced statistics to try to address social problems. Joe Walsh, who works at the University of Chicago's Center for Data Science and Public Policy, is a self-described "data scientist for social good." He undertakes projects such as predicting enrollment in Chicago's public schools. When we spoke in the fall of 2014, he was working on a study to determine what homes in which urban neighborhoods posed the highest risk of lead poisoning. "Then," he explained, "we know where to start remediation."

Walsh betrays a similar high-mindedness when it comes to his favorite sport, hockey. He grew up in metro Detroit when the Red Wings were the alpha stars of the NHL, winning the Stanley Cup three times between 1997 and 2002. His favorite player was Steve Yzerman, aka Stevie Y, aka the Captain, a skilled, graceful, fluid center who scored goals prolifically before transitioning to a defensive leader. Upon retiring, Yzerman was, predictably, enshrined in the Hall of Fame.

Walsh, unlike some of his friends, had decidedly less regard for Bob Probert, the Red Wings' ruthless (and near toothless) enforcer. Apart from his role as a one-man crime wave—his many arrests included ones for cocaine possession and for crashing his motorcycle with a BAC three times the legal limit—Probert was known for his on-ice fighting. Dropping the gloves with regularity, he racked up penalty minutes as if shopping in bulk.

Probert and his teammate Joey Kocur made up Detroit's Bruise Brothers. Walsh was skeptical of the high regard in which Wings fans held the pair. "Honestly," he says, "I would prefer to see fighting removed from hockey, and I don't think it helps a team win games, and there's a good bit of evidence supporting that."

Still, Walsh watched enough hockey to know that fighting played a prominent role in the game, from an entertainment standpoint but also in terms of apparent in-game momentum. And, true to form, he was curious about the data. *Who's better than who?* is something we ask all the time, whether it's for college football teams or horses at the racetrack," Walsh says. "Well, who's a better fighter than who? I wondered whether that kind of analysis had been done for hockey."

Walsh tooled around the cult website hockeyfights.com, stripped the data, ran his analysis, and found something interesting. More than 100,000 hockey fights were indexed on the site, and fans were able to vote on the winner of each brawl. For more than 6,000 of these fights, at least 10 users had voted on the winner. And in these 6,000 throwdowns with what Walsh deemed a statistically meaningful number of votes, the winner was 20 percent more likely to have been the fighter from the home team.

According to Walsh's data:

A full 25 percent of the fights ended in a draw.

Of the remainder, road players won 35 percent, while home players won 41 percent.

Pick any NHL player with a minimum of five fights at home and five fights away, and he is almost two-thirds more likely to have a better home record. Sometimes dramatically so. Tony Twist, a notorious enforcer in the '90s, mostly for the St. Louis Blues, was 7-1-1 fighting at home and 1-2-4 fighting on the road. Sean Avery, the human rash who retired in 2012? He was 16-4-9 at home and 4-8-21 on the road. The overall difference by team was striking as well.

Oh, and Bob Probert? He illustrated the difference as well as anyone else. According to the hockeyfights.com database, Probert had 240 fights in his NHL career, 64 of which had enough votes to allow for meaningful statistical analysis. Of those, he won 76 percent at home and 56 percent on the road.

On October 11, 2014, Walsh reached out to Jon via Twitter: @Scorecasting @jon_wertheim Data from @hockeyfights shows home fighters 20 percent more likely to win; refs have no influence on result.

With that, the gloves were dropped.

FIRST, some backstory: In their book, *Scorecasting*, Jon and his co-conspirator, University of Chicago economist Tobias Moskowitz, addressed the issue of home field advantage. For all the myths in sports, home field (and ice and court and even course) advantage is not one of them. It is real. It is remarkably consistent over time and among sports. From Japanese baseball to Brazilian soccer to the NBA, home teams *in every major sport*, cumulatively over time, win more often than not.

As to the question *Why?* Well, that's where the myths come in. Reflexively, we might think that the advantage owes to the partiality of fans, who are, at once, supportive of the home team and inhospitable to the visitors. It's easier to play in front of a cosseting audience than a hostile crowd, right?

Not really—there's very little to suggest that individual performance diminishes on the road. Think about those crazed fans waving and clapping Thunderstix when road players shoot free throws. Yet, cumulatively, NBA players make the same percentage of shots—down to the decimal, 75.9 percent—on the road as at home. (And this doesn't vary depending on the time within the game, either.) In baseball, a pitcher's control doesn't change according to where the game is played. During NHL shootouts, when you'd expect the crowd to be at its most raucous, road teams actually win slightly *more often* than home teams. In football the distances of punts and made field goals are virtually identical for home and road teams. And despite the crowd trying to make play-calling inaudible, visiting quarterbacks actually rate slightly *better* than home QBs.

Okay, then, another explanation: It's the rigors of travel that doom the visitors. When one team sleeps in its own beds and the other sleeps on lumpy pillows between interruptions from the couple fighting in the adjacent hotel room, well, that influences performance. Right? Not really. How do we know? In games for which the "visiting" team travels no farther than the home team—Cubs vs. White Sox; Lakers vs. Clippers—the home advantage remains constant. Likewise, road teams don't lose more often when they travel greater distances. Over time the Knicks, for example, fare no better on the road against the Nets or Sixers than they do against the Portland Trail Blazers or Sacramento Kings, on the opposite coast. The results would be different, of course, if those long flights and jet lag were driving the disadvantage.

A third (again, thoroughly plausible) explanation is that home teams benefit from the unique characteristics of their "home" and can even build a team to take advantage of their surroundings. Playing before the short outfield porches in Wrigley Field, the Cubs can gain an edge by stocking their outfield with power hitters. Meanwhile the Mets, playing half their games in Citi Field, home to one of baseball's most capacious outfields, can get a leg up by building their team around pitching. In football the Packers and Bills can fill their roster with players accustomed to the cold. And so forth.

But there's little empirical support for this. We looked at the most obvious case—"hitter-friendly" ballparks versus "pitcher-friendly" ballparks—and found that teams in hitters' parks, presumably stacked with sluggers, don't outhit their visitors by more than teams in pitchers' parks outhit theirs. There's not much anecdotal support, either. Maybe the best cold-weather NFL player of all time? Brett Favre, who grew up in . . . southern Mississippi. (Nor do deception and "dark arts"—sign stealing, groundskeeping she-nanigans, locker-room sabotage, and for that matter underinflated footballs—help to explain home advantage. At one time they might have, but because of standardized league rules, surveillance tech-nology, and stiff punishments for cheating, it would be hard to pull off such skulduggery today.)[1]

Scorecasting argued instead that it is officials' bias that really drives the home advantage. Home teams strike out less and walk more in baseball and are called for fewer fouls in basketball and soc-cer. In football, home teams are called for fewer penalties (although the differential has declined since the challenge system arrived), especially on the most "valuable" penalties, such as those resulting in a first down. (Since the advent of replay, the NFL's general home advantage has dwindled as well.)

None of this implies that the officials are instructed to rule in favor of the home team or that they're corrupt in any way. But they are human, subject to the same social pressures as all of us. In study after study, psychologists have found that social influence has a powerful effect on behavior. When 50,000 people are telling you to make a call a certain way, you're inclined to comply to avoid upset-ting the masses. Likewise, a wealth of research suggests that during times of uncertainty, we rely on cues from crowds to figure out the "correct" solutions to ambiguous problems. Forced to make a split-second decision, an official might easily resolve his ambivalence by relying on the crowd, even as an unconscious tiebreaker of sorts.

YET Joe Walsh's research on hockey fights puzzled us. Here was an instance in sports that—by its very essence—was isolated from officiating. Yet the home fighter was significantly more successful. Why would this be?

---

1.   Sam and his family live in the Boston area, so for their continued safety, here we resist making a gratuitous New England Patriots joke.

We called Walsh, who could scarcely have been more genial and curious. First, he was quick to admit that this wasn't the most rigorous research undertaking. He had based the definition of "winning" each fight on the votes of fans. Perhaps voting for the winner of a fight—inherently subjective to begin with—was more likely among hockey fans who had seen the fight live rather than on television; thus, home players would be favored. Yet the data suggested that the fans judging the winners were distributed throughout North America. In many cases these were high-volume, equal-opportunity voters; the same hockeyfights.com users cast votes on dozens, even hundreds, of fights involving players from all NHL teams.

Sam Page, a sharp young hockey writer at *Sports Illustrated,* suggested that the home team might fare better in fights than the road team because the visitors make their line changes first. "The home coach can react to the road coach's deployments," he reasoned.

But then—in the manner of a hockey player circling and declining to drop the gloves—Sam backed away from his hypothesis. On second thought, he said, under hockey's unwritten code, both players have to agree to a fight. So even if a home team put an enforcer on the ice to counter an opposing lineup, the ensuing fight would have to be consensual, minimizing any advantage by virtue of the last line change.

Then we came across a bit of science.

In his doctoral dissertation in zoology (didn't see that coming, did you?) at the University of Wisconsin, Matthew Fuxjager studied the fighting habits of territorial mice. What he noticed: When mice fought at home, they were more aggressive and won more often. A lot more often. And having prior experience at winning jacked up the home advantage even further.

For his first experiment, Fuxjager gave mice three winning experiences (fights against smaller mice) in their home cage. Then he gave half of these mice another fight in their home cage and the other half a fight in an unfamiliar cage—all against bigger mice. The mice that had the fourth fight in their home cage won 100 percent of the time. Among the mice that had the fourth fight in the unfamiliar cage? They won a paltry *40 percent* of the time.[2]

Fuxjager found a similar result among mice without previous winning experience. He subjected such rookies to a single fight, again against larger opponents. Half of the mice had their first fight in their home cage, whereas the other half debuted in an unfamiliar cage. In these maiden fights, mice won 40 percent of the time in their home environment but only 10 percent of the time away from home.

Beyond wins and losses, the mice also exhibited different brain chemistry when fighting at home. The testosterone that courses through the body acts through androgen receptors, basically bodily sensors. The more receptors there are, the greater the effect of testosterone. In Fuxjager's studies, regardless of where a fight occurred, there was an increase in androgen receptors in one region of the brain. But in two brain regions—the nucleus accumbens and the central tegmental area, which govern motivation and reward reinforcement, respectively—the receptor level increased only if the mouse had its dispute at home.

Even *after* the battle, there was an observable spike in testosterone in the mice that won fights at home. When the same mouse won fights in an unfamiliar cage, no demonstrable testosterone release occurred after the encounter.

"For the mice, a home fight is a more important fight," says Fuxjager, now a professor of biology at Wake Forest. "They want to protect their home turf. They want to protect their resources. They want to protect their mate or their offspring. They're more motivated, and there's a different physiological effect that comes with

---

2. When word of this study first trickled out, Fuxjager received angry communiqués from the local PETA chapter. At Fuxjager's request, we pause here to note that this was not the rodent version of Fight Club. In fact, no mice were harmed in the making of this science. These were territorial disputes, simulating the kind of conflicts mice would naturally have in the wild. They would nip at each other but wouldn't draw blood, much less kill each other. It was clear, though, which mouse won each dispute, because it remained in the space while the loser retreated.

that. It's clear that winning at home has different effects on physiology than winning in other environments."

While the hockey goon isn't dropping his gloves at center ice to protect his offspring, he may be subject to changes in brain chemistry similar to those found in the mice. When he fights in a familiar environment, he might be more sensitive to testosterone, and his rewards circuit might be stimulated in a way that his opponent's isn't. As in the mice, this surge of testosterone could lead to a heightened level of aggression and, in turn, a heightened rate of success in fights at home.

FUXJAGER also observed a longer-lasting consequence in his research. When it comes to fighting, there is a winner effect: The more often mice won, the more likely they were to seek out fights. In other words, *winning fights is addictive.*

Again, the evidence is in the brain circuitry. Regardless of whether the fights were at home or away, winning mice exhibited more androgen sensitivity and more activity in the regions of the brain that modulate social aggression, motivation, and reward. And these neurological changes lasted for several days after the fights, which means, says Fuxjager, that long-term changes in brain circuitry could motivate these mice to seek more fighting opportunities. "You win a fight at home, and you increase [the] sensitivity of these brain regions to testosterone. Then the testosterone acts and makes you hungry for more fighting."

This should give us pause when we valorize NHL goons, or even when we excuse them as an ineradicable part of hockey culture. An enforcer is likely to fight because it's his designated role on the team, because he has experience, because he has confidence. But he's also likely to fight because his brain chemistry—his risk-reward circuitry—becomes different from that of his teammates.

In the case of Probert, he fought early and often, starting in junior hockey. By his rookie season with the Red Wings he had already been in innumerable fights; his taste for battle was well cultivated, as perhaps was his neurological drive to fight. In his first

NHL season he tallied 23 penalty minutes for each of the eight goals he scored.

Probert's 398 penalty minutes in the 1987–88 season rank as one of the highest totals in NHL history. And when he retired in 2002, he had logged 3,300 penalty minutes, fifth most of all time. Given what we know about the altered brain chemistry that comes with fighting—the effect of risk-taking, the rewiring of the pleasure centers—it seems reasonable to wonder whether such tendencies were also reflected in his risky off-ice behavior, such as his cocaine use and a motorcycle DUI.

Bob Probert died on July 5, 2010, at age 45. The cause of death was heart failure. Yet by that time Probert was showing signs of memory loss and a short temper—so much so that he agreed to donate brain-tissue samples to researchers at Boston University. They determined that he suffered from the same degenerative disease, chronic traumatic encephalopathy (CTE), that's become so tragically common among NFL players. You inevitably wonder how much was owed to the rewiring that came with fighting—both at home and away?

The Curse of the Expert

Life was good for Andy Roddick in the fall of 2003. He had won the U.S. Open men's singles title after celebrating his 21st birthday during the tournament. He had a charming celebrity girlfriend and millions in endorsements, and he would finish the year as the top-ranked tennis player in the world.

But, by accident of birth, Roddick had the misfortune of being a contemporary of Roger Federer. By 2004 the Swiss maestro had married his exquisite talent to a maturing disposition, and he was beginning his ascent of the sport. Often Federer's victories came at Roddick's expense. (In their 24 head-to-head matches, Federer would win 21 times.) Roddick's fortunes were dealt another blow a few years later when Rafael Nadal achieved cruising altitude. Nadal, a teenager from the Spanish island of Mallorca, played something resembling a tribal dialect of tennis, a funky cognate predicated on lefty spins and angles that defied physics and geometry in equal measure.

Roddick remained an elite player, but he sometimes felt akin to the fifth Beatle or the sixth of those burger-making guys. And by 2006 it had gotten worse: He was losing early and often, his confidence disintegrating. After dropping a match to a lesser light at an event in California, Roddick lamented, "We all have the ability. I think it has to do with confidence more than anything. I think that comes through at big moments. . . . Why would I feel confident right now? If that was the case, I don't think we'd be sitting here having this funeral-like press conference. It's just weird because, you know . . . I used to hit for a half hour and then go eat Cheetos the rest of the day. Now I'm really trying to make it happen, being professional, really going for it. And I miss my Cheetos."

That spring Roddick didn't get out of the first round of the French Open. A few weeks later, at Wimbledon—where, two years running, he had reached the final only to lose, naturally, to Federer—Roddick lost in the third round to a British teenager with an unruly head of hair. In retrospect there was no shame in that defeat; a few years later, shorn and polished, Andy Murray would become the first British male since the 1930s to win Wimbledon. But Roddick, lacking in self-belief and expelled from the top 10 that day, was adrift.

When he returned to the United States, he announced that he was hiring a new coach. The choice was—at once—inspired, intriguing, and bizarre: Jimmy Connors.

While Connors had always been a profoundly polarizing force, his bona fides as a player were never in question. Here was one of the most accomplished men ever to grip a racket. In a career that spanned more than 20 years, Connors won a record 109 singles titles. There were more powerful players and more natural athletes, but none had Connors's taste for battle.

Connors hadn't done much coaching, but he explained that he would bring his singular intensity to bear with Roddick. How could he help? "It's not always in the game," Connors said at the time. "It's the intangibles that could make the difference, along with a few tweaks here and there. I'm not sitting down there breaking down and criticizing everything. I'm just trying to make him the best that he can be."

It was unclear what, besides attitude, Connors brought to the proverbial table. Before Roddick called, Connors hadn't followed tennis and didn't know much about the top, say, 100 players on the ATP Tour. Fair enough. But even after a few months with Roddick, Connors had done little to familiarize himself with the field.

Technique wasn't Connors's strong suit, either. Nor was he a particularly gifted strategist. His discussions about tactics would often devolve into terse coachspeak and sports homilies. *Never quit fighting. . . . Worry about yourself and not the guy on the other side of the net. . . . It's a marathon, not a sprint.* Connors would later admit that he knew, instinctively, what he wanted Roddick to do, but that he had a hard time communicating his thoughts.

For a while, anyway, Connors's mere presence and aura were enough. Roddick won a summer event in Cincinnati. At the U.S. Open he reached the singles final. While he fell to Federer (no surprise there), he was back in the top 10, projecting self-belief and blasting the ball with abandon. Lack of Cheetos notwithstanding, it was a lot like old times.

But by early 2008, Roddick's relationship with Connors had run its course. They split amicably. Roddick then announced that Larry Stefanki would succeed Connors. Stefanki and Connors had been contemporaries on the circuit. They were both born in Illinois and moved to California. But the comparisons ended there.

As a player, Stefanki was a journeyman who won one title. While Connors routinely cruised through tournament draws and departed with the trophy, Stefanki posted a lifetime pro record of 52-87 and earned less than $300,000 total, roughly 3 percent of Connors's career prize money. Stefanki was as contemplative and measured—mystical, almost—as Connors was brash and outspoken.

Stefanki had coached a number of other players, and Roddick had known him casually. But Roddick didn't realize just how radically different the new coaching regime would be. Stefanki arrived for work the first day armed with a notebook. When Roddick asked what it was, Stefanki said he had taken some notes at Roddick's previous match. "It was just meticulous," Roddick recalls. "He was hitting on things I'd never thought about before."

Because he'd coached other men on the circuit, Stefanki knew the field and the players' tendencies in a way that Connors didn't. And he approached coaching not as a quirky diversion but as a true second career. He prepared diligently, embraced technology, and tried to find ways to innovate. He noticed nuances.

Beyond that, Stefanki could articulate his thoughts and verbalize precisely what he saw and what he wished Roddick would do differently. Stefanki never came close to replicating Connors's success on the court and was not in the same phylum as a player, but he was exponentially better at seeing the game and explaining it.

When Roddick compares his coaches, he stresses that he's not throwing Connors under the tour bus. "Jimmy was a shot in the arm, which is exactly what I needed at that time," he says. "Larry was more of a long-term play, the guy who was going to help put me in the place where I'd have the best chance of winning."

And Roddick is sympathetic to Connors's shortcomings. "I can't teach tennis for shit," Roddick says. "If a nine-year-old asks me how to serve, I would have absolutely no idea what to say. 'Just hit the ball, kid.' I'm telling you, I would be totally worthless. I don't even know if I could explain how to grip the racket."

There is, of course, a certain irony to it all. Why would Jimmy Connors, a figure on tennis's Mount Rushmore, struggle to explain the simplest concepts, while Larry Stefanki, a pro tennis commoner who won fewer than half his career matches, had the savant-like ability to see the game within the game and to explain it in easily graspable terms?

Turns out this is a common phenomenon. Surely you've heard the expression "Those who can't do, teach." (And maybe you've heard the follow-up, usually attributed to Woody Allen: "And those who can't teach, teach gym.") Well, here's an important corollary: Those who *can* do often can't teach.

The better we get at a task, the worse we often become at articulating what we're doing. So it is that the Great Ones are often beset by what is sometimes called the *curse of expertise*: They struggle to communicate what has always come naturally to them. When the Pro Bowl quarterback who threw the game-winning touchdown shrugs after being asked by the sideline reporter, "How did you it?" he's not necessarily being coy. When track star Gwen Torrence was once asked to explain her sprinting virtuosity, and she said, "I don't know; the gun goes off and I run as fast as I can, just like I've been doing for as long as I can remember," she might have been speaking candidly.

They can't put into words what they just did any more than you and I can offer an informative description of how we walk down the street. ("I dunno, Erin, I just kinda put one foot in front of the other. Take it one step at a time, you know?") Why is it so hard? Because, as Andy Roddick noted, being an expert at *doing* something doesn't always translate into being an expert at *explaining how* to do it.

This is an important conclusion with implications for teaching, mentoring, and business training. It's also one that gets us a bit closer to understanding one of the great mysteries in sports: Why do the best players often make the worst coaches, and vice versa?

THERE are plenty of examples of this in golf, tennis, boxing, and other individual sports. But the curse of expertise expresses itself in team sports as well. You could argue (not unreasonably) that team sports provide a more complicated dynamic, that the coach of a team is more akin to a military general or a CEO than to an instructor or a tutor, and that you have to control for quality of talent and payroll level when assessing team coaching performance. And yet in team sports, too, the history is unambiguous: The list of elite players who have fared poorly as coaches is too long to chronicle fully here.

Try to recall an A-list athlete from a team sport who turned to coaching and came anywhere near replicating his or her success as a player. Maybe Bill Russell. *Maybe.* He was successful as a player-coach, sure, but otherwise he boasted a sub-.500 coaching record. Beyond Russell, it's tough. Elgin Baylor turned in a coaching record of 86-135. Even discounting that he worked for the sad-sack New Orleans Jazz franchise (an excellent apprenticeship for his subsequent tenure as a Los Angeles Clippers executive), this was hardly a second career worthy of his excellence as a player. Another NBA Hall of Famer from Baylor and Russell's era, Bob Cousy, fared little better, going 141-207 as coach of the Cincinnati Royals and the Kansas City–Omaha Kings in the early '70s.

More recently, Magic Johnson coached the Los Angeles Lakers for 16 games near the end of the 1993–94 season. At one point he turned to an assistant and asked rhetorically, "What have I gotten myself into?" Magic's former teammate (and fellow Hall of Famer) James Worthy later commented, "I remember pulling Magic Johnson to the side. I was like, 'You're Magic. Anthony Peeler might take three years to learn what you do in a week.'" Coach Johnson lost five of his first six games and resigned after the season, his career coaching record a dismal 5-11.

Of course, you can't talk about Magic without mentioning Larry Bird, and Bird might be the closest you'll find to an elite player turned successful coach (excluding the player-coach variety). He boasted a .687 winning percentage with the Pacers and was voted NBA Coach of the Year his first season. But he didn't last long; his entire coaching career spanned just three seasons. Isiah Thomas's record as a coach and executive was unquestionably impressive, but more in the way of *my, what an impressive multicar pileup*. Look beyond his pedestrian .456 winning percentage and you'll find a remarkable litany of lawsuits and salary-cap mismanagement, not to mention the bankrupting of an entire league, the CBA.

While Michael Jordan never coached, he might be the ultimate illustration of the lack of correlation between playing excellence and post-retirement sports success. He joined the Washington Wizards in 2000 as president of basketball operations; in 2001 he came out of retirement to play for the team. This period should have doubled as a celebratory send-off for an unrivaled player: Jordan as the wise veteran who, at age 40, had lost his primacy as a player but was imparting his wisdom to the next generation. But it wasn't like that at all. Instead there was a palpable friction between Jordan and the other Wizards, virtually all of whom had worshipped him before he became their boss/teammate.

Jordan was less a mentor than a tormentor. He could not grasp why these younger players couldn't perform as he once had. Eyes ablaze, he cursed at them with disgust. He was particularly rough on Kwame Brown, whom Jordan had selected with the first pick in the 2001 NBA draft. (According to *The Washington Post*, Jordan was known to call Brown a "flaming faggot," among other terms of endearment, often reducing the player to tears.) Owing to a personality conflict with Jordan, swingman Rip Hamilton was traded to Detroit, where he would become an NBA champion and All-Star. "Michael was tough," Wizards assistant John Bach told *Sports Illustrated*. "But that's just who he is, attempting to make [his teammates] better."

But that's the thing: He didn't make his teammates better. Jon covered the NBA at the time and recalls that it was a fool's errand trying to get those teammates to identify specific pearls of wisdom His Airness was dispensing to them. It became clear that Jordan's attitude reflected the Nike catchphrase he helped to popularize: Just Do It. He didn't (couldn't?) share pointers or technical expertise. He simply wanted Popeye Jones and Tyronn Lue and Jahidi White and other teammates imbued with only a fraction of his talent to do as he did. And when they didn't (couldn't?), Jordan got pissed.

Even worse than Jordan's record as a mentor and motivator with Washington was his performance as a talent evaluator. In the front office of the Wizards and later the Charlotte Bobcats, Jordan drafted or acquired a list of high-profile busts that includes not only Brown but also Adam Morrison and DeSagana Diop. He traded away Hamilton and Tyson Chandler, which didn't help Jordan's teams much but did help the Pistons and Mavericks win *their* championships. That Jordan could be as great as he was on the court but as lousy as he's been in the front office suggests that experts not only have difficulty explaining how they do what they do but can also have difficulty assessing talent in others.

In the NBA, it seems to be the journeymen, the basketball Stefankis, who fare best as coaches. As we began to write this chapter in the summer of 2014, four teams remained in the NBA playoffs: Indiana, Miami, Oklahoma City, and San Antonio. Pacers coach Frank Vogel played for Juniata College in Pennsylvania before transferring to Kentucky, where he was on the jayvee team but, more important, was a student manager for the varsity under Rick Pitino. Spurs coach Gregg Popovich was captain of his team at the Air Force Academy but never played a minute in the NBA. Nor did Eric Spoelstra, the Miami coach, who played for the University of Portland. Scott Brooks, then of Oklahoma City, enjoyed a 10-year NBA career, but by his own admission he was a marginal player, averaging fewer than five points per game.

Basketball is not the only team sport in which the top coaches were not top players. As his nickname, the Great One, suggests, Wayne Gretzky was a singular hockey player, a winner of 10 scoring titles, nine Hart Trophy (MVP) awards, and four Stanley Cups. He was something other than great as a coach, however. During his four seasons behind the bench of the Phoenix Coyotes, Gretzky posted a record of 143-161-24.

How about baseball? Ted Williams, the peerless hitter, batted .406 in 1941, the last year a major-league batter crossed the .400 threshold. Yet as manager of the Washington Senators,[1] Williams had a winning percentage that was scarcely higher, .429, as his teams went 273-364 over four forgettable seasons. He was recently named by a website one of the "10 Worst Managers in MLB History." Pete Rose stands out as a perennial all-star with some managing success, namely a .525 career winning percentage and 1985 Manager of the Year honors. Of course, his managerial stint stands out for other reasons as well, suggesting that perhaps one key to a successful transition from star player to star manager is, shall we say, extracurricular financial incentive.

As exceptional a major-league pitcher as Bob Gibson was, he was exceptionally subpar as a major-league pitching coach. The Hall of Fame fireballer was famous for strolling to the mound to counsel one of his pitchers and hissing, *Just throw the damn ball over the damn plate.* As the reliever Steve Bedrosian, who toiled under Gibson in Atlanta, complained to *The Philadelphia Inquirer*, "Bob Gibson was the kind of coach that believed you always should throw hard. But he wanted everyone to bring it all the time. And he said when you feel tired and don't think you have a good fastball, you had to grunt a little more."

The most successful baseball managers often seem to have been marginal players, sometimes good enough to make the majors—and in the case of Joe Torre, even win an MVP award during one atypically excellent season—but seldom stars. Same goes for those who

---

1. Who became the Texas Rangers in 1971, Williams's final year at the helm.

populate their coaching staffs. Consider this: The 1976 California Angels batted .235 as a team. For decades this stood as the worst collective average for an American League team in the era of the designated hitter. Yet a remarkable *five* hitters on that historically inept team—Bobby Bonds, Tommy Davis, Mike Easler, Adrian Garrett, and Ron Jackson—would become major-league hitting coaches.

TO be fair, so far we've been cherry-picking names. We thought of great players who failed as coaches, and we assumed that the readiness with which such examples sprung to mind confirmed the proposition. What would a more rigorous look at the numbers tell us? We set out to answer this question for the world of baseball.

As of the time we're writing this, the active manager with the highest career winning percentage is the Cardinals' Mike Matheny, at .563. As a player, Matheny had career "slash" stats (batting average/on-base percentage/slugging percentage) of .239/.293/.344, well below league averages during his era. His career WAR (Wins Above Replacement), a metric designed to quantify how many wins a player is worth to his team beyond how an average minor-league replacement would have performed, was essentially zero. Negative 0.3, to be precise—a number akin to Bluto Blutarski's GPA, suggesting that had the baseball gods replaced Matheny with an unknown Triple-A call-up, his teams would never have known the difference.

Second among active managers in winning percentage: Joe Girardi, just a notch below Matheny at .562. Girardi was a major-league catcher and did make an All-Star team. His RBI triple off Greg Maddux in the 1996 World Series gave the Yankees a lead they wouldn't relinquish in their first title clincher in two decades. But the statistics paint Girardi as another middle-of-the road contributor. His slash stats were also below league averages: .267/.315/.350. His career WAR of 5.7 means that over a 15-year career, the sum total of his player value translated into just 0.4 extra wins per season for the teams he played on.

But we're still not making a particularly rigorous statistical case. Poring over the careers of individual managers isn't much more persuasive than our cherry-picking earlier. We can tell you that the manager with the highest career winning percentage of all time, Joe McCarthy, never made it to the majors. We can tell you that even his *minor-league* hitting stats were unimpressive—almost smack-dab in the middle of the Mathenys and Girardis. But without analyses that aggregate across entire groups of managers, we can't offer an informed assessment of whether the most successful managers tend to be journeyman players or whether that just *seems* to be the case. So let's look at some aggregated data.

Of the 30 active MLB managers as of Opening Day 2015, three were pitchers (Bud Black, John Farrell, Bryan Price). Three isn't enough for a meaningful statistical analysis, so we'll stick to hitters. Of the 27 remaining managers, four (Terry Collins, Fredi González, Joe Maddon, Buck Showalter) never played in the majors, and one (Jeff Banister, the first-year manager of the Texas Rangers) batted only once in the big leagues (a single; career batting average: 1.000!). That leaves us with a dataset of 22 active managers with enough of a playing-career sample to analyze. We then looked up *Baseball Reference*'s contemporary league averages[2] throughout the playing career of each manager. This allowed us to compare each manager's hitting stats to the performance of his average peer. By our calculations, the league average slash-stat line during the playing careers of our 22 managers was .266/.334/.408. The average player performance of the 22 active managers themselves was .254/.320/.376.

2015 MLB Managers' Playing Statistics

Manager	BA	OBP	SLG
Ausmus, Brad	.251	.325	.344
Bochy, Bruce	.239	.298	.388
Cash, Kevin	.183	.248	.278

---

2. Defined by *Baseball Reference* as the performance that a league average non-pitcher would have had in the same season in the same ballparks.

Francona, Terry	.274	.300	.351
Gibbons, John	.220	.316	.360
Girardi, Joe	.267	.315	.350
Hale, Chip	.277	.346	.363
Hinch, A. J.	.219	.280	.356
Hurdle, Clint	.259	.341	.403
Matheny, Mike	.239	.293	.344
Mattingly, Don	.307	.358	.471
McClendon, Lloyd	.244	.325	.381
Melvin, Bob	.233	.268	.337
Molitor, Paul	.306	.369	.448
Redmond, Mike	.287	.342	.358
Roenicke, Ron	.238	.353	.338
Sandberg, Ryne	.285	.344	.452
Scioscia, Mike	.259	.344	.356
Ventura, Robin	.267	.362	.444
Weiss, Walt	.258	.351	.326
Williams, Matt	.268	.317	.489
Yost, Ned	.212	.237	.329

Note: shaded box = statistic below contemporary league average for that individual's playing career.

Not listed are active managers at the start of the 2015 season who were pitchers (Bud Black, John Farrell, Bryan Price), who never made it to the majors as players (Terry Collins, Fredi González, Joe Maddon, Buck Showalter), or who had only one big-league at-bat (Jeff Banister).

In other words, among active managers in 2015 who had major-league at-bats, their playing career batting average was 12 points below the league average, on-base percentage was 14 points below average, and slugging percentage was 32 points below average. So if the question is who *gets* managerial jobs these days, the answer seems to be: journeymen with somewhat below-average career statistics.

In fact, there's some basis for suggesting that today's managers are players with *disappointing* careers. Twelve active managers in 2015 were first-round draft choices. The career slash-stat line for this subset of managers who were once highly touted prospects is just as unimpressive: .253/.321/.381.

But, you might (and should) ask, what about the *most successful* managers? What do their playing statistics look like? Of course, there's no one way to assess managerial success—you can look at career winning percentage, World Series titles, winning with multiple teams, longevity, etc. We decided to study managers who have been deemed the most successful by their peers and the sportswriters who covered them. There are currently 22 managers in the Baseball Hall of Fame. One, Tommy Lasorda, was a pitcher. Three (Joe McCarthy, Frank Selee, Earl Weaver) never made it to the majors as players. A fourth, Walter Alston, made it to the big leagues but batted only once (alas, a strikeout). That leaves us with a sample of 17.

Back to *Baseball Reference*: The league average slash-stat line, aggregating across the playing careers of all 17 of these Hall of Fame managers, was .269/.335/.382. The numbers these elite managers themselves put up were .262/.335/.346. Simply put: Hall of Fame baseball managers were mediocre to below-average major-league ballplayers.

Hall of Fame Managers' Playing Statistics

Manager	BA	OBP	SLG
Anderson, Sparky	.218	.282	.249
Cox, Bobby	.225	.310	.309
Durocher, Leo	.247	.299	.320
Hanlon, Ned	.260	.325	.340
Harris, Bucky	.274	.352	.354
Herzog, Whitey	.257	.354	.365

Huggins, Miller	.265	.382	.314
La Russa, Tony	.199	.292	.250
Lopez, Al	.261	.326	.337
Mack, Connie	.244	.305	.300
McGraw, John	.334	.466	.410
McKechnie, Bill	.251	.301	.313
Robinson, Wilbert	.273	.316	.346
Southworth, Billy	.297	.359	.415
Stengel, Casey	.284	.356	.410
Torre, Joe	.297	.365	.452
Williams, Dick	.260	.312	.392

Note: shaded box = statistic below contemporary league average for that individual's playing career.

Not listed are HOF managers who were pitchers (Tommy Lasorda), or who never made it to the majors as players (Joe McCarthy, Frank Selee, Earl Weaver), or who had only one big-league at-bat (Walter Alston).

Finally, we can also ask the same question the other way around. Instead of *What kind of players were the greatest managers ever?*, how about *What kind of managers were the greatest players ever?* The song remains the same: not so hot. Of the 240 baseball players inducted into the Hall of Fame, 36 went on to manage (we're excluding those who did so only as player-managers). They compiled a career managerial winning percentage of just .461.[3] Historically, Hall of Fame baseball players make below-average managers.

ADMITTEDLY, there's no single explanation for what's going on here. In the spring of 2015, ESPN posed the question to then-rookie Twins manager Paul Molitor, himself a Hall of Fame player. Moli-

---

3. This number excludes seasons in which these 36 Hall of Famers served as player-managers (which 20 of them did at least once). Including those seasons doesn't make their managerial performance *that* much better: The cumulative winning percentage rises slightly, to .478.

tor's response: "I don't really know why more guys haven't tried. Maybe they don't have the need or are afraid of the commitment or afraid of failure."

For one thing, personality likely plays a role. Perhaps a certain level of egotism, self-confidence, and self-discipline is required to attain the highest levels of athletic success; perhaps some of these traits don't translate into success in coaching. Much as great pitchers are rarely great hitters, maybe playing and coaching prowess are skill sets that rarely overlap.

Money is also relevant. The most elite of the elite athletes may have little financial incentive to get into coaching. Larry Stefanki earned $300,000 in his career; Jimmy Connors made more than $8 million. Maybe it shouldn't surprise us to learn which of the two was more motivated to take up and refine the coaching trade. Those numbers have only skyrocketed: Roger Federer will retire with a net worth deep into nine figures; LeBron James has already earned more than $130 million in salary before the age of 30, not even counting his piles of endorsement money. It's hard to envision men with similarly expansive portfolios putting in long hours after retirement breaking down batting-practice video with minor-league prospects in Toledo or ironing out the putting kinks of a young player on the back practice green.

Still, the most celebrated, successful, and well-compensated players of past eras have often given it a shot, whether as coaches, front-office execs, or both: Gretzky. Various NBA Dream Teamers, from Magic to Bird to Jordan. And the stories of their failures—or, at least, lack of sustained success—often share themes: Roddick thinks Connors struggled to explain his craft. Jordan couldn't articulate what, exactly, he wanted his teammates and draftees to do. Bob Gibson just said to throw harder (and grunt louder).

All of these examples are consistent with the research conclusion that there's a *curse of expertise*. The same tendencies that improve our performance in one domain don't always help us explain it in another—in fact, sometimes they make it harder. For example, recent studies have demonstrated that expert athletes have a remarkable ability to predict outcomes on their field/court/pitch based on minimal movements by their opponents. In this research, respondents are shown video clips leading up to a critical athletic moment: the seconds before a basketball jump shot or a soccer penalty kick. The video then stops milliseconds before the ball is released or kicked, and the viewer is asked to predict the outcome. Will the jumper go in the basket? Will the penalty-taker choose to aim for the right or the left post?

Experts outperform novices on tasks like these. But they don't usually realize why. It's the smallest details—how open the penalty-taker's hips are positioned moments before contact—that make a difference, and while the expert's brain becomes fine-tuned enough to pick these up, the expert herself often doesn't know it.

As a team of Italian neuroscientists studying basketball perceptions concluded, "Achieving excellence in sports may be related to the fine-tuning of specific anticipatory . . . mechanisms that endow elite athletes' brains with the ability to predict others' actions ahead of their realization." Of course, experts can't share with others these skills that they themselves don't realize or fully appreciate.

Interestingly, it's not just visual experience that contributes to this form of expertise. It's *motor* experience, too. As in experience going up for a rebound after a missed jumper, or taking (or trying to stop) a penalty kick. So-called experts whose experience is more observational—fans, sports media—don't fare as well on these anticipatory tasks. Functional MRI (magnetic resonance imaging) studies of the brain show that when the expert athlete views a scene like this, he or she experiences increased activation not only in regions of the brain associated with perception but also in those associated with motor skill. In other words, the expert brain figures out more quickly what its opponent is doing and then also starts preparing the body to respond promptly to this forecasted action.

In fact, in one study of experienced soccer forwards and goalkeepers, distracting magnetic stimulation of brain regions associated with motor representation undermined experts' (but not non-experts') abilities to anticipate where penalty kicks were headed. So being an elite athlete requires exceptional refinement of perceptual *and* motor skills, not to mention extraordinary inter-action between the two systems. How, exactly, are the Great Ones supposed to impart these well-honed and automatized tendencies of the brain to others?

You don't even have to drill down to the neural level to identify differences between experts and others. Just talking to and observing experts reveals how differently they see and interact with the world. For example, one aspect of expertise is learning how to skip steps. Non-experts have to work through a rote checklist of procedures in order to accomplish a goal; experts figure out shortcuts, sometimes even without recognizing that they've done so.

Another component of expertise is developing a more abstract mental picture of how things work. In one study of military electricians, what separated the more skilled technicians from their less skilled colleagues was the ability to create a mental model of how a device worked. This allowed them to make a series of specific observations and quickly deduce a list of potential diagnoses and a plan for proceeding.

Non-experts were more likely to describe the same device as a group of unrelated parts and to rely on trial and error (switching different parts in and out) to solve problems. In short, research demonstrates that "the way experts store and process information may make it difficult for them to share that expertise with others regardless of whether or not they are motivated to do so."

So experts see—and mentally organize—the world differently from the rest of us. And they often don't realize it. In fact, failure to recognize how less skilled others are experiencing things is one of the major obstacles to the transmission of expertise. Witness the fruitlessness of a Bob Gibson mound visit or a Michael Jordan mentoring session. Or, for that matter, the college-educated adult flustered by his inability to help his kid with math homework or the IT assistant stymied in her efforts to talk employees through basic computing tasks. If you can't see what's going on from the viewpoint of those who are less expert than you, you can't instruct effectively.

Consider a series of studies conducted at Stanford in which researcher Pamela Hinds compared the predictions of expert and non-expert LEGO builders. Yes, that's right, expert LEGO builders. Hinds knew she had experts on her hands because her research assistants conducted the training themselves: They had college students build four LEGO Star Wars V-Wing fighters—sans instruction manual, guided only by a visual model of the final product—in a marathon training session. Two weeks later, they asked these newly minted experts to assemble a fifth V-Wing fighter. (Apparently the Imperial LEGO troops were getting ready to mount quite the aerial assault.) In just two weeks this group had become very well versed in all things V-Wing-related.

But Hinds wasn't interested in their actual expertise. What she really wanted to know was whether they were able to remember, with accuracy, what the task had been like before they became experts. How easily could these savvy LEGOers put themselves back into the mindset of novices lacking V-Wing experience? Remember, it was only two weeks earlier that *they* had been beginners. If these supposed experts had already forgotten what it felt like to be less skilled and less experienced, imagine the mindset gulf that must exist between the Hall-of-Famer-turned-coach and the unpolished rookies on his roster.

Hinds asked her expert builders to estimate how long it would take a novice to assemble a LEGO V-Wing for the first time. The experts' estimate was eight minutes. In reality, though, the average novice took 12 minutes, 50 percent longer than the experts had predicted. And remember, the experts themselves had been novices just two weeks earlier, when it had taken *them* just over 12 minutes to build the ship for the first time without an instruction manual. All that the experts had to do to give a reasonable estimate was remember their own experience from a scant 10–14 days ago. They couldn't. Elite performers in all walks of life don't realize (or recall) how challenging their domain can be for non-elite performers.

• • •

SO we have these two conclusions regarding the curse of expertise: 1) elite performers see the world in complex ways that are difficult to recognize, much less articulate; and 2) elite performers struggle to put themselves in the shoes of those less skilled than they are.

Then, as if that weren't enough to threaten any link between athletic and coaching success, along comes more recent research indicating that *the mere act of explaining how to perform an athletic feat can make you worse at performing it yourself*. For a study they conducted in 2008, psychologists Mike Anderson and Kristin Flegal recruited a group of expert golfers and a group of beginning golfers to practice putting on a flat green. After a few dozen putts, the subjects were divided into two groups. In one, the participants were asked to spend a few minutes discussing their putts. The other group was given an unrelated distractor task.

After that, the golfers began putting again. Among the experts, those who had spent time talking about their putting now needed twice as many attempts to maneuver the ball into the hole as those who had not spent their break discussing how to putt. The novices, on the other hand, were not adversely affected by talking about their putting. In fact, some performed marginally better after the discussion.

As Sian Beilock, a psychology professor at the University of Chicago, puts it: "For well-learned activities like taking a free throw, hitting a simple putt, or playing a cadence [in music] that you have performed a thousand times in the past, thinking too much about the step-by-step processes of what you are doing can be detrimental."

In other words, we were wrong earlier when we compared the crossover between athletic and coaching performance to the limited relationship between a National Leaguer's pitching and hitting abilities. The analogy doesn't work—things are even *bleaker* for the elite athlete who wants to coach than they are for the big-league hurler who has to hit. The comparison would be apt only if each act of pitching a baseball somehow made a player just a tiny bit worse as a hitter. It's not just that there's a tenuous link between on-field prowess and coaching success. Being too good at one actually comes at the expense of the other.

What wide-ranging lessons are provided by this "curse of expertise" research? Well, first and foremost, now we know how to predict the next wave of elite managers simply by looking at the statistics of active players. The average playing career OPS (on-base plus slugging) of Hall of Fame managers is .681. Ladies and gentlemen, presenting your managerial Hall of Fame class of 2050: Brandon Inge (OPS of .685), Kurt Suzuki (.682), and Elvis Andrus (.677).

Okay, so that isn't really how this works. But it does appear that a baseball team in need of a manager should look to Girardis rather than Jeters. That an orchestra searching for a conductor might be better off with a capable musician who was never a first-chair virtuoso. And that just as LEGO savants quickly forget what life was like before they mastered their plastic-block universe and everything became awesome, so, too, do a short memory and failure to empathize impede the corporate manager's ability to effectively understand and mentor employees.

In even more concrete terms, researchers have begun to identify specific steps that experts can take to overcome this so-called curse. For one, collecting data helps. Experts' assumptions about which aspects of a task will be particularly challenging for novices aren't always on target. When teachers, for example, use frequent quizzes or other assessments to find out which concepts are giving their students the most trouble, they're able to tailor instruction more effectively.

Another useful strategy is to turn the expert-novice relationship into a two-way street. As detailed earlier, asking experts to articulate exactly how they do things can backfire—expertise often relies upon tacit knowledge that's difficult to put into words (and delicate enough to be disrupted by the mere act of describing it). Setting up an apprenticeship model in which the novice gets to shadow and observe the expert as she goes about her work turns out to be much more effective.

And, of course, the ultimate solution is anything that will

prompt experts to think about their own performance trajectory with more accuracy and understanding. Confronting them with evidence of their pre-expertise performance or asking them to write out a brief reflection on what they struggled with as novices can be an effective way to reinforce the mental link between their own past and the present of those they are instructing. Alas, easier said than done, since jotting down notes often goes together with expertise as seamlessly as . . . well, jotting down notes goes with Jimmy Connors. But the point remains: The curse of expertise can be surmounted with the right combination of mindset and strategy.

DON'T feel too bad for Jimmy Connors, though. In 2013 he was still living the good life at his estate in Santa Barbara. Aside from promoting his controversial memoir, he was largely out of the public eye. In a rare interview—for an ESPN *30 for 30* documentary that explored what made Connors so repugnant and alluring at the same time—he admitted that "tennis wasn't on the brain much."

But suddenly, midway through the summer, he got a call from Maria Sharapova. Not unlike Andy Roddick seven years earlier, Sharapova was wrestling with her form and motivation. In particular, she struggled against Serena Williams, who had beaten her 13 straight times, dating back eight years. Sharapova needed a change, and she needed a charge. Would Connors be her coach?

He agreed. He hadn't coached since parting with Roddick. And however little he knew about the men's game, he knew even less about women's tennis. If this had been match.com, the compatibility scores between Sharapova and Connors would have been low.

But, hey, who knows? As one tennis scribe predicted optimistically, "Upon further review, maybe it's not such an odd couple. Like Connors, Sharapova predicates her game largely on grit, compensating for a lack of raw talent or innate athleticism with a certain competitive zeal and an appetite for the fight." (Okay, that irrationally optimistic voice was Jon's.)

The first tournament of the Sharapova-Connors partnership

was in Cincinnati, the same event at which Roddick and Connors had their initial success. It went—how to put this?—decidedly less well. Sharapova lost her first match under Connors's tutelage. And promptly fired him.

The damage control was handled expertly. Sharapova declared, "It's not the right fit for this time in my career." The deposed coach took to Twitter, @JimmyConnors assuring everyone that he was fine: "Back home in SB—family, pups, and home cooking. Oh—I forgot, and a vodka on the rocks." There was never much of an explanation for the breakup, though months later Sharapova's agent told Jon, "Once they started working together a little bit, it wasn't clear to Maria what Jimmy had to offer."

As Connors's replacement, Sharapova hired Sven Groeneveld. His career-high pro ranking: No. 826.

As for Cooperstown, 2014 proved to be a banner year for managers, with Bobby Cox, Tony La Russa, and Joe Torre getting their day in the sun at the Hall of Fame. Of course, the honors were not for their playing careers. Torre's playing days were the best of the trio, by far. He won the National League MVP in 1971 with a phenomenal season in which he batted .363 and drove in 137 runs, numbers he'd never come close to approaching again. Far less impressive were the careers of Cox (.225 hitter over two brief seasons with the Yankees) and La Russa (.199 average in just 176 big-league at-bats spread out over six seasons with four teams).

Indeed, La Russa talked about the discrepancy between these numbers and his managerial record during his induction speech, even owning up to a touch of sheepishness about being feted at the pantheon of the game's greatest performers: "It's uncomfortable because I didn't make it as a player," he said. "Not even close."

He then related the tale of his being introduced to the Chamber of Commerce in the town where he had his first managerial job, a minor-league gig. Paul Richards, himself another mediocre player turned successful coach and executive, had the duty of introducing the rookie skipper to fans in Knoxville. "Well, if you're wondering about this boy that's going to manage this team," La Russa started, channeling Richards's Texas drawl. "You've heard that the worst player makes the best manager? This young player has a chance to be an *outstanding* manager."

After pondering his punch line for a moment amid the audience's laughter, La Russa concluded, "You know, it always hurts to hear the truth." Or, for that matter, to see it written in the heartless agate type of a slash-statistics line.

Acting on Impulse

WHY WE AREN'T SO DIFFERENT FROM THE
SPORTS HOTHEAD (L-O-B, CRABTREE!)

That Tony Stewart can maneuver a race car has never been in dispute. But Stewart's reputation for skilled and clever driving—for finding the perfect calibration of power and control—is rivaled by another reputation. When he races, he is, in sports parlance, a hothead. Not for nothing is Stewart nicknamed Smoke. Long as he is on talent, he is short on fuse.

In a prescient 2002 *Sports Illustrated* feature story titled "Road Rage: Tony Stewart Can Handle Everything—Except Himself," the brilliant writer Jeff MacGregor put it like this: "For sure, they say, he's one helluva driver, maybe the best on the track. But he can also be broody and hotheaded, they'll say. He runs a little tight, like a car that won't turn and wants to run into the wall. He is, in other words, flawed and fully human." Again, that was in 2002, years before Stewart flung his helmet at the windshield of a rival driver. Before he punched an Australian racetrack owner. And long before he crossed paths with Kevin Ward Jr.

Ward was, by his own reckoning, something of a hothead, too. Though more than 20 years younger than Stewart, he cut a similar figure. Growing up in upstate New York, near the Canadian border, Ward was a sprint-car fiend who regularly cut class in high school to enter auto races. He didn't suffer from a lack of self-confidence. Regardless of the weather or the time of day, he wore sunglasses. Ward "lived his life," wrote the New York *Daily News*, "with the throttle open and a foot to the floor."

On August 9, 2014, Stewart and Ward were among the 22 drivers in a 25-lap dirt-track race at Canandaigua Motorsports Park in upstate New York. For Ward, it was one of the biggest races of his young career. For Stewart, it was a return to his racing roots. He was in the area for the so-called Sunday money, NASCAR's Sprint Cup race at Watkins Glen. But, as he tends to do, he was happy to mix it up in his open-wheel sprint car the night before the "real" race. If this was the equivalent of Derek Jeter playing in a Long Island beer league the night before a Yankees game, so be it. It was part of Stewart's Everyman appeal.

If you were following sports (or the national news) at all that summer, you likely recall what happened next. Stewart ran Ward into a corner, causing him to crash, although it was not a huge wreck. In what might be called professional-grade road rage, Ward unbuckled his seat belt, got out of his car, and walked onto the track, looking for Stewart and his number 14 car, gesturing as if to say, "Lemme at him." It was an act not uncommon in racing. In fact, it recalled Stewart's 2012 confrontation with Matt Kenseth at Bristol Motor Speedway, which was punctuated by the notorious helmet throw.

As Ward gesticulated wildly on the track during the caution lap, other drivers strafed by. But right at the time when Ward should've come into Stewart's line of sight, Stewart seemed to gun his engine. The number 14 car fishtailed. Its right rear wheel struck Ward, dragged him under the car, and then ejected him into the air 50 feet down the track, where he landed and lay motionless. Shortly thereafter, Ward was declared dead at a local hospital. According to the coroner's report, the cause of death was "massive blunt trauma."

Without blaming the victim, think about the degree to which sound judgment deserted Ward. In the middle of a night race, wearing a black suit, black helmet, and black visor, with cars orbiting at the speed of interstate traffic, the man climbed onto a busy oval looking for a fight.

And what of Stewart, revving his engine from the safety of his vehicle as a human being stood perilously close to the side of the track? By the end of the following month, a grand jury in Ontario County, New York, had declined to indict Stewart in Ward's death. And in the summer of 2015, just days shy of the incident's one-year anniversary, Ward's family filed a wrongful-death lawsuit against Stewart in Lewis County Supreme Court. To this day, public sentiment remains mixed.

TO watch sports is to witness all manner of impulsive behavior. Along with stars and scrubs, wise veterans and callow rookies, clubhouse cancers and glue guys, *hotheads* are an archetype, a species of fauna native to sports. They are the jocks who let their primal instincts overwhelm their rational cores. They are the athletes (and occasionally coaches) whose decision-making trees seem to lack a few branches. They are the football players who get flagged for mindless 15-yard personal fouls, the hockey goons provoked into retaliation that leads to a power-play goal, the agitators who just can't seem to resist a good fight (or bite).

The French soccer player Zinedine Zidane was—as his affectionate nickname Zizou suggests—a beloved star during his gilded 17-season career, a midfielder esteemed for his poise and elegance. At least that was his reputation until the 2006 World Cup. In the final game of the tournament—and, tragically though not coincidentally, the final game of his career—Zidane infamously head-butted the chest of a goading Italian player in the waning minutes. It was a crucial lapse in cool that helped Italy clinch the Cup. It also redefined Zidane's legacy, especially outside Europe.

Not that Zidane has a monopoly on World Cup hotheadedness. Perhaps the seminal image of the 2014 event was not the Cup-winning goal by Germany's Mario Götze or Brazil's humiliation at home, but rather the vampiric Uruguayan striker Luis Suárez *biting* the shoulder of Italian defender Giorgio Chiellini. It earned Suárez a four-month FIFA suspension, in large part because it was not the first time he had made a mid-game snack of human flesh.[1]

And, of course, no discussion of opponent-biting would be complete without a token reference to Mike Tyson, who chomped on the ear of Evander Holyfield not once but twice during their 1997 heavyweight title fight.

More instances of athletes being divorced from poise: Roger Clemens throwing a bat at Mike Piazza during a 2000 World Series game. Serena Williams threatening to $@&%ing shove a tennis ball down a lineswoman's $@&%ing throat at the 2009 U.S. Open. Ron Artest, then with the Indiana Pacers (before his commitment to World Peace, in both name and deed) running into the stands to fight a fan during an NBA game in Detroit, sparking the so-called Malice at the Palace and earning a record 73-game suspension. John Tudor of the St. Louis Cardinals punching a different fan—of the electric rotating variety—after he was shelled during a 1985 World Series game. (The cut to Tudor's finger required stitches, though not as many as the 15 that Amar'e Stoudemire, then a New York Knicks star, needed after punching a glass case housing a fire extinguisher after a 2013 loss to the Miami Heat. BLOODY IDIOT was the obligatory headline in the next day's *New York Post*.)

It's not just athletes who fly off the handle, either. Woody Hayes, the longtime Ohio State football coach, once slugged an opposing player at the 1978 Gator Bowl. (Like Zidane's head butt, Hayes's punch would mark the end of a career and redefine a legacy.) It's hockey coaches challenging their counterparts through the Plexiglas partition (or in the case of the famously choleric Mike Keenan, physically challenging an NHL timekeeper). It's Joshua Adams, a Mississippi high school basketball ref, reacting to relentless goading during a game by fatally punching a coach outside the gym in 2014.

No sooner had the 2013 NFC Championship Game ended than Richard Sherman, the Seattle Seahawks' most voluble player, headed

---

1. It was hard not to admire the creativity of Suárez's explanation: "I hit my face against the player, leaving a small bruise on my cheek and a strong pain in my teeth."

toward Fox sideline reporter Erin Andrews, who was brandishing a microphone. Moments earlier, Sherman, an All-Pro cornerback, had blanketed San Francisco 49ers receiver Michael Crabtree, tipping away a last-minute end zone pass and causing a game-sealing interception. Andrews asked Sherman about the final play, and, well, you probably know what came next. Sherman glared into the camera and fired off the verbal equivalent of shrapnel.

"Well, I'm the best corner in the game! When you try me with a sorry receiver like Crabtree, that's the result you're going to get," he shouted in an angry rasp. Twitching in obvious agitation, Sherman took a quick breath and continued, "Don't you ever talk about me!"

Wait, what? Andrews stammered and asked Sherman to identify who had been talking about him. The player barked: "Crabtree. Don't you open your mouth about the best, or I'll shut it for you real quick. L-O-B!"[2]

This soliloquy was more WWE than NFL. It was jarring to virtually everyone, but to no one more than Andrews, who stammered a bit more before clumsily handing off to her colleagues back in the broadcast booth. It was, at once, excruciating and gripping television.

Sherman's oration would supersede the game itself. It would produce innumerable GIFs and Internet memes. "Sherman's Epic Rant," re-created by Kermit the Frog and Miss Piggy, would become a YouTube sensation. The reaction would overwhelm social media and turn into a national referendum with deeper themes. *Sherman was a thug. Sherman was a goon.* No, wait. *Sherman was simply an entertainer playing the role of the heel. The critics were racist.*

Sherman's background helped make the story compelling. While he was extraverted in the extreme—famous for spewing prodigious amounts of trash talk and for confronting ESPN's chief peacock, Skip Bayless—Sherman was also a communications major in college and was known as one of the more thoughtful and self-aware

---

2. For those who don't speak fluent Seahawk, that's L-O-B as in Legion of Boom, the preferred nickname of Seattle's fearsome secondary.

figures in the NFL. What had happened to *that* guy? Where was the articulate Stanford grad during the postgame interview with Andrews?

No one really knew, certainly not Sherman himself. Almost a month to the day after the San Francisco game, he cut a decidedly different figure as he sat at a table in a steakhouse at the Fontainebleau Hotel in Miami Beach. He was at the resort to host a *Sports Illustrated* function commemorating the 2014 Swimsuit Issue. Seattle had won the Super Bowl and been feted with a parade. Sherman had been injured in that game and was contemplating his rehab. He was surrounded by models as well as men in suits from the magazine. The rapper Flo Rida was set to perform nearby. Still, Sherman's Epic Rant was *the* conversation topic. "It still kind of cracks me up," the player said. "I look at that person and say, 'That's not me.' It mystifies, man."

It shouldn't. Sherman's tirade may have been out of character, but, like so many examples of athletic hotheadedness, it was consistent with what research tells us about human nature. Those who have studied the effects of physiological arousal on thought and behavior report that we seem to have two personalities: one for cool conditions and one for when we are gripped by hot passion.

DAN Ariely and George Loewenstein are pioneering researchers in an interdisciplinary field known as behavioral economics. Ariely, a best-selling author and experimental psychologist (whose work on the allure of the free we discuss on page 4), now teaches at Duke's Fuqua School of Business. Loewenstein earned his Ph.D. in economics and holds an endowed chair in the Department of Social and Decision Sciences at Carnegie Mellon. In decades of published research, the two scholars have tackled a wide range of issues related to decision-making, including irrationality, empathy, dishonesty, and negotiation strategy. They also have a thing or two to teach us about what might be up with Tony Stewart and Richard Sherman.

One of the major conclusions to emerge from both researchers' work is that human nature is surprisingly state-dependent. That is, depending on the circumstances, we think and act like very different people. (Or, to invoke the title of Sam's previous book, *Situations Matter*.) For example, we operate in a "hot state" of mind (and body) when we're angry, hungry, in pain, or generally aroused. Other times we're in a "cold state." Our thought processes and behavioral tendencies vary dramatically from one state to the other, often in ways that we don't fully appreciate. Cold-state self has a hard time predicting how hot-state self will react, and vice versa.

In 2006, Ariely and Loewenstein collaborated on a paper titled "The Heat of the Moment," in which they set out to investigate one aspect of the so-called hot state: how we think when we're physiologically aroused. They focused on sexual arousal. So we have to offer a disclaimer: The details of the study we're about to describe would get an R rating from the Motion Picture Association of America. (We'll add a second disclaimer: The question of how sexual arousal differs from athletic/competitive arousal is an important one to which we'll return shortly.)

In Ariely and Loewenstein's study, male students at UC Berkeley were recruited for an experiment that they knew would involve masturbation. Each was given a laptop to borrow for 24 hours, allowing him to complete the study in private. Each student was also given a small keypad that could be held in one hand, freeing up the other hand to, as the authors describe it, "self-stimulate," but only to a "sub-orgasmic level of arousal."

Participants were instructed to run a program on the laptop that would present a series of questions. In some of the sessions, the men answered these questions in a non-aroused state. In others, the program also cycled through a set of erotic photographs, and the men answered the questions via keypad while self-stimulating. This allowed researchers to explore differences in how the men tended to think when in a hot state and when in a cold state.

The questions fell into three categories. Category One: sexual risk-taking. The men were asked about their tendencies and attitudes regarding unprotected sex. For example: Would you always use a condom if you didn't know the sexual history of a new partner? And to what extent does a condom decrease sexual pleasure?

Category Two involved willingness to engage in morally problematic behavior to procure sex. For instance: Would you tell a woman you love her or encourage her to drink more to increase the chances of having sex with her?

Category Three stuck to simple questions about sexual attraction: Would it be fun to get tied up by your partner? Spanked by an attractive woman? Can you imagine having sex with a 50-year-old? How about 60? Would you consider sexual congress with an animal? And so forth.

Ariely and Loewenstein found that men's responses to questions in all three categories varied widely depending on arousal level. In a "cool," unaroused state, 42 percent found women's shoes erotic. In a "hot" state, 65 percent did. When aroused, respondents thought it would be significantly more fun to have sex with someone they hated or with someone extremely fat; they also reported being more likely to have sex without a condom, or to pay for a fancy dinner in hopes of facilitating a sexual encounter. As for sex with a 60-year-old, it appealed to only 7 percent of the college-age subjccts—until they were aroused, when the percentage jumped to 23.

Is it just men who react like this? No. Follow-up studies indicated that when aroused, women, too, object less to risky sexual behavior. And another question: Is this true only for sex? Daily personal experience suggests not: Arousal can change who we are in a variety of situations. Most of us don't fantasize about hitting a stranger's car with a golf club . . . until our blood boils after said stranger cuts us off in traffic. You're a demure and measured soccer mom . . . until the ref blows a call and you start screaming from the sidelines. You feel antagonized on social media and respond with a profane tweet. You get caught up in the heat of competition at a school auction and bid a small fortune for a collage of kindergarteners' handprints. Even outside the bedroom we seem to become different people when our bodies run hot.

But how about a more scientific answer? Does research really allow us to jump from conclusions about sexual stimulation to an assertion that physiological arousal stoked the fires that led Kevin

Ward Jr. to confront a speeding race car on foot, caused Richard Sherman's Vesuvian eruption beside Erin Andrews, and triggered various soccer stars to head-butt and bite their way into red-card ignominy? Studies of the brain suggest that the difference between sexual and competitive arousal may not be that large at all.

Consider a brain-imaging study conducted at Massachusetts General Hospital in Boston, in which healthy male participants went through what's known as a PET scan. PET stands for *positron emission tomography*, and the test works by detecting low levels of radiation released from a substance—called a tracer—that has been introduced into the body. The PET scanner monitors signals that are emitted by the tracer as it is absorbed by the body. A computer then creates a 3-D map of the tissue or organ in question. Physicians use a PET scan to assess the function of an organ. Neuroscience researchers have also turned to PET, using it, for example, to measure how different stimuli cause changes in blood flow in different regions of the brain.

Before showing up for the scan, each participant in the Mass General study was asked to write out descriptions of several autobiographical events. One had to be a "maximally pleasant" sexual encounter. Another involved "maximally pleasant" competitive arousal, such as scoring a game-clinching goal or winning a team championship. Yet other descriptions detailed more mundane, non-arousing events for baseline control comparisons.

A member of the research team read aloud and recorded, in a neutral tone of voice, the narratives written by each participant. This allowed the researchers to play back the audio to participants as they lay still in the PET scanner (picture the head resting in the center of a giant square doughnut). It also gave them control over what each subject was thinking about at any point during the course of the study. One by one, the audio-recorded narratives were played for the participant, who was instructed to close his eyes and imagine as vividly as possible the event described. Lying there as repeated images were taken of his brain—changes in blood flow in a particular region are considered evidence of corresponding changes in neural activity—each participant listened to his own story of sexual pleasure, his story about competitive glory, and a series of less arousing anecdotes.

The study results indicated that sexual and competitive arousal produce a number of parallel responses in the brain. Arousing thoughts of both types led to increased blood flow in the anterior cingulate cortex and anterior temporal cortex, regions of the brain often involved in emotion-related processes. Both forms of arousal led to *decreased* blood flow in what are known as heteromodal association areas: regions that receive and integrate signals sent by sensory and motor areas of the brain, allowing for higher-level thought, judgment, and expression. And in a much lower-tech outcome, participants reported their own estimates of their physiological arousal while hearing the sexual and competition stories (8.9 and 8.8 out of 10, respectively).

There's a danger of reading too much into the brain images taken during a PET scan study. It would be an oversimplification to argue on the basis of these changes in blood flow that both sexual and competitive arousal make brains more emotional. Or that both forms of arousal shut down the brain areas responsible for thoughtful and deliberative judgment. Or that winning your co-ed softball league feels just as good as sex. (It depends on the sex. And the softball league.) But the Mass General study does suggest that various hot states can have similar effects on the brain—that the riskier attitudes and lower standards espoused by Ariely and Loewenstein's self-stimulators might share characteristics with the thoughts and actions of athletic hotheads.

In fact, there's a case to be made that the arousal fueled by competition, exertion, and adrenaline might have *even more* of an impact on our thought processes than sexual arousal does. We spoke with Dr. Michael Lardon, a faculty member in the Department of Psychiatry at UC San Diego and consulting psychiatrist to U.S. Olympic teams at their Chula Vista, California, training center. Lardon is an expert on how the brain and body interact during athletic competition. He has worked with dozens of elite athletes, including Olympic medalists and Super Bowl and World Series champions. (In an interesting side note, Lardon's college roommate, at Stanford, was also a bit of an expert on elite performance: Eric Heiden, a five-time gold medalist in speed skating and now a physician himself.)

Lardon walked us through the basic effects of arousal. "Think of the brain as a series of highways," he explained. "You've got the thalamus—you can think of that as a relay station; the cortex, a place where consciousness, attention, and processing occur; and the amygdala, which also helps with decisions but plays a big role in all emotional response."

Under non-arousing circumstances, Lardon said, the following oversimplified series of events might occur: We perceive a stimulus in our environment; it's relayed to the thalamus; the cortex helps us digest it and ponder, at least briefly, the potential repercussions of how we might respond; the amygdala weighs in if an emotional response is called for; and we respond. Following this example, Lardon continued, "you decide that it's best not to give the umpire the finger because there are consequences, so you don't do it. . . . You just don't go crazy."

Arousal, Lardon said, "short-circuits that pathway," making us more prone to outbursts (such as flipping off that ump). When the arousal is sexual, emotion and imagery inundate the cortex, "revving it up," as Lardon put it. In the midst of this bombardment of excitement? The cortex is flooded, distorting rational thinking. "Bottom line is, you don't think the best," said Lardon.

But in many respects, the effects of competitive arousal are potentially *more* dramatic, Lardon suggested to us. Referring to the thalamus, the brain's relay station, "the fight-or-flight type response blows open the gate—going directly to the amygdala, or 'fear factory'—and we don't really go through the cortex at all," he explained. So while the brain ordinarily takes the high road from thalamus to cortex to amygdala, a tense and anxiety-producing situation sends us down the lower express route from thalamus directly to amygdala.

From an evolutionary perspective, this rerouting switch has served us well: When the prehistoric caveman saw the dangerous bear, he didn't stop to ponder various courses of action; the amygdala told him to be fearful and run (and not necessarily in that order). But when the modern caveman takes a questionable called third strike in the late innings of a playoff nail-biter, he blows open this very same gate. And bypassing the cortex means an increased chance that the batter, too, gets bypassed—for the duration of the game, after being ejected for cursing out the ump.

SO sexual arousal and the arousal of the last-minute goal-line stand are not the same thing, but their behavioral effects and neural processes often run in parallel paths. Consider a Week 3 NFL game between St. Louis and Dallas in September 2014. While the Rams were blowing a three-touchdown lead at home in a game they'd eventually lose to the Cowboys 34–31, TV cameras caught St. Louis tight end Jared Cook on the sideline shoving his own teammate, quarterback Austin Davis.

"I was heated, like anybody else," Cook said after the game. Then he took to Twitter to further explain, inadvertently yet directly quoting Ariely and Loewenstein's sexual arousal paper: "My actions from today's game were truly a mistake—unintentional and in the heat of the moment."

Perhaps you're still a skeptic, believing that Richard Sherman didn't fall victim to a short-circuited thalamus but instead carefully orchestrated his postgame rant for the sake of publicity. Research suggests the contrary, though, that Sherman was probably unaware of just how riled up he was when he took to the mic—much as Jared Cook was when he "unintentionally" shoved a teammate. The rest of us, too, often fail to realize how skewed our preferences become in a hot state. A wealth of studies argue convincingly that we often misattribute the sources of our arousal or simply fail to recognize arousal's influence in the moment.

The truth is, we're pretty poor prognosticators of how various experiences and altered states will affect us. And that's a conclusion with implications not only for the Pro Bowl cornerback but also for consumers, employees, and board members making non-televised decisions every day.

Arousal can make us take unnecessary risks. We know this

from Ariely and Loewenstein: Their aroused participants weren't just more attracted to anything that moved—their actual risk-assessment process was also impaired. They expressed more negative attitudes about condoms; they underestimated the importance of using birth control with a new partner who had an unknown sexual history.

In another study, researchers at Iowa State asked men to estimate the risk of contracting a sexually transmitted disease from a series of hypothetical new partners. Perceptions of risk dropped significantly when the photos of the women in question were sexually arousing. And arousal has also been implicated in risky financial decisions, though it remains unclear whether arousal is the cause or rather a symptom that reflects the stress and high stakes involved in making such choices.

Arousal can make us worse negotiators, leaving us angry or envious and undermining our ability to get what we want. In one set of studies at MIT Business School, researchers put individuals through their paces on a treadmill before turning them loose to negotiate. They found that physiological arousal has a polarizing effect on perceptions of negotiation outcome. For people who came into the study with a positive view of negotiating, being aroused increased their post-negotiation satisfaction. But for those who dreaded the back-and-forth of negotiating, being aroused left them less satisfied; they interpreted their physical symptoms as signs of frustration and displeasure.

And arousal can make us dumber. That's the idea behind using scantily clad male and female models to move product. But the same goes for non-sexual arousal. In one consumer study, participants were given a seven-minute exercise task. It wasn't the most demanding of physical challenges—repeatedly stepping onto and off a seven-inch-high block—but it was enough to get the heart pumping. Afterward they were asked to evaluate a series of magazine ads for various products. Some participants reviewed the ads almost immediately after the exercise period, while their pulse and blood pressure were still elevated. Others saw the ads after a seven-minute cool-down period. The potential consumers in a hot state made less rational assessments of the ads. They were more swayed by superficial characteristics, such as whether or not an ad included a celebrity endorsement. Their cooler-state contemporaries, on the other hand, were more thoughtful, considering the strength of the arguments and information presented about each product.

What can we do about all of this? There are ways to impede arousal. Among teenagers, motor vehicle accidents are the leading cause of death. Teen drivers crash at almost the twice the rate of 20- to 24-year-olds, three times the rate of 25- to 29-year-olds, and four times the rate of 30- to 69-year-olds.

What's more, when two teens are in the car, the risk of a crash nearly doubles. When three or more teens are in the car, the risk increases fourfold. Inexperience and impulsive behavior are a potentially lethal combination. Dan Ariely has offered the intriguing suggestion that we install precautionary devices to offset teenage arousal: When, for instance, a teen is driving above a certain speed threshold, the music automatically switches from Top 40 to classical.

Of course, others have an interest in coming up with creative ways to *accelerate* the effects of arousal. Among car dealers, there's a time-honored tradition—if you want to call it that—of encouraging prospective customers to break the speed limit when they're out on a test drive. Why? Because the exhilaration that comes from doing 100 mph on the interstate might lead them to make what would be, in every sense of the phrase, an impulse purchase.

Likewise casinos, those masters of manipulation, go to great lengths to foster an atmosphere of arousal. Note the noise (often piped in) and the seizure-inducing lights. Hunger makes us more inclined to impulsive behavior; therefore, as widely available as drink is on the casino floor, there's often a scarcity of food.

And the same goes for matters of the heart. When Jon was in college, his psychology professor (now the university president) noted that savvy psych grad students often tried to take their dates to hockey games, where fights might break out, or to horror movies—things that got the blood pumping and induced a hot state of mind. Note, too, that if you think there's a cute guy/girl at the gym when you walk in and your pulse is at baseline level, he or she will look even more appealing to you when you're on the elliptical machine and your heart is racing.

In short, whether in the bedroom, between the sidelines, or at the corporate conference table, the hot-state "you" doesn't think or act the same way as the cool-state "you." More from Ariely, this time in his book *Predictably Irrational*: "Even the most brilliant and rational person, in the heat of passion, seems to be absolutely and completely divorced from the person he thought he was. Moreover, it is not just that people make wrong predictions about themselves— their predictions are wrong by a wide margin."

Why should athletes and coaches be any different? In fact, we'd propose that some of the very same attributes that make athletes elite performers also make them especially prone to outbursts. Lightning reflexes, impulsive decision-making, reckless abandon, aggressiveness . . . these are terms in heavy rotation when sportswriters describe the makeup of heavyweight champions and quicksilver NBA players. Intensely competitive and arousing situations can fuel the fire for individuals who already tend to run hot.

We would submit that Richard Sherman was unlikely to have predicted how he would act when interviewed in the immediate, emotional aftermath of the biggest game of his career. That Kevin Ward Jr. gave little thought beforehand to how he'd respond if his car were run into the corner. That Luis Suárez would've sworn up and down that he'd never bite an opponent . . . again. And that we, too, are often in the dark when it comes to guessing how we'll react when the heat gets turned up.

Why Athletes Don't Need an Empty Bed Before Competition

Asked what he would have been if not a soccer player, the British striker Peter Crouch paused for a moment. Then he replied memorably, "A virgin." Jason Giambi, the baseball slugger, had a slightly less decorous take on the considerable overlap between sex and sports. While playing for the Oakland A's, he wore a T-shirt underneath his No. 16 jersey that bore this bit of (horn)doggerel: *Party Like a Rock Star. Hammer Like a Porn Star. Rake Like an All-Star.* When Wilt Chamberlain famously boasted of having slept with 20,000 women, it triggered a round of guffaws—as well as a memorable *Saturday Night Live* sketch starring M.C. Hammer. ("I remember Cheryl. Number 13,906. But in my heart she was number 2,078. Cheryl was so full of life, love, and laughter.")

Entire forests have been felled—and innumerable pixels have been consumed—in discussions of athletes and their virility. Capaciously muscled, physically fit players in their athletic prime are often also in their sexual primes as well.

But the more we've learned about athletes and their heroic carnal appetites—from Tiger Woods to NBA player Gary Payton (who sired two sons, Gary Jr. and Gary II, within four months of each other) to the litany of athletes who have circulated images of their proverbial "junk" on social media—the more Chamberlain's numerical claim sounds not like laughable hyperbole but like an indiscreet boast. It recalls the old joke about the hardest part of playing in the NBA: trying to keep a straight face while you tell your significant other how much you'll miss her before departing on a road trip. Or, as a colleague of Jon's once put it, "Joe DiMaggio had a hearty appetite for chorus girls, but, lucky for his legacy, Thedirty.com was not around to chronicle his bedroom exploits."

Yet there *is* a time when some athletes have been uncharacteristically celibate: before competition. This dates to the ancient Olympics, when Plato warned competitors to refrain from sexual intimacy, lest they tire themselves out. More than a few years later, Burgess Meredith, in his role as Mickey the trainer, warned Rocky Balboa: "Women weaken legs." Muhammad Ali and Mike Tyson seem to have agreed, each having taken vows of chastity in the weeks preceding fights. (Ali's theory was that ejaculation sapped a man of valuable testosterone.) While coaching the Buffalo Bills, Marv Levy reportedly decreed before the team's four Super Bowls that his players were to avoid their wives and girlfriends. (Lot of good that did the Bills.)

This belief persists, at least in some corners. During the 2014 World Cup, several teams barred their players from having sex on grounds that it might undercut performance. "There will be no sex in Brazil," asserted Safet Susic, the coach of Bosnia-Herzegovina's national team. "This is not a holiday trip. We are there to play football." Miguel Herrera, Mexico's coach, was even harsher, telling the newspaper *Reforma*, "If a player cannot endure a month or 20 days without having intercourse, then [he is] not prepared to be a professional." (That Herrera's team had been rocked by a prostitution scandal may have had something to do with this stance.)

But is this myth or science? Is there any evidence that intercourse saps an athlete of strength and stamina? Does sex before competition affect performance?

One of the first efforts to document the effects of sex on athletic performance was conducted by exercise physiologists Tommy Boone and Stephanie Gilmore. For a study that was published in 1995, they recruited 11 male volunteers to complete two sessions of a "maximal treadmill test," in which the speed and grade of the machine were increased every three minutes until a participant was unable to continue. The sessions were scheduled one week apart. For one session, participants were instructed to have sexual inter-course 12 hours before arriving at the lab; for the other, they were under strict no-sex orders the night before. (The research team did not know which session was which, so as not to bias its interpreta-tion of the data.)

Across a wide range of physiological measures, the researchers found *no difference* between the post-sex and post-abstinence tread-mill sessions. Aerobic power, heart rate, blood pressure, respira-tion . . . none of these varied significantly. In the no-sex baseline sessions, the men were able to stay on the treadmill an average of 13 minutes. The average for sessions 12 hours after sex? Also 13 minutes.

Five years later, a team of Spanish and Swiss researchers con-ducted a follow-up study, this one with a sample of higher-level athletes. The group included cyclists, long-distance runners, weight-lifters, hockey players, and soccer players, all with experience in international competition. Again, the athletes completed a series of stress tests on several days, both after having had sex and after having abstained. The tests were run several times each day: either two and 10 hours after sex or in the morning and afternoon after a sexless night. The tests themselves involved riding a stationary bike until exhaustion—the difficulty level gradually increased until the athlete could not continue—in some instances while simultane-ously solving mental math problems.

As in the previous study, recent sex had no discernible impact on performance. Both when the athletes tried to achieve maximal physical exertion and when they tried to muster the concentration needed for the math task, their recent intimacies (or lack thereof) had no apparent effect. There was a slight (though not statistically significant) tendency for a somewhat slower post-workout recovery period two hours after sex, leading researchers to conclude that "the recovery capacity of an athlete could be affected if he had sexual in-tercourse two hours before a competition." Other than that, there was no evidence that sex undermines later performance.

To be frank: This reservoir of research literature isn't the deepest. There are only a handful of studies, each with a relatively small number of participants. And all the papers we uncovered focused on male athletes; we know even less about how recent sex affects women's performance. But the published research paints a consistent story: The presumption that sex will undermine athletic performance is more urban legend—an old coaches' tale, so to speak—than scientific fact.

Some science even suggests that if sex has any influence, it probably *benefits* performance. In one study involving women (but not athletes), researchers at Rutgers looked at the physical aftereffects of vaginal stimulation. They found that women who had just had an orgasm demonstrated a huge jump in pain tolerance (between 75 and 100 percent!).

As for Ali's notion that sex saps a boxer's testosterone? Well . . . not so much. Emmanuele Jannini, an Italian endocrinologist who specializes in research related to sex, proposes precisely the opposite: Testosterone *increases* post-coitus. "After three months without sex, which is not so uncommon for some athletes, testosterone dramatically drops to levels close to children's levels," Jannini explained. In a one-two combination to the midsection of Ali's abstinence theory, the endocrinologist added sarcastically, "Do you think this may be useful for a boxer?"[1]

But it's not just physical concerns that lead some athletes and coaches to embrace the doctrine of pre-competition abstinence. What about the underlying psychology of sex? Here's Marty Liquori, once the world's top-ranked 5,000-meter runner: "Sex makes you happy, and happy people don't run a 3:47 mile."

Well, one could just as easily argue the opposite. Consider the suggestion of Samantha McGlone—future Olympic triathlete—and her co-author Ian Shrier, a sports medicine researcher, in a paper

---

1. Though, to be fair, Jannini's conclusion seems to have been based on a study of men dealing with impotence-related problems. Who knows how much we can generalize from it? Again, this isn't the most robust research literature.

published in 2000 in the *Clinical Journal of Sport Medicine*. "If athletes are too anxious and restless the night before an event," they write, "then sex may be a relaxing distraction." Here's Pliny the Elder making essentially the same point in 77 CE: "Athletes when sluggish are revitalized by lovemaking."

The role of expectation is not to be dismissed, either. If you buy the idea that abstinence adds some juice to your fastball or shaves a few seconds off your pace, it may just do that. Believe that sex will *boost* athletic performance? Indulging may provide that extra bit of confidence or needed jolt. Athletes are creatures of routine, notoriously superstitious, so perhaps the best advice in preparing for a big competition is just to keep dancing with whoever brung you to the ball.

Most athletes don't seem to believe that sex is a performance un-enhancer. In a recent survey, researchers in Slovakia and Serbia polled long-distance runners and race-walkers about their post-coital athletic capabilities. Close to 90 percent said that they experienced no deficits in athletic performance after having sex the night before. In fact almost half saw no problem with sexual activity *just 30 minutes* before a race.

At the Vancouver Winter Olympics, 2,000 virile athletes from around the world were lodged together in a self-contained village for two weeks. Before the Games were over, members of the Vancouver organizing committee had to make an emergency call for additional condoms, as the original inventory was already depleted.

Then there's Ronda Rousey, the UFC doyenne. Before a 2012 fight, she told an interviewer that, yes, she is sexually active before fights. "For girls it raises your testosterone, so I try to have as much sex as possible before I fight," she said. Then, with an approximation of comic timing, she added: "Not with like *everybody*. I don't put out like a Craigslist ad or anything, but if I got a steady I'm going to be like, 'Yo, fight time's coming up.'"

We're confident that most coaches who endorse abstinence before competition aren't basing their stance on strict scrutiny of the scientific literature. After all, according to McGlone and Shrier, your average romp between married partners burns fewer than 50 calories, equivalent to a leisurely walk around the block or up two flights of stairs. A literal roll in the hay seems more likely to lead to exhaustion (and injury) than a figurative one.

On the contrary, it doesn't take a conspiracy theorist to suggest that a ban on sex is less about the sex than about the pursuit. "No sex allowed" might amount to coachspeak for "Get some sleep, don't hurt yourself, and don't do anything stupid."

It was Casey Stengel, the hidebound Yankees manager, who had it right. "Being with a woman all night never hurt no professional baseball player," he said. "It's staying up all night looking for a woman that does him in."

Why the Coach's Seat Is *Always* Hot

The 1916 Philadelphia Athletics weren't simply a bad baseball team. They were a historically bad baseball team. Couldn't hit. Couldn't pitch. Couldn't field. Fate was their nemesis as well. Predating a time of political correctness, the Athletics employed for five seasons a mascot/batboy/good-luck charm with a physical deformity: a local teenager, Louis Van Zelst. The players would superstitiously touch Louis's hunched back before batting. Alas, Louis seemed to bring the team little in the way of good fortune, and his own luck turned out to be even worse than that of his downtrodden employers, as he passed away from Bright's disease in the winter of 1915.

The Athletics finished the 1916 season 36-117, for a miserable winning percentage of .235, lowest in the modern era. Only a handful of other Major League teams have lost more games—and they did so over a longer, 162-game schedule. The Athletics had been in last place of the American League the previous season, and they would finish in last place each of the next five seasons as well.

Through it all, though, the team's manager would keep his job.

It's axiomatic in sports: Records are made to be broken. But Connie Mack's managerial career is a parade of records that, with virtual certainty, will never be topped. When he reached the tail end of an undistinguished career as a Major League player (.244 batting average), Mack was named player-manager of the Pittsburgh Pirates.

When he retired, he left Pittsburgh and helped lead a minor-league team in Milwaukee. In 1901 he accepted a job as manager, treasurer, and part-time owner of a new franchise, the Philadelphia Athletics.

Mack would win a record 3,731 major-league games, including five World Series titles. It sounds impressive. It *is* impressive—the second-most-successful manager, John McGraw, won nearly 1,000 fewer games. But some context: Mack's win total was spread over 50 seasons. That's right. Five-zero. Mack managed the Athletics from 1901 to 1950, through one depression, two world wars, and nine presidential administrations, from McKinley to Truman and through six terms' worth of Roosevelts. During Mack's managerial tenure with a single club, the U.S. population doubled and the domestic GNP increased almost tenfold.

More remarkable still might be Mack's major-league record for lost games: 3,948. For all his teams' successes, Mack had a career losing record (.486). Offsetting the five World Series titles, his teams finished in last place 17 times.

If 17 last-place finishes without being fired sounds like roughly 16 more than a manager would expect today, well, consider that Mack managed in a very different era, with a decidedly more patient sports culture. Franchises were not worth billions. There was no sports talk radio—in Philadelphia's case, no WIP—to foment fan dissatisfaction. (*This is Alex from Swarthmore. Long time, first time, Howard. And I gotta tell ya, it's time to sack Mack!*) There were no social media campaigns (#ConnieSux) or GIFs to punctuate every misstep.

Mack helped assure his longevity with his easygoing carriage. Wearing a solemn expression and a three-piece suit, he cut a dignified figure and built consensus and support. A "players' manager," we'd call him today. He refrained from swearing or drinking but accommodated players who were less temperate. Unlike the managers of other teams, he never imposed curfews or bed checks.

The door to Mack's oval-shaped office at Shibe Park was always open. At one point various Athletics players complained to the manager about the carousing of the team's star pitcher, Rube Waddell. "Rube is not as black as he is painted," Mack replied diplomatically, "although he will never be mistaken for one of Raphael's cherubim." (In part because of this immoderate lifestyle, Waddell died at age 37; Mack helped pay for the headstone.)

Mostly, though, Mack's job security was protected by the convenient fact that he had an ownership stake in the team. The Athletics were often in dire financial straits. More than once Philadelphia won the World Series only to gut the roster when players became too expensive—presaging the Florida Marlins nearly a century later. But replacing the manager was never deemed an appropriate or prudent personnel move.

Eventually Mack's body and mind revolted. Managing into his 80s, Mack was known to fall asleep in the dugout, leaving it to his coaches to decide whether to pinch-hit or leave a starting pitcher in the game. Mack had a hard time recalling the names of his players. The Athletics ignored his bizarre outbursts, and by the end, other coaches often overruled his less sensible decisions. When Connie Mack finally stepped down, he remained defiant. "I'm not quitting because I'm getting old," he remarked after the 1950 season. "I'm quitting because I think people want me to." He was 87.

Envision Mack's career today, and it inspires chuckles, if not belly laughs. Fifty consecutive seasons coaching one team? Surviving seven straight seasons of finishing dead last in the league? Managing into your late 80s?

Today the coach or manager of a pro sports team doesn't sit on a bench; he sits on a perpetual hot seat. The term *embattled coach* is damn near redundant. Beset by pressure from ownership to win, bedeviled by the unrealistic expectations of the media and fans, betrayed by underachieving players with fat, often guaranteed contracts, the contemporary bench boss is constantly under siege.

As his base of power and his job security steadily erode, the coach has come to resemble a well-paid temp—a Kelly Girl in Armani or a Bose headset—who can take his team to the brink of a title yet must still be prepared to clean out his office whenever the boss's number appears on his caller ID. In fact, you would be hard-pressed to name a profession with more turnover, more *churn*, to use the voguish term. The *reductio ad absurdum* might have come a decade ago when the Denver Nuggets' public relations staff simultaneously lobbied for Jeff Bzdelik among Coach of the Year voters *and* prepared a press release welcoming a potential successor.

NFL players might have the shortest half-lives in sports, but their median career length of just over three years[1] is still longer than the average tenure of a head coach. Prior to the 2015 NFL season, 14 teams had changed head coaches at least once over the past two seasons.

The day after the last Sunday of the NFL regular season has been christened Black Monday, when many head coaches are told to hand in their playbooks and parking passes. Not that they constitute the definitive list of the fired. Other NFL coaches work into the playoffs and are *then* jettisoned for taking their team insufficiently deep into the postseason. The Denver Broncos reached the Super Bowl in February 2014 and turned in a 12-4 regular season the following fall. Yet the day after a 2015 playoff loss to the Colts, the team announced that "by mutual agreement" it was parting ways with head coach John Fox.

Coaches in the NBA can relate. As we write this in the spring of 2015, Oklahoma City Thunder coach Scott Brooks has just moved from the hot seat to the unemployment line, which might seem harsh given the .620 winning percentage he compiled over seven seasons. (Then again, he fared better than his immediate predecessor. P. J. Carlesimo was fired after just 13 games.) And in Chicago, Tom Thibodeau also endured an exit interview, never mind that the Bulls team he coached had just won 50 games and reached the Eastern Conference finals.

Big-time college sports don't offer much more security. One example among dozens: Bo Pelini was recently fired as Nebraska's football coach after a 9-3 campaign. And in baseball, as of Opening Day 2015 the average tenure of a manager with his current team was just three seasons. (Remove from the equation the 15 full seasons that Mike Scioscia has been with the Angels, and the average drops to just a shade over two and a half.)

"The line [determining] how a coach is perceived is so thin and

---

1.   This oft-trafficked statistic is put out by the NFL Players Association (i.e., labor). The NFL itself (i.e., management) contends that the average career length is roughly six years, based on players who make a club's Week 1 roster in their rookie season.

so fluid," former college basketball coach Fran Fraschilla, now a TV analyst, told Jon. "I always go back to what Jeff Van Gundy told me a long time ago: 'Biggest game of the year. You're down one. You get a good shot. The ball is in the air. It hangs there. Good coach or bad coach? Good coach or bad coach? Good coach or bad coach?'"

There's an element of labor economics here, too. Players' salaries continue to escalate. A generation ago, if a player argued with a coach, he'd risk being deemed a malcontent. Today the more likely framing is: The coach has "lost the locker room." Management might also contend that because of free agency and salary-cap restrictions, it doesn't have the luxury of long-term planning. And when a faltering team needs a change and the players are locked into high-priced contracts, firing the coach is the only way to make a change.

The real question is: Does it work? Get past the splashy introductory press conference and its buzzwords, *fresh energy* and *new philosophy* and *culture change*. Does the new coach outperform the one who just got fired?

For such a simple question, finding an answer is surprisingly complicated. For starters, how to best assess team performance? Wins? Improved quality of play? Some managerial equivalent of WAR, Wins Above Replacement? Postseason appearances? Don't forget that when a team changes coaches, it often overhauls its roster as well, so does better (or worse) performance the next season reflect the new coach or the new players?

And what about dumb luck? It's the pachyderm in the room that can flatten even the most well-researched and -financed front-office plans: Freak injuries, bad hops, blown calls, and other vagaries often tip the balance in the pursuit of a successful season. The football team that recovers an unusually high share of its own fumbles one year is unlikely to repeat the feat the next. The pitching staff that this season yields an abnormally low BABIP (batting average on balls in play) will, likely, be less lucky next season. (And vice versa.) We risk reading too much into year-by-year change when much of it owes to simple fluctuations of fortune.

When Michael Roach, a professor of economics and finance at Middle Tennessee State University, studied the effects of NFL coaching changes, he sought to address these issues. He cast a broad net, aggregating data not for just a handful of teams or seasons but rather for every team across 18 years in the current salary-cap era. He distinguished between coaching changes precipitated by a firing and those following a retirement. He included three measures of team performance: wins, point differential, and playoff appearances. He even came up with a mathematical way to estimate and control for the effects of season-to-season luck.[2]

NFL Coaching Tenure and Team Performance

Tenure (Seasons)	Wins	Point Differential	Odds of Playoffs
1	7.1	-33.9	26%
2	7.5	-13.3	34%
3	7.8	-4.3	34%
4	8.4	17.2	41%
5	9.0	24.4	51%
6	8.8	28.6	56%
7	9.4	41.9	52%
8	9.0	37.8	47%
9	8.9	33.0	43%
10+	8.8	26.5	51%

(Adapted from Roach, 2013)

---

2.   Indeed, Roach found strong evidence of what he refers to as "mean reversion" in the NFL, so that teams that finish below .500 one season perform, on average, better the next season. (The opposite goes for teams above .500.) For example, in the 1995–2012 time window that Roach examined, a five-win team tended to win 2.1 more games the following year, regardless of whether it changed coaches. The average four-win team won 3.1 more times the next season, and so forth. Such regression to the mean reflects luck evening out, but it also owes to various NFL competitive-balance measures (losing teams get higher draft picks and weaker schedules), not to mention an increased motivation to go out and sign better players.

One of the first analyses that Roach conducted was a crude one that looked at how an NFL coach's tenure predicts his team's level of success. The simple answer: The longer a coach has been around, the more successful his team is. As the table on page 116 illustrates, in his first year with a franchise the average NFL coach wins seven games, gets outscored by 34 points, and has just a 26 percent chance of making the playoffs.[3] The numbers get a bit better with each successive year, but it's not until a coach's fourth season at the helm that the average team breaks .500 and scores more points than it allows. The only problem? The average NFL coach doesn't make it to the end of a fourth season.

By Roach's own admission, though, this data table suffers from a chicken-and-egg problem. Does longevity lead to better coaching, with a longer tenure giving a coach enough time to install his scheme, gain the trust of his coordinators and players, and learn from early mistakes? Perhaps. But it's just as likely that good coaching leads to longevity—that coaches who succeed stick around, and those who don't get the pink slip.

To truly assess the effects of coaching changes, Roach needed to use a more rigorous regression analysis, one that accounted not only for annual fluctuations in luck but also for other factors that contribute heavily to a team's performance, such as strength of schedule. So that's what he did with 18 years of NFL data. The statistical conclusion couldn't have been more straightforward: "The results clearly indicate that on average teams are making themselves worse off by firing their coaches."

How much worse? According to Roach's model, a team that fired its coach reduced its win total the following year by 0.8 victories. The team's point differential decreased by 27 points. Its odds of making the playoffs dropped by 12 percent.

This conclusion is not limited to the NFL. Recently, political scientists at the University of Colorado and Loyola University Chicago conducted a similar analysis for college football. They examined

---

3.   In a league in which 37.5 percent (12/32) of teams currently qualify for the postseason.

data from Division I football schools between 1997 and 2010, noting
a total of 263 coaching changes at 115 universities. Analysis indicated
that for teams already performing poorly, "coach replacements have
little effect on team performance." The news was even worse for
more middling teams: "replacing the head coach appears to result in
worse performance over subsequent years than comparable teams
who retained their coach."

Indeed, our sport-by-sport review of research on coaching
changes sounds like a broken record:

- According to fivethirtyeight.com, coaching tenures are even
  shorter in professional hockey than in baseball and football,
  clocking in at an average of 2.4 seasons. Yet NHL teams that fire
  their coaches perform exactly the same as those that don't, in
  terms of winning percentage and playoff success.

- In baseball, coaching changes appear to have a small effect:
  Teams perform worse after they make the move during the
  season (as opposed to over the winter) or when they hire from
  outside the organization (as opposed to promoting from within).

- Soccer? Midseason managerial changes in English association
  football lead clubs to underperform over the next several
  months. Switching countries (and focusing only on a top-tier
  league), analysis of Italy's Serie A reveals no evidence that
  coaching changes have positive effects on teams' results.

- Basketball? Coaching changes were found to have no reliable
  effect on team performance either in the NBA or in college.

As comically out-of-date as the saga of Connie Mack sounds,
maybe the Philadelphia Athletics and their manager-for-a-half-
century were onto something.

·   ·   ·

SO coaching changes aren't all that they're cracked up to be. Why not? With regard to football, Roach puts forth a few ideas. NFL rosters and game plans are fairly complex, even compared to those of other sports. Teams carry 53 players plus a practice squad; up to 45 of those players can participate in any given game, as part of the offensive, defensive, and/or special-teams units. When offensive playbooks and defensive schemes change, it's reasonable to expect a steep learning curve and a turbulent transition. "Orchestrating so many individuals with so many different assignments is a massive undertaking," says Roach. In fact, he compares the coach of an NFL team to the head of a small company.

Which is an enlightening analogy, because it turns out that the effects of replacing an NFL coach look remarkably similar to those of replacing a corporate CEO. Take, for example, Kmart. In the mid-1990s, the rise of Walmart, Target, and other competitors made for tough times at the Kmart Corporation. Its stock price dropped almost 75 percent in just a few years, leading the board of directors to dismiss CEO Joseph Antonini, a longtime company veteran. His replacement was Floyd Hall, an outsider with executive experience at the Grand Union grocery chain, B. Dalton Booksellers, and Target. This buoyed shareholders' morale and Wall Street valuations. Kmart stock spiked 8 percent. The great American comeback story was on.

But then it wasn't. Kmart's stock plummeted again. Floyd Hall's bold response? An unlikely partnership with Martha Stewart. By 2000 the board had seen enough, replacing Hall with another outsider. (The awkward marriage with Stewart would endure for almost another decade.) Within two years Kmart filed for bankruptcy, Hall having moved on to new adventures as the owner of a minor-league baseball team in New Jersey.

Kmart is not alone, according to Margarethe Wiersema, professor of management at the Merage School of Business at the University of California, Irvine. A few years ago, Wiersema conducted a study of CEO turnover within the 500 largest public companies in the U.S. over a 24-month period. Her objective was the same as

Roach's had been in his NFL analyses: to determine how a change in leadership at the top would affect an organization's performance.

Wiersema's outcome measures were a bit different from Roach's, of course. (Think profits instead of wins; return on assets instead of point differential.) But her findings were strikingly similar. From her article: "I found that companies with CEO dismissals experienced no significant improvement in their operating earnings or their stock performance." Specifically, company earnings averaged 11.2 percent before the dismissal of a CEO and 11.8 percent after, a difference that wasn't statistically meaningful. Return on assets averaged 2.6 percent before dismissal and 2.4 percent after.

Just as important, Wiersema's data allowed her to explain this apparent lack of improvement. For one, she found that dismissing a CEO sets off a crisis that the board of directors isn't always equipped to handle. In the face of yet another quarter of disappointing earnings—much like another losing season—there's pressure to make a change at the top decisively and quickly. The problem is that it's much easier and faster to fire someone than it is to identify and woo the right replacement.

Wiersema also concluded that in selecting a new CEO, boards typically pay more attention to placating their present (and potential) investors than they do to fixing the problems that plagued the company in the first place. The allure of the quick fix often leads to the sexy outside hire. But as Wiersema notes, "External candidates, although they appeal to Wall Street, are often less likely than insiders to understand the company's problems." At least at first. And investors—much like fan bases, beat writers, and "hands-on" team owners—aren't always willing to wait patiently for the turnaround.

This lack of effectiveness of leadership changes—on sidelines and in boardrooms—also leads to the question, *Why?* As in, why do teams (and businesses) keep making this move when it doesn't promote success? If firing the coach is anything but a sure bet for improved performance, why does the coaching carousel seem to spin faster with each passing year?

One explanation will be instantly (and painfully) familiar to anyone who has ever rooted for a team run by Donald Sterling, Jeffrey Loria, or Cincinnati's Brown family: the dirty little secret that, sometimes, winning isn't ownership's top priority. A coaching change has the potential to pique fans' interest and cause a short-term surge in ticket sales, regardless of the outcome on the field. Some changes, in fact, are made less for the line score than for the bottom line. Sterling once fired Mike Dunleavy while the coach was in the fourth year of a five-year, $22 million contract, and during Dunleavy's arbitration hearing to collect on his contract—he ultimately succeeded—it became clear that Sterling had fired the coach primarily to cut costs.

Other front offices may be aware that they're playing (and paying) a long shot, but they're still willing to take the risk. Statistics tell us that the effects of a coaching change will likely be a net zero or even a few extra losses in the short term. But what's the alternative? Waiting for incremental improvement? Counting on mean reversion, the steady return to mediocrity? Odds are, your new coaching hire will ultimately be labeled a failure, but there's the outside chance that you *could* strike Belichickian gold.

But the best explanation might be the psychological appeal of at least doing *something*. Known in more academic circles as *action bias*, the concept is straightforward: Faced with uncertainty or ambiguous problems, we would often rather do something than nothing—even if it's counterproductive. Standing pat feels akin to giving up. So we act.

Action bias figures prominently in financial mistakes. In an academic paper with an excellent title—"Trading Is Hazardous to Your Wealth"—Brad Barber and Terrance Odean, then finance professors at the University of California, Davis, argued that investors routinely hurt their portfolios with excessive trading. The market goes up, and investors don't want to feel as if they're just standing passively on the sidelines, so they depart from their long-term strategies and goals and try to capitalize. The market goes down, and investors don't want to feel as if they're fiddling while Rome burns, so they sell off positions, incurring transaction costs and tax liabilities in the process. In both cases they typically would be better served doing nothing. But the impulse to act, to *do something*, proves irresistible.

Other examples: The physician who, unable to diagnose a condition, decides to prescribe at least some course of treatment rather than wait to collect more evidence. The rookie police officer at the scene of a near brawl who hasn't yet learned to hold back and monitor developments, jumping right in instead and escalating violence rather than preventing it. The U.S. politician who, confident that another nation's domestic unrest calls for *some* sort of American intervention, doesn't wait to see if the situation will run its course organically.

Action bias also explains a great deal in sports. Such as why a football coach inevitably calls a time-out before an opposing kicker's late-game field-goal attempt. There's little statistical evidence that "icing the kicker" is an effective strategy. But, *hey, at least we tried something*. Likewise, there's little to suggest that distracting an opposing free-throw shooter works. But better for fans behind the baseline to wave maniacally and stomp their feet and yell epithets than to stand by idly. Action bias explains why so many poker players stay in the game when they should fold, and why blackjack players overplay hands, hitting when they should stick.

A few years ago, Israeli researchers conducted a statistical analysis of hundreds of penalty kicks in top soccer leagues worldwide. Such situations are unenviable for even the best goalkeepers: The kick comes from just 12 yards away, at speeds approaching 100 mph. The keeper has little choice but to guess which way to jump before the ball is struck and hope to get lucky. And even when he or she *does* guess correctly, a save is anything but guaranteed. In the Israelis' dataset, goalies stopped only 14.7 percent of penalties taken.

The researchers found that goalkeepers' most frequent strategy was to guess left, jumping to that side 49.3 percent of the time. They jumped to the right side 44.4 percent of the time. On only 6.3 percent of kicks did the keeper stay put in the center of the goal.

This hardly seems surprising. "You rarely see a goalkeeper stand in the middle and make a save," says Danny Cepero, former keeper for Major League Soccer's New York Red Bulls. And if a goalie does stay put, there are potential costs. Assuming the shot goes by on one side or the other, "you look like a fool," says Cepero. Indeed, when the Israeli researchers interviewed several dozen professional keepers, asking for their reactions to various hypothetical scenarios, the goalies reported that they'd feel bad after guessing wrong and giving up a penalty-kick goal, but they'd feel much worse about staying in the center as a ball went into the net to either side of them.

By now you can probably guess what the actual game data indicate. The keepers would make more saves by staying put. That 14.7 percent overall save rate we cited earlier? Breaking it down by keepers' decisions, it's 14.2 percent when guessing left and 12.6 percent when guessing right. This number spikes to a healthy 33.3 percent, though, on penalties when the goalie stays in the center of the goal (and then reacts to the ball). In other words, even though statistically it's the wrong decision, most goalkeepers choose to guess a post, to do *something* because they're worried that the consequences of appearing to do nothing would be worse.

Sounds a lot like a front office firing a head coach or a board of directors replacing a CEO. Intuition and concerns about fan/shareholder reaction aside, sometimes the best move is no move at all.

WE noted before that, on average, the (famously brief) tenure of NFL players is still longer than that of their head coaches. But that's somewhat misleading. The average NFL player performs for barely three years and then must consider a new career. The NFL head coach? He might be lucky to last two seasons before he's terminated, but then he's often summoned to begin a new tour of duty with another team.

John Fox, the coach who was unceremoniously dumped by the Broncos one year after a Super Bowl appearance? Within the week he had been hired as the new coach of the Chicago Bears. On Black

Monday of 2014, Rex Ryan was fired as coach of the New York Jets after the team's miserable 4-12 season. He not only didn't have to wait long to get a new job; he didn't even have to leave the state. Within two weeks Ryan was announced as the new head coach of the Buffalo Bills.

Fans of other pro sports are likely to relate. In the NBA, George Karl was fired by the Cleveland Cavaliers, Golden State Warriors, Seattle SuperSonics, Milwaukee Bucks, and Denver Nuggets. Yet when the Sacramento Kings were looking to make a coaching change in February 2015, Karl was their top choice, and fans rejoiced when he took the job. (Spoiler alert: It took all of four months for reports to emerge that Kings management was already considering firing Karl.) Farther south in California, Byron Scott, coach of the Lakers, was working on his fourth NBA head coaching job over just 13 full seasons.

When baseball fans note that Billy Martin was fired five times by the Yankees, it's often proffered as evidence of the instability of the owner, George Steinbrenner. But it's worth noting that four other teams (Twins, Tigers, Rangers, A's) hired and fired Martin as well. (Martin's hockey analogue might be Mike Keenan, who coached for eight NHL franchises.) And don't forget the Toronto Blue Jays, who in 2008 decided to replace manager John Gibbons with Cito Gaston, a second-termer who had helmed the team to its two World Series titles in the early 1990s. Gaston managed for three more seasons until the Jays hired John Farrell, who lasted only two years before leaving to win a World Series with the Boston Red Sox. Farrell's replacement in Toronto in 2013? None other than the man who had started this double-elimination game of musical chairs, John Gibbons.

In fact, it is the rare coach or manager who gets only one chance. Punctuating his remarks with his familiar cackle, Red Auerbach once put it this way to Jon: "They're so lousy they deserve to get fired midseason, but they're so good another team wants them right away."

This culture of retreads flies in the face of logic. Why keep giving opportunities to workers who, in many cases, have underachieved in their previous positions? The answer seems to be that while general managers are eager to show off a willingness to do *something*, they're not eager to do something crazy.

Like many of us faced with tough decisions, those who hire head coaches tend to be risk-averse. Or in the words of Daniel Kahneman, the Nobel Prize–winning psychologist: "For most people, the fear of losing $100 is more intense than the hope of gaining $150." Yes, the allure of discovering and landing the next great coach is great. But not as great as the risk posed to the job security of the GM who swings for the fences with an unconventional hire . . . and misses.

To their credit, some franchises recently have tried to overcome this bias for the familiar coach, declining to give in to the tendency to recycle. In basketball, for example, in the past few seasons teams have hired head coaches with no prior NBA bench experience, including David Blatt, Derek Fisher, Steve Kerr, Jason Kidd, and Brad Stevens. The Oklahoma City Thunder replaced Scott Brooks with Billy Donovan, who had been terrifically successful at the University of Florida but had never before coached in the NBA. The Philadelphia Flyers hired University of North Dakota head coach Dave Hakstol, the first college hockey coach to make the jump to the NHL since Herb Brooks in 1981. The Florida Marlins replaced their manager with former scout and GM Dan Jennings, a man with zero managerial experience in either the major or minor leagues. Some of these hires will work out better than others, of course.

The Pittsburgh Pirates once offered John Wooden a job as the team's manager. Wooden was in the midst of his unrivaled reign as UCLA's basketball coach. The rationale: Wooden, who had once coached college baseball and was a fan of the game, was an exceptional leader, motivator, and strategist, and that would compensate for whatever baseball-specific knowledge gaps he might have. Wooden declined the offer, but it was an inspired bit of thinking by the Pirates.

But we're not entirely there yet. As we write this, the Pirates are managed by Clint Hurdle, available because he had been fired by the

Rockies. Hurdle was preceded for three years by John Russell, the team's previous third-base coach. Before Russell, the team was led for just two seasons by Jim Tracy, who'd previously been fired by the Dodgers when they hired former Red Sox manager Grady Little for a two-year stint. . . .

Why So Many Successful Ultra-Endurance Athletes Are Also Successful Recovering Addicts

Timothy Olson's status as a world-class athlete is belied by his appearance. When he heads off on training runs from his base in Boulder, Colorado, he usually wears only a T-shirt that's invariably soaked within minutes, a pair of shorts, a pair of running shoes, and a bandanna to cover his thatch of dirty-blond hair.

Olson also camouflages his lofty stature with his demeanor: He's all humility and courtesy. He speaks so quietly that friends say they have to lean in to hear him. His running shoes? They were supplied by his sponsor, The North Face, but Olson is reluctant to tell you this for fear that he'll come across as boastful.

But any doubt of his elite standing is removed when he begins to run. His style is a mix of violence and grace. His legs pump furiously, his arms cleave the air, his ponytail trails behind him like the tail on a kite. Yet he is a study in efficiency: no wasted movement, gears purring in synchrony. And he sustains this style for hours at a time.

There are runs. There are long runs. Then there are Timothy Olson training runs. Olson, one of the world's top ultrarunners, will cover a stretch of road that, for the rest of us, would require gallons of gasoline—and possibly an oil change. On this day, as the morning sun starts to creep over the Rocky Mountains, Olson announces casually that he plans to run "30 or 40" miles, treating with nonchalance a 10-mile margin of error that, for many, would constitute a week's accomplishment. And he'll do this a few more times this week. Then again, when you're accustomed to winning 100-mile endurance races with times under 15 hours—essentially four straight sub-four-hour marathons—well, what's an extra 10 miles, give or take?

Besides, these distances are negligible compared to the vast psychological expanse Olson has traveled to get to where he is today.

Olson grew up in Amherst, a blink-and-you-miss-it burg in the agricultural midsection of Wisconsin. With social options at a minimum, he and his friends ran through tracks and mazes they'd carved into the cornfields. In high school Olson made the cross-country team. He was proficient—he recalls that his personal record for a 5K race was around 16 minutes—and running was fun. It was also in keeping with his strict religious upbringing, which was predicated on self-improvement.

But it was at this same time that Olson fell into the tight grip of drug and alcohol addiction. "I was lost, I was confused, I didn't know what I wanted to do with my life," he says, "so I was making a bunch of wrong decisions." He enrolled in college but dropped out. He watched as friends and acquaintances overdosed. He saw others hauled to prison for drug offenses; one of them committed suicide in his cell. Soon Olson, too, was arrested, and he served a short stint on a drug-related charge.

Rock bottom? That's hard to pinpoint. But he might have hit it one morning at age 22. Trying desperately to sober up in the shower, he pondered suicide and began to cry. Soon he was sobbing convulsively. "I wanted to die," he says, "but deep inside there was this internal battle that would not let me give in. I felt like I needed to prove the world wrong, and prove myself wrong. I decided to stop being weak and start living."

That meant quitting hard drugs. That also meant running. While re-enrolling in college, Olson volunteered to coach the cross-country team at his old high school. He rediscovered the joy of the sport. The self-reliance. The pacing. The intimate conversation between the mind and the body. The incremental gains. The freedom.

He began adding distance to his runs. Then he began to add elevation and inclines and trails. In 2007, he embarked on a road trip around the West, running up and down and at altitude and into his future wife, Krista, also a runner. They would get engaged, fittingly, during a half-marathon.

Around this time Olson realized that he had the aptitude and fortitude to be a strong runner. A really strong runner. He and Krista moved to Ashland, Oregon, in part for its natural beauty, in part because of its strong running community. Hal Koerner, an ultrarunner of distinction, owns the local running shop. Anton Krupicka and Jenn Shelton, both of whom were mentioned in Christopher McDougall's best-selling book *Born to Run*, are based in Ashland. Same for brothers Eric and Kyle Skaggs.

One day Olson decided to join a group for a 50K run along a local river. "It was a very rough experience," he recalls. "I never bonked so hard. I was hallucinating. It was crazy. A lot of people would say, 'I'm going to go find a fun sport, play basketball with my buddies, not try to kill myself like I'm doing here.' But I just really liked it. I was definitely working through some stuff mentally, emotionally. But also I just really liked running. It led to this peace, this well-being."

He stuck with it, and soon he was running longer distances in shorter times. In 2011, at 28, he won his first 100-mile race. In 2012 he not only won the prestigious Western States 100-mile Endurance Run but also posted the first sub-15-hour time, clocking a new course record of 14:46. Not long after this he relocated to Boulder, where he could train full-time in nature and at altitude. When we first spoke to Olson, in December 2014, he had just completed a 50-mile race in California in 6:42:54, finishing first out of the 112 entrants in his age category, 30–34.

Olson has trained in the Canary Islands and in Chamonix, France. He's raced all over the world, sometimes taking along Krista and their young son. "Honestly," he says, "I'm still trying to process everything that's happened to me over the last ten years. But it's been an amazing run." Literally.

• • •

JUST as Olson graciously shared his history with us, he hasn't shied from sharing it with the greater running community. In 2012 he wrote a post for the site irunfar.com titled "My Path to Contentment: From Addict to Awakened Ultrarunner." In it he told his deeply confessional story with bracing candor: "Running was my lifesaver. I first started back running to detox, clean out my body and pass that fun, pee-in-a-cup drug test. I ran to forget, I ran for peace, I ran because it was all I could do and it healed me. Running helped me look inside myself, forgive myself, trust myself, and learn from my past. Running let out all sorts of emotions; I found myself crying, laughing, screaming and puking through this road of recovery."

Olson braced himself for the comments section, usually an online dustbin for cynicism and snark from trolls delighting in the misfortunes of others. He was pleasantly surprised, though, by the reader response. There were many notes of encouragement and congratulation. Still more striking: the large subset of kindred spirits. A smattering:

- David wrote: *I can relate to your story on many levels. We should chat sometime. . . .*

- Olga: *Absolutely awesome. I know of many ultrarunners [who have] found [salvation] in this sport, a replacement of sorts, a cleansing experience. My own son is going through a stage of peeing in a cup and living on probation and parole after serving, and as his awakening is slowly happening, he keeps saying he wants to be like me.*

- Seamus: *Great piece! I definitely have a similar story. . . . I notice, however, that the more I run, the better my life is when I'm not running. Best part: I'm getting much better. I'm about to attempt my first 50 [mile race] in 9 days. Reading this is getting me amped!*

- Jess: *I have been down that same road.*

• Richard: *I have a very similar story involving alcoholism. The disease kept me from running a step for three-and-a-half years, but I returned to run a 3:03 marathon last fall past the age of 52.*

Olson already knew that others had gravitated to endurance sports as they tried to squelch various personal demons. But this threw it all into sharp relief. "People really connected to me," he says. "Maybe more so [because] I've had success in running, and they look up to me. But then they realize that I'm just a schmuck, like a lot of people, who wanted to turn my life around. I feel like there's just been a huge swing of people okay with telling their stories."

Spend only a few moments online going down the endurance-sports rabbit hole, and it's hard not to be struck by the high incidence of recovering addicts. Blake Anderson of Chico, California, is a star on the Ironman triathlon circuit. He also speaks about his past, starting with experimentation with marijuana that led to experimentation with cocaine, which led to full-blown drug and alcohol addiction. He didn't connect with a formal recovery program, but as he told his local newspaper, he found a different path to sobriety. He says, "My meetings are every time I lace up my running shoes; every time I clip my cleats into the pedals on my bike; every time I crush those laps in the pool."

Rich Roll was a former college swimmer and a successful litigator at a prominent law firm in southern California—until he developed what he calls "a mean case of alcoholism." His days began with a vodka tonic in the shower. "What started out as all fun and games," he writes on his website, "morphed into scenes out of *Leaving Las Vegas*." Why does he have a website? Because, after spending 100 days in an Oregon treatment center, he became one of the top endurance-sports athletes. A veteran of the Ultraman (a three-day event on the Big Island of Hawaii consisting of a 10K ocean swim, a bike ride of more than 260 miles, and a double-marathon run), he was named one of the "25 Fittest Men in the World" by *Men's Fitness*.

In northwest Ohio, Todd Crandell runs a counseling program, Racing for Recovery, predicated on the use of exercise to help recovering addicts lead healthier lives. Besides being a licensed chemical dependency counselor, Crandell has lived through addiction. He says that his promising hockey career was cut short by drug and alcohol abuse that lasted for 13 years. He then discovered extreme physical fitness. He's entered dozens of Ironman triathlons, and, like Roll, he's completed the Ultraman in Hawaii.

It doesn't take a licensed psychologist to suggest that many ultrarunners seem to be swapping one addiction for another (albeit far healthier) one. Here's Timothy Olson's take: *"I'll use this as an addiction instead of that* wasn't my [conscious] thought process, but subconsciously it felt good. I'd go for a big run and I'd come back feeling pretty damn high. It was natural. It was a good thing."

He's right. And it goes deeper than that. Why the apparent overlap between successful ultra-endurance competition and successful recovery from addiction? Research doesn't provide one clear answer. The ultra-endurance movement remains a relatively young phenomenon; there haven't been scores of studies documenting the magnitude of the relationship between addiction and ultra competition, or pinpointing what might account for it. So, at the risk of oversimplification, we'll settle for pondering a few hypotheses.

For one thing, addicts in recovery are often encouraged to stop thinking about drugs and to manage their intrusive thoughts and impulses. "You not only train them to forcibly distract themselves," says Dr. John Krystal, chair of the Department of Psychiatry at Yale and an expert in alcoholism, "you teach them to make themselves *do something*."

Krystal told us that much as we would like to think we can override the primitive, lower part of our brain with higher-brain conscious thought, it seldom works out that way. "When we're trying to control powerful urges and feelings," he said, "it helps to not just rely on higher thinking but to become engaged in something else." It's not quite trading one addiction for another, but it's close. "You're substituting one powerful and maladaptive source of support with another kind of support that is more constructive but also very powerful," said Krystal. Some addicts in recovery become very drawn to religion, for example. But it's easy to see how serious running would fit the bill too.

Similarly, addicts in search of sobriety are encouraged to change contexts and try to protect themselves from the usual traps. Engaging with a hard-core running community makes sense. It's the antithesis of a self-destructive activity; it's rewarding; and it's unlikely to overlap with people and situations that evoke drug use.

There's likely a neurochemical explanation, too. There are clear parallels between the biological pathways underlying the brain's responses to drugs and to exercise. We checked in again with Dr. Michael Lardon, consulting psychiatrist at the U.S. Olympic training center in Chula Vista, California. Lardon talked to us about the generally positive effects that exercise has on the brain, particularly the endocannabinoid system, a group of receptors that help regulate balance, or homeostasis, throughout the body. "When you exercise a lot," Lardon explained, "you engage this system." And when you engage this system? "You feel better. You get an elevation in mood as [the exercise] works on the mood centers of the brain. It increases the levels of proteins that have an antidepressant effect."

Note the name of this important regulatory system: *endocannabinoid*. As in, endogenous cannabinoid. As in, a system that received its name 20 years ago from scientists trying to discover the pathways through which the cannabis plant exerts its effects on the human body. Just to be clear, we asked Lardon, we're talking about exercise and drug use operating through the same sort of mechanism? "Right," he said. "There's experimental evidence with animal models. . . . When they get certain drugs, animals that usually exercise a lot will exercise less. There's a litany of studies that show that exercise engages this same reward pathway."

Exercise also triggers the release of various chemical messengers, most notably endorphins in the reward center of the brain. Endorphins, or stress hormones, played a key role in evolution, helping us survive stressful situations and making strenuous activity possible. Endorphins also, in simple terms, make us feel really good. Running great distances can produce a euphoric high. So can taking drugs and drinking alcohol. "Endorphins are like heroin in the sense that they dull the pain of battle and injury and things like that," says Dr. Charles O'Brien at the University of Pennsylvania. O'Brien, one of the world's most prominent addiction researchers, runs his own center for addiction treatment. He told us: "We use an opiate receptor blocker to treat alcoholism. When [patients] are on the receptor blocker, they don't get that endorphin high, and it helps them to stop drinking."

It also stands to reason that the personality type prone to experimenting with drugs has a general tendency to seek out new experiences and physical sensations—such as running great distances. A half century ago, psychologist Marvin Zuckerman created a written test to assess such a personality type. It included suggestions such as:

- "I like wild, uninhibited parties."

- "I can't stand watching a movie that I've seen before."

- "When you can predict almost everything a person will do and say, he or she must be a bore."

Over the years Zuckerman's sensation-seeking scale has been correlated with a number of personality characteristics and behaviors. People who score high on it tend to be uninhibited, impulsive, and nonconforming. They're typically open to new adventures. They report a wider range of experiences with sex and drugs.

There's little research examining Zuckerman-scale scores among ultra-endurance athletes, but sensation-seeking has been linked to participation in high-risk sports (such as mountaineering and skydiving). And the personality-type hypothesis is consistent with the intuition that only a certain kind of person would even consider entering the pain cave associated with ultra endurance or taking the risks inherent in pushing one's body to its outer limits of performance under the most extreme circumstances—*bonking*, to use Olson's term. In other words, these are individuals of a particular

constitution drawn to endeavors that activate particular brain systems.

Maybe the most intriguing research we came across was that of a
Yale colleague of Krystal's, Dr. Philip Corlett, who specializes in the
neuroscience of alcoholism. His research suggests that people with
a family history of alcoholism have a general tendency to develop
not just addictions but also habits. In some cases their feelings of
euphoria can be triggered by the *act of pursuing* a stimulus around
them, rather than by how good the stimulus itself makes them feel.

Corlett noticed that when alcoholics early in their drinking careers were shown a picture of a drink, it triggered their *nucleus accumbens*, the part of the brain that governs motivation and reward. But
once they had been drinking for a long time, being shown a picture
of a beer (or their preferred drink) engaged a part of the brain usually associated with motor action rather than with pleasure. Corlett
says, "The action itself—what they did habitually, without thinking
of the outcome—became a means to an end. Picking up the drink
was [as important] as how good the drink tasted."[1]

Corlett tested this with an intriguing study. His subjects were
not heavy drinkers but came from families with a history of alcoholism. They were told they would be playing a game that would
either give them a reward or enable them to avoid punishment. The
game entailed looking at a series of pictures on a screen and pushing a corresponding button as quickly as they could. When their
responses were quick enough, they were rewarded not with alcohol but with a shot of Gatorade, delivered into their mouths by a
computer-controlled infusion pump. If they didn't push the button
quickly enough, they got a shot of a bitter-tasting liquid instead.

What Corlett found: Participants learned the associations between the images and the correct buttons to push more quickly
when they had a family history of alcoholism. It wasn't so much

---

1.   Consider smokers who turn to vaping—using e-cigarettes, which simulate much of
the sensation of smoking—in an effort to quit their habit. They're essentially hoping
that they're as addicted to the physical acts of holding a cigarette, inhaling, and exhaling
as they are to the nicotine in tobacco.

that they were driven by the reward of the drink—remember, these individuals weren't alcoholics, and the computerized pump had only Gatorade on tap. Rather, they seem to have inherited a brain that finds the *pursuit* of reward to be invigorating. Explains Corlett: "It's not the actual outcome that they're working for. Their behaviors are elicited more rapidly and efficiently by the cues in the environment that guide you and tell you what to do."

Corlett's deduction from this research is that it's not necessarily the "runner's high" or the neurochemistry that comes with ultra-running that is so appealing to some people (including, it seems, those born with a predisposition to addiction, even if they themselves are not addicts). Rather, it's the *ritual*—the training time, the act of preparation, the repetitive action.

Of course, Corlett's data are from individuals who have only a family history of alcoholism. Among those who have personally gone down the paths of addiction and recovery? The allure of the ritual pursuit seems even stronger. Corlett says, "It might also be the case that [recovered addicts] have a brain that is sensitive to the possibility of any kind of a reward and that drives vigorous action toward that reward, but it isn't necessarily as sensitive to the reward itself." Or, in plainer terms: "Once you've gone through addiction, it's easier for your brain to replace one set of habits with another set of habits."

Which is to say, when Timothy Olson takes inventory of his inspiring transition and says, "I have an addictive personality; I got into running really good, and it became kind of that crutch," he shows that he knows himself well. Perhaps better than he realizes.

Why Giving Every Little League Kid a Trophy Is Such a Lousy Idea

They sit atop faux marble bases. And they sit on shelves, bookcases, and mantels. But lately sports trophies have also come to sit in boxes, bins, and storage lockers. They have lost so much value, they're the Weimar currency of our age. Why? Because supply keeps pace with demand. Everyone who's spent time in the youth-sports ecosystem knows that trophies are ubiquitous. Everyone gets one—regardless of effort or outcome.

There is no question that this movement has been a boon to trophy manufacturers. By some reports, the American Youth Soccer Organization spends more than 10 percent of its annual operating budget on figurines and plaques. Trophy sales amount to a more-than-$3 billion industry in North America alone.

Yet whether this has been a boon to our kids . . . well, that's a knottier matter. In a recent poll, 57 percent of Americans agreed that only kids on winning teams should get trophies. James Harrison, NFL linebacker, recently made national news by vowing to return his sons' participation trophies. In an Instagram post punctuated by #harrisonfamilyvalues, the Steeler Pro Bowler announced that his boys would have to wait to "earn a real trophy."

As illustrated by Rush Limbaugh's vocal endorsement of Harrison's post, political conservatives are particularly likely to bemoan the participation trophy as the tin-plated totem of a weakening

American work ethic. *Too much praise and too many trophies make us soft and entitled,* the thinking goes. *Time to give the proverbial stiff-arm to the trophy epidemic.* Or as Glenn Beck said: "Please stop teaching my children that everyone gets a trophy just for participating. . . . There are losers in life."

But one can also object to the ubiquitous participation award without adopting a Darwinian (Beckian?) focus on classifying "winners" and "losers." We'd propose that the biggest risk posed by trophy culture isn't that too much praise makes kids soft. Rather, it's that we're not praising our kids correctly.

To illustrate this, allow us to take you on a field trip to South Bend, Indiana, at the dawn of the 1980s. We'll look in on a college hockey program struggling on the precipice of extinction and on a research-based effort to turn the team around. This was no *Full Metal Jacket*–like attempt to make the players winners by first breaking them down, harping on their limitations, and showing them why they were losers. On the contrary, this is a comeback story in which praise—the right kind of praise—plays a starring role.

FOR as often as we mention the storied tradition of Notre Dame athletics, little of the mythology centers around games played on ice. Yet in recent years, the Irish hockey team has emerged as one of the school's most successful programs and an unlikely national college powerhouse. The Irish qualified for the NCAA tournament six times between 2007 and 2014, twice reaching the Frozen Four, the sport's equivalent of the Final Four in college basketball.

Not far from Notre Dame's vaunted football stadium is the Compton Family Ice Arena, as swanky a venue as you'll find in college hockey, flush with its own Irish pub. The playing rink is named in honor of Charles (Lefty) Smith, and for good reason. Lefty, the Knute Rockne of Notre Dame hockey, took over the team in 1968 and was its head coach for 19 seasons. Widely admired on campus, he felt that his duties and obligations went well beyond line changes and teaching the neutral-zone trap. All 126 players who completed their eligibility under Lefty earned their college degrees.

After stepping down as coach, he stayed in the athletic department and remained close to the hockey program. In 2012, three days after his retirement from Notre Dame, he passed away at age 81.

Unlike the football program, though, the Irish hockey team is a more recent success story. For decades it skated back and forth between varsity and club status, and in the early '80s Lefty's teams started to go sideways. Despite heralded recruits and stars such as Dave Poulin (who would go on to play 13 seasons in the NHL), the Irish struggled. In 1979–80, the team won 14 of its first 16 games, and the season was pregnant with promise. But things took a hairpin turn, with several long losing streaks culminating in a final record of 18-19-1. The Irish then endured losing seasons of 18-20-1 and 13-21-2. Lefty was puzzled, and the seniors were left groping for any solution that might help them finish their college careers on a winning note.

The co-captains of the team approached some of their psychology professors and explained the team's failure to fulfill the potential of its celebrated recruiting class. It was an inspired, if unusual, course of action. (We struggle to imagine, say, Johnny Manziel bemoaning the plight of his team at a Texas A&M faculty meeting.)

Two of the psychologists, Charles Crowell and Chris Anderson, specialized in behavioral management within organizations. As Crowell put it, "We're taking principles out of the psych lab and into real-world settings like classrooms and workplaces." Their overarching theory: Organizational success doesn't happen by accident. And a number of interventions can accelerate activities that, in concert, increase the chance of a desired outcome.

At the time, Crowell and Anderson were working with a bank trying to improve its customer satisfaction. They studied the way tellers interacted with customers, which served as a baseline. The research goal was to improve on that baseline. So, first, they intervened by coming up with 10 phrases that tellers should use with customers to improve their banking experience. Then the researchers intervened again, developing charts to indicate which tellers were hitting the 10 targeted phrases, so that employees could see their own data and improve accordingly. And then they intervened a third time, praising the tellers who had reached certain predetermined goals. Before long, as more and more tellers started to adjust their behavior, the bank saw an uptick in customer satisfaction.

After hearing the hockey players' lament, the professors—as psychologists tend to do—asked the captains to engage in a bit of self-diagnosis. *What was the team's biggest on-ice limitation? If the co-captains could change one thing about the way the team played, what would it be?*

Their answer: checking. The captains said that increasing legal body checks was critical to improving the team's performance. More checking would disrupt opponents more and create more opportunities for Notre Dame to regain control of the puck. This would lead to more Irish goals, which would lead to more victories.

So, much as they did with the bank tellers, the psychologists devised a three-pronged intervention to increase what they came to refer to as the *hit rate*: the number of legal checks per minute of ice time. "The idea was that if we could improve the hit rate," recalls Crowell, "the wins would take care of themselves."

The first step was to create a *player feedback intervention*. Each Monday following a weekend home game, the captains posted graphs in the locker room showing each player's hit rate, much as Crowell and Anderson had done with the bank tellers' use of customer-friendly phrases. (The research team computed the hit rates after poring over game film.)

Second, in the middle portion of the season, the researchers moved on to *individualized goal setting*. This intervention required meetings between the captains and each player during which the player was asked to come up with a challenging but achievable hit-rate objective. This target was then added to each player's locker room graph in the form of a bold line, giving him a goal to aim for in each game (and to compare his performance to afterward).

Finally, the researchers introduced *performance-contingent praise*. For the last two games of the season—a number increased to six games in a follow-up study the next year—Coach Smith spent a few minutes during the pregame dinners lavishing public recognition on specific players based on their hit rates. Crowell, who's still a professor at Notre Dame, recalls that Lefty was "reluctant at first," but the coach played along. His praise was specific to the checking. It wasn't "great job out there" or "hell of a game." It was targeted praise for specific players whose stats indicated that they had been aggressive. "Great job on the boards, Number 68," or "Hell of a difference you made out there on the ice with those three checks in the third period."

The effects of these interventions were impressive.[1] They led to improved player performance, in the form of an overall 82 percent increase in hit rate. The Irish played more aggressively, but it was a controlled aggression: Researchers found no evidence of an increase in penalty minutes after any of the interventions; only clean hits were on the rise. Most important, the 1981–82 Irish finished 23-15-2, giving their graduating seniors their first winning season.

What helped turn Notre Dame hockey around? Concrete feedback. Specific goals tied to performance. And praise linked directly to increased effort. By the end of the intervention period, Lefty Smith was only too happy to dish out specific praise to those who had earned it.

Apart from helping Notre Dame hockey win games (and helping Notre Dame psychologists publish a research paper), this study tells us something interesting about praise and performance more generally. "It needs to be *targeted*," says Crowell. "Saying something broad like 'You were great today' may make someone feel good, but that's about it. If you really want positive reinforcement to change behavior, you need to be specific about what you're acknowledging."

WHICH brings us back to where we started, to the Little League diamonds and youth soccer fields in today's era of the participation trophy. Of course, youth sports are about more than wins and

---

1. This improvement was measured against a pre-intervention baseline. Given that the "praise mandate" took place over only two games, the change in hit rate after the praise intervention was not statistically significant in the first season. But it was statistically reliable in the follow-up study run the next season, in which praise was offered at six pregame meetings.

losses. For some children, especially the youngest, the participation trophy might be the dangling carrot needed to get them to see the season through to completion. But as players mature, league goals shift away from simply having fun to principles of teamwork, personal esteem, and, yes, performance between the lines. Then the participation trophy starts to feel laughably out of place.

So instead we should praise our kids for winning, right? Not so fast. The language of clear *winners* and *losers* is no better than the hollow, automatic praise of trophy culture.

According to Stanford psychologist Carol Dweck, praise—even heaps of it—can be a good thing, but it has to be the right kind. The problem is that we tend to praise in fixed, dispositional terms. Preschooler brings home a colorful painting? We reply, *My, what a great artist you are*. Middle-schooler with a straight-A report card? *You're so smart* is the natural response.

This type of praise is rewarding and motivating only so long as the going stays good. When performance hits its inevitable bumps in the road, kids—accustomed to thinking of themselves as great artists, students, and athletes—naturally start to infer that those fixed labels no longer apply. So they stop trying as hard. Because what's the point of banging your head against what you believe to be the rigid limit of your capabilities?

In one study, Dweck and a colleague observed as a fifth-grade teacher varied the type of praise given to students who had just taken a test. Some students were praised for intelligence ("You must be smart at these problems"). Others were praised for effort ("You must have worked hard at these problems"). As expected, the students praised in terms of fixed intelligence were more likely to agree later with statements such as *Your intelligence is something basic that you can't really change*.

Next, the students were offered a choice between two academic tasks, one challenging and one easy. The intelligence-praised kids opted for the easy task that posed little risk to their newly fragile sense of self. But the effort-praised kids more often chose the challenging task that offered the potential to learn something new. And when they completed a subsequent series of tasks? It was the effort-praised students who performed better. The intelligence-praised kids struggled, gave up more easily, and were more likely to be dishonest about how well they had done.

Praise *can* boost performance in the classroom, just as it can on the home ice of South Bend—but not when it's based on simply showing up, and not when it frames success in terms of fixed levels of aptitude. To maximize impact, *praise has to be linked to effort*.

In other words, contrary to intuition, it's problematic to tell a kid she's a natural athlete. Or that he's a winner. Because when performance-based praise or reward is framed in terms of fixed ability, the stage is set not for perseverance but for future letdown. It's those kids praised for *effort* who are more likely to show grit and less likely to skirt a challenge down the road. To lapse into coach-speak: They're the ones who develop stick-to-it-iveness when the going gets tough.

So, no, you certainly don't have to give trophies to every kid in the youth sports league, especially if your primary goals include improved performance. And if you want to name an MVP on the team you're coaching? Go for it. But be sure to give out Most Improved and Best Hustle awards, too.

Or if you do subscribe to the every-kid-needs-to-get-something idea, come up with an individualized award for each player that emphasizes some effort-related aspect of his or her performance. This isn't as easy as handing each kid the same mass-produced trophy (trust us; we know from experience).[2] But it's definitely worth *your* effort if your coaching goals go beyond the final game of the season.

---

2. Coach Sam's personal favorite from last Little League season: the always coveted *Best job hustling over from LF to back up throws to 3B* award.

Why Rooting for the Mets Is Like Building That IKEA Desk

The year was 1737. A young author/inventor/printer had recently turned 31 and was serving in the Pennsylvania legislature. The year before, Ben Franklin had earned a promotion to clerk of the General Assembly. Now he had been put forth for reappointment. But while his initial elevation to the role had gone unopposed, this second nomination was contentious.

A new member of the legislature made a long speech against Franklin in an effort to throw support to another candidate. Franklin won the vote anyway, a result that he amusingly referred to in his autobiography as the outcome "more agreeable to me."[1]

The smear campaign had failed. Still, it had rankled Franklin. This newcomer who had spoken out in his disfavor was wealthy, well educated, and poised for a powerful career of his own. Accordingly, Franklin thought it wise to strike up an alliance with him rather than a rivalry. Never opposed to experimentation, Franklin used an unusual strategy to accomplish his goal. He decided that the best way to turn his adversary into a friend wasn't flattery, bribery, or "paying any servile respect to him." Rather,

---

1.   After all—as he went on to write with an honesty and self-deprecation that have all but vanished from politics—the clerk position paid more.

Franklin decided to win over his opponent by asking *him* for a favor.

"Having heard that he had in his library a certain very scarce and curious book, I wrote a note to him, expressing my desire of perusing that book, and requesting he would do me the favour of lending it to me for a few days," Franklin later wrote. "He sent it immediately, and I return'd it in about a week with another note, expressing strongly my sense of the favor. When we next met in the House, he spoke to me (which he had never done before), and with great civility; and he ever after manifested a readiness to serve me on all occasions."

A colonial-era Jedi mind trick? Perhaps. A precursor to Phil Jackson's lending books to Kobe and Shaq? Maybe. Franklin, though, saw it as quite intuitive reasoning that "He that has once done you a kindness will be more ready to do you another, than he whom you yourself have obliged."

In other words, when you go to the trouble of doing a favor for someone else, it feels like a waste of your time unless the recipient is worthwhile. Thus, whether you thought so previously or not, you persuade yourself that the person you helped must be a pretty good guy.

THE year was 1959. Another young man, this one a psychology Ph.D. student at Stanford named Elliot Aronson, was asking college women to talk to him about sex. All in the name of science, of course.

Aronson and his fellow grad student Jud Mills were interested in the psychological effects of going through an initiation. They recruited 63 Stanford women for a study that they described as being about the psychology of sex. More precisely, each student was told that she would be joining a group that had already met regularly for several weeks, and she would be taking the place of a woman who had dropped out because of a scheduling conflict.

Because these group discussions were about sex, Aronson and Mills explained to each participant, the research team first had to make sure that she was comfortable talking publicly about such matters. "Although most people are interested in sex," they noted in elegantly phrased understatement, "they tend to be a little shy when it comes to discussing it." Therefore, the researchers continued, "it is extremely important to arrange things so that the members of the discussion group can talk as freely and frankly as possible."

The solution that Aronson and Mills claimed to have come up with to achieve such freedom and frankness was inventive enough, we're sure, to have brought a smile to Ben Franklin's face: a screening process known as the "embarrassment test." It entailed having the woman read material with sexual content aloud in the presence of a researcher—Aronson himself—who ostensibly would determine her suitability for the group discussion by assessing things such as verbal hesitation, blushing, and other signs of discomfort.

In fact there were two versions of the embarrassment test, one milder than the other. Female participants were assigned to one at random. In the mild test, a woman had to read aloud—in front of this male graduate researcher—from a series of 3-by-5 index cards. Printed on each was a word or phrase that was related to sex but wasn't obscene. *Virgin* or *sexual intercourse*, for example.

In the other version of the test, the ante was upped. Here, again in Aronson's presence, the woman had to read aloud vivid descriptions of sexual activity from several novels, *Lady Chatterley's Lover* among them. Participants in this test also had index cards to read, and the words on them *were* obscene. In what is surely the lewdest use of a Latin abbreviation ever to grace the pages of a scientific journal, the published research paper provides these details: "*e.g.*, fuck, cock, and screw."

All but one of the female recruits agreed to take whichever embarrassment test they were assigned. Regardless of her performance, Aronson then told each woman that she had "passed." Her prize? Entrée into this group about which she had heard so much. Indeed, right there on the spot, Aronson gave each woman the chance to eavesdrop on the conversation going on in another room.

Alas, despite the buildup, the group discussion was a likely letdown. It proved not to be an engaging conversation about sexual mores among liberated and articulate fellow Stanford students. Instead, it was a boring, clinical exchange about bird plumage displays. And migration patterns. And dogs in heat. It wasn't a spontaneous give-and-take; it was a scripted discussion intended by the researchers to be lifeless. As Aronson himself would explain years later, "The discussion was as slow, boring, and turgid as I could make it."

It was a classic bait-and-switch. One could hardly have blamed the participants if they had been angry by the end of the study. But the women weren't upset. Not at all. For that matter, when asked to rate the boring discussion they had listened in on, the women who went through the initiation said it was more interesting than did a separate control group who never heard anything about an embarrassment test. And the more severe the initiation, the more the women actually claimed that they liked the group and were excited about becoming a part of it.

Why? Because the women in Aronson and Mills's study relied on an assumption shared by most of us—that we voluntarily subject ourselves to unpleasantness only if, in the end, there's something of value in it for us. The thought that they might have suffered through such embarrassment for nothing was hard for these Stanford women to accept. So, without even realizing it, they lied to themselves, their psyches inflating the appeal of the group.

THE year is 2015. Yet another young man, this one a New Yorker, Jon's son, roots for his beloved Mets despite no evidence that they will reciprocate his affection by performing with any semblance of consistent competence. For reasons the boy never quite articulated to his father's satisfaction, he gravitated to the team at an early age. This afforded him membership in a tribe that wears orange and blue, speaks of 1986 with hushed reverence, and feels a spike of adrenaline when a large plastic apple emerges, all too infrequently, behind center field. It has given the boy reason to stay up late on summer nights. It has also fostered in him an intimate relationship with failure.

Loyalty to the Mets lays bare the great undercarriage of sports, a blight more widespread than PEDs, Thunderstix, and opt-out clauses. We speak, of course, of losing. Sports is a zero-sum game. Every time one baseball team records the final out—the players converging near the mound to slap palms and butts—another team marches forlornly to the clubhouse, spikes clacking almost mournfully on the concrete. For every fighter whose fatigued arm is raised in triumph by the referee, another fighter looks down at the canvas. (Or worse, up at the arena lighting fixtures.)

For every ritually excellent NFL team, there are the Lions, Raiders, and Browns. For every Harlem Globetrotter, there is a Washington General. For every Serena Williams, there is an Arantxa Rus, a Dutch player who not long ago tied the WTA record for consecutive defeats. Scandinavian proverb: The winner takes it all. We don't hoist the losers on our shoulders or fete them with parades or enrich them with signature-brand shoe endorsements. But losers not only exist; they exist in equal measure to winners. When Ralph Waldo Emerson wrote, "I am defeated all the time; yet to victory, I am born," at least he realized the inevitable math. If there weren't losers, it wouldn't be competition.

Losing, like winning, has its own set of characteristics. In the case of the Mets, there has been over the past two decades a numbing predictability in both the micro and the macro. The season begins with promise and hope in spring training. By early summer, as the team drifts south in the standings, hope has been largely extinguished.

And before 2015 these rhythms would also replicate themselves over the course of nine innings. Games at Citi Field began with anticipation and possibility. Then, the inevitable letdown. Like your favorite band in concert, the pre-2015 Mets had a set list: mental lapse in the field, squandered opportunity at the plate, shaky relief pitching. By the last few innings, as fans left and the brakes on the nearby subway trains became more audible, torpor set in. Unlike in the Wall Street disclaimer, past performance *was* indicative of future results.

But here is something else that's predictable: Fans will be drawn to this team and others like it, even when they're losing. Maybe fewer fans than if the team were contending, but there will be thousands and thousands of return customers, Jon's son among them.

They know what they're signing up for: Before the 2015 season when the team's PR department tried to generate Twitter interest using the hashtag #IAmAMetsFanBecause, the team's loyal fan base came through with responses that ached with self-awareness. Such as #IAmAMetsFanBecause *I am an idiot*. And because: *endless suffering builds strong character*. And, of course, because: *I hate myself*.

Ben Wertheim was only 13 in 2015, but he had already been through an impressive run of misery. In 2007, his first season as a fan, the Mets had one of the greatest late-season collapses in baseball history. The next year, Ben watched the team miss out on the playoffs by losing its final game at Shea Stadium. He also watched Oliver Perez misdirect pitches;[2] Jason Bay hit little besides air molecules; Jose Reyes and R. A. Dickey win a batting title and a Cy Young Award, respectively, and then leave town.

And it's not as if there wasn't always an alternative. The same distance from Ben's Manhattan apartment as Citi Field, there is a nameless American League franchise with a rich history of winning, that regards sub-.500 seasons much the way English Premier League teams regard relegation. But the Mets' relentless losing never diminished Ben's loyalty. "I don't know," he once said, shrugging. "It'll make it more fun when they win."

Did it ever. Completely unexpectedly, Ben's theory was confirmed in 2015. Through 96 games of the season, the Mets were 48–48, a likable but unthreatening team, missing their one legitimate star, the injured David Wright, and their anticipated closer, Jenrry Mejia, who'd (again) managed to violate baseball's drug policy. Then, faster than you can say *Syndergaard*, the Mets started doing a convincing impersonation of their 1986 forebears. Belying its youth, the starting pitching staff was, collectively, almost ruthless in its accuracy. Jeurys Familia emerged as a bullpen leading man. A series of uncharacteristically shrewd personnel moves had the effect of upgrading the lineup, not least the acquisition of Yoenis Cespedes, who hit 17 home runs in his 57 games with the team.

---

2. At a salary of $12 million.

By late September, the Mets had clinched the team's first playoff appearance in nearly a decade. And they kept winning. New York beat the favored Los Angeles Dodgers in the first playoff round, taking the decisive fifth game on the road. Then, in a battle of misbegotten franchises, the Mets swept the Cubs in the NLCS. The pitching remained sharp. Daniel Murphy, an unremarkable second baseman who had never hit more than 14 home runs in an entire season, suddenly looked like the second coming of Babe Ruth, smacking 7 home runs in the first 9 postseason games. The decision-making of the team's manager, Terry Collins, was unimpeachable.

And then, just like that, it all went to hell. Playing the Kansas City Royals in the World Series, the Mets reverted to playing like . . . the Mets. The five games comprised a carnival of blown leads and base-running blunders and directionless throws. Routine ground balls squirted under gloves. Bats went cold. Cespedes injured himself by hitting a foul ball directly into his kneecap. Murphy tallied more fielding errors than hits. Capitulating to the prideful player's demands, Collins let his tired starting pitcher, Matt Harvey, remain in the game for too long in the series clincher. As Frank Thomas put it, without apparent irony, on the Fox broadcast, "The Mets have nothing to hold their heads down for, except they didn't play that well and they gave away this World Series."

Fans were disappointed to see such a pleasant surprise of a season end so unceremoniously. They were left pondering whether this was the beginning of a halcyon era or a cosmic aberration—with the team due to revert to losing prodigiously and using Groupon to sell tickets. But above all there was joy. The fan base—Ben Wertheim among them—was giddy about the season. It wasn't simply that faith had been rewarded. It was that the previous suffering had imbued the experience with extra sweetness.

THE Founding Father, the Stanford researcher, and the doe-eyed Mets fan: The very different stories of these very different young men share an important if not readily apparent theme. In all three instances, we see behavior that seems less than rational: Franklin's adversary comes around and becomes a friend even though *he's* the one who has to make the effort of doing a favor. Aronson's Stanford students claim they were intrigued by a conversation, even though it was extraordinarily and intentionally boring. Jon's son insisted on rooting for the Mets, even though they are, well, the Mets. There's a common thread here that helps explain seemingly counterintuitive behavior.

The term *effort justification* was coined and then popularized by social psychologists, Aronson among them.[3] The idea is that when people make sacrifices to pursue a goal, the effort exerted is often validated by elevating the attractiveness of the goal. In other words, we often come to love that which we suffer to achieve. Examples of effort justification are all around us.

Case in point: the IKEA effect. That's the apt name that Mike Norton, of Harvard Business School, and his colleagues recently gave to the finding that people inflate their valuation of self-made products. The researchers' studies demonstrated that subjects saw their own creations—whether they assembled boxes, folded origami, or built with LEGOs—as worth more than other people did. Once again, it's all about effort.

This aspect of the IKEA business model is brilliant. Not only does the company get out of having to assemble all those Arkelstorps and Fjälkinges, but once we've navigated the hieroglyphic instructions and glued our last dowel (and resisted the periodic urge to gash our foreheads with those Allen wrenches in frustration),

---

3. Indeed, we talked recently with Aronson, and he suggested that his study was, in many respects, a scientific examination of the very type of assumption Ben Franklin made. How can we know for sure that it was the effort of lending the book that thawed the ice between the colonial politicians? Maybe it was just Franklin's winning personality. But the Aronson-Mills study persuades us that it had a lot to do with effort, because all the Stanford women interacted with the same guy (Aronson) under controlled circumstances. The only difference between the experimental trials was the severity of the embarrassment test. So the finding that women who took the more salacious test liked the discussion group the most must reflect something about the initiation itself, and not something unique about Aronson.

we don't mind so much that the Godmorgon is a bit rickety or the Bjursnäs is crooked. Because we exerted ourselves to complete the task, we value the result more.

This isn't true just with Swedish furniture. When the "early adopters" camp out overnight at the Apple Store, awaiting the release of the next iToy, it boosts their attachment to the device. The extreme lengths to which they go to obtain the product invariably influence their assessment, because only a fool would wait for hours to buy something mediocre. Similarly, when we have to secure an invitation to use a product, it becomes that much more attractive.

Remember when Google first released gmail, and getting your own account meant persuading a friend who was among the chosen ones to share one of her golden tickets with you? Treating a free e-mail account the same way we would a backstage concert pass was a savvy strategy for bolstering allegiance to something that would, in short order, be available to anyone. Even when it comes to personal finance, it helps to keep effort justification in mind: We tend to overvalue those stocks and securities in our portfolio that we worked especially hard to find. We overestimate the value of a property to which we've devoted hours of sweat-soaked do-it-yourself home improvement.

Speaking of sweat, effort justification also looms large when it comes to exercise: if you're looking to tone your physique, you should join a gym. No kidding, right? But, really, you should *join* a gym. As in, pay a membership fee. Why? Effort justification. Far be it from us to undercut Groucho Marx, but most of us *do* want to belong to clubs that would have us as members. When we pay for access, we often come to value a group more than when the access comes for free.[4]

Now that you're at the gym, embarking on the human hamster wheel that is the treadmill, you'll probably want a new pair of

---

4. While there's no research on the matter, you wonder whether the odious and extortionate concept of Personal Seat Licenses—buying the right to buy tickets—doesn't owe something to effort justification.

shoes, too. But did you know that you can design them yourself online, an option that Nike, in particular, has popularized? Again, when we exert the effort to customize products (even via some low-impact pointing and clicking), we value them more. Much like the IKEA business model, this is, on its face, counterintuitive. When the manufacturer doesn't, well, *manufacture*, shouldn't we hold the product in lower esteem? When we have to do some of the work ourselves, shouldn't we value the product less? But this type of thinking doesn't account for effort justification. Our investment of time and energy in the design leads us to confer more, not less, value on the shoes.

We even value companies more when we see *them* exert effort. In one series of studies, Ryan Buell and Mike Norton—yes, Mr. IKEA again—reported that consumers prefer a travel website that takes several seconds longer and shows on its status bar all the options it's checking as opposed to one that gives the same result instantaneously. *Hey, look how hard they're working*, we seem to tell ourselves. *If these folks took their time and devoted more effort than the competition, they must deserve my business.*

THE implications of effort justification are wide-ranging, not just limited to the worlds of consumer goods and self-improvement. Effort justification also provides a compelling (and disturbing) explanation for why hazing and other initiation rites are so tough to stamp out—no matter how hard universities, the military, sports teams, and other organizations try. The more brutal the fraternity and sorority hazing, the more loyalty its members subsequently show.

By extrapolation, then, effort justification might explain the appeal of the hard-ass coach. Jon grew up in Bloomington, Indiana, during the meaty years of Bob Knight's reign as tyrannical coach of the Hoosiers basketball team. Knight's reputation for exceptional coaching—to wit: three NCAA titles from 1976 to '87 and an Olympic gold medal in '84—was rivaled by his reputation for exceptional bullying, megalomania, and what might charitably be called "harsh labor conditions."

Knight stalked officials and cursed prodigiously and hurled chairs across the court and pushed assistant coaches into bookshelves and stuffed a fan into a garbage can and once, in Puerto Rico, was accused of hitting a policeman before a team practice. Here's how Knight described his mystique to *Esquire* magazine: "I guess that people are attracted, or whatever, to a no-bullshit guy who tells people to shove it up their ass when he thinks it's appropriate." Bear in mind that this was in 1988, the year Indiana was the defending NCAA champion.

But some of Knight's most intense eruptions were reserved for his own players. Having come to Indiana after coaching at West Point, he ran his program like a military unit. He demanded perfection, and when the players came up short, there was hell to pay. Beyond the wind sprints and the punitive practices at unholy hours and the misogynistic nicknames—"Pussy" was a Knight favorite—there was conduct that would now get a coach fired on the spot. To stress what Knight perceived to be the soft play of forward Daryl Thomas (as well as expose his own Neanderthal gender attitudes), Knight once dangled a tampon in Thomas's locker.

In a particularly irascible mood during practice one day, Knight went so far as to choke a player, Neil Reed. A videotape of the incident surfaced. Perhaps most tellingly, no one reacted as if this were extraordinary. And in what might have been Knight's most antisocial act of all—which is really saying something—he once retreated to a bathroom stall during halftime of a game and emerged brandishing soiled toilet paper, a visual aid to help offer his assessment of the team's play.

But, at least through the mid-'90s, Knight never had trouble recruiting players. "Oh, we all grew up wanting to play for Coach Knight," recalls Steve Alford, an Indiana all-American and now a prominent college coach. That Knight could be brutal, far more so than coaches at other programs, was, perversely, part of the appeal. A. J. Guyton, a quick-beyond-reason guard who played for Knight from 1996 to 2000, put it like this in a 2014 Facebook post: "I attended IU because there was an opportunity to play & people said I couldn't make it under Coach Knight."

More remarkable, still, might be the attitudes of players who survived four years under Knight. He had leached the fun out basketball and bent their spirit and heaped on them rations of verbal and emotional abuse. But hundreds of former players were—and remain—intensely loyal to their coach. As *Sports Illustrated* once wrote, Knight is "the object of near fanatical devotion from his former players." Instead of speaking of "surviving" the experience, they speak of their years at Indiana in the most glowing terms imaginable.

We're not suggesting that the only way for a coach to breed players' loyalty is via Stockholm Syndrome or by adopting the role of sadistic movie-cliché drill sergeant. Loyalty is tough to quantify, and gentler coaching souls also have devoted acolytes. But you'd be hard-pressed to argue that those who played for, say, Lute Olson or Billy Donovan or Thad Matta are *more* loyal than the men who played under Knight (even though those other players were treated much more hospitably than were the Hoosiers).

Rather, we're suggesting that it is precisely *because* Knight's players made extraordinary sacrifices—sacrifices that would not have been required at Arizona or Florida or Ohio State—that they have this unwavering sense of loyalty, of kinship, and of "cherishing the experience," a phrase that former Hoosiers use repeatedly. It all reads like the aforementioned movie cliché: The soldiers love their drill sergeant in spite of (nay, because of!) his sadism. While Knight may not have known the term *effort justification* (and never would have used it without splicing in at least one f-bomb), his m.o. suggests that he didn't merely grasp the principle; it was an underpinning of his success.

Effort justification can work in reverse, too. Which is to say that coaches and teams often assign greater subjective value to players who have been especially challenging or labor-intensive. Listen to college basketball coaches on Senior Night and, inevitably, they spend the most time gushing over the players who "gave me fits" or "turned my hair gray," the kids who nearly transferred or flunked out but persevered to the end.

As we write this in the summer of 2015,[5] Robert Griffin III, d/b/a RG3, has once again been named the starting quarterback for Washington's NFL team. Which mystifies and angers a good many of the team's fans, media, and even former players. Griffin, the 2011 Heisman Trophy winner, was the second player picked in the 2012 NFL Draft. He made a sparkling debut that fall, drawing comparisons to everyone from Michael Vick to Barack Obama (the former because of his speed, the latter because he symbolized post-racial hope and change in Washington).

Yet after that auspicious beginning, Griffin's next several years were filled with equal parts drama and melodrama—and little winning. Late in his rookie season he suffered a knee injury. Two weeks later, though his doctor had not cleared him to return, the quarterback played again. At the (unconscionable) behest of then Redskins coach Mike Shanahan, Griffin also played in the wild-card playoff game, in which he reinjured his right knee, requiring surgery to repair both the ACL and the LCL.

Clearly restricted in mobility, he was far less successful in his second season. His statistics plummeted, he scored zero touchdowns (versus seven his rookie season), and Washington won just 3 of 16 games. Depending on whose spin you accept, Shanahan either resigned or was fired—but not before leaking the opinion that Griffin suffered from "insecurity." Washington hired Jay Gruden as coach before the 2014 season, during which Griffin dislocated his left ankle in Week 2 (on a play in which he was untouched) and was carted off the field. He would return to play in seven of the team's last eight games, finishing the season with more interceptions thrown than touchdowns.

Adding still another source of tension and intrigue: Griffin's

---

5.   Recognizing full well that by the time you read this, several new twists, turns, proclamations, injuries, and Twitter wars may have been added to the RG3 saga . . .

backup, Kirk Cousins, is regarded as one of the NFL's most capable understudies. Joe Theismann, the venerable former Washington quarterback, put it like this during a 2014 preseason game on the Redskins Broadcast Network: "Let's stop beating around the bush. Kirk Cousins has played much better at the quarterback position than Robert Griffin III has. . . . Now, if there was a quarterback competition, it wouldn't be a competition. Kirk Cousins would be the man." And yet another QB on the roster, Colt McCoy, may have had the best season of all three in 2014. But still, as the 2015 season approaches, Griffin (if healthy) has been named the starter. Again.

An economist might explain that the reason Griffin keeps on keeping his starting job is the "sunk cost fallacy": Redskins ownership has made an investment in him and is hell-bent on sticking with it, even to the team's long-term detriment. (Much as you and I might be tempted to eat that three-day-old sushi we bought or to attend an outdoor concert despite being sick—"Hey, we already paid for it.") The psychologist would add to this the idea of effort justification. The Redskins have already suffered abundantly with Griffin: through the unfulfilled early promise; the losses; the injuries and rehabilitation; the hirings and firings related to their quarterback's performance. All of this *sturm und drang* has imbued ownership with extra loyalty to Griffin and distorted estimation of his value. At this point, Dan Snyder seems to be enamored with RG3 precisely *because* he has invested in him, rather than being invested in him because he's enamored with the QB's performance.

The same happens in individual sports. The harder you work to shoot a round of golf under par, the more value you're likely to confer on the milestone. The more you had to labor to haul in that marlin on the fishing trip, the more likely you are to invest in taxidermy. The more intense the struggle to complete the marathon, the more pride you're likely to take in the achievement. The weight room bromide *no pain, no gain* doesn't quite capture it. It's more like, *pain distorts our subjective value of the gain*. Which, admittedly, is far less catchy.

The struggle can be long-term, too. R. A. Dickey won the National League Cy Young Award in 2012. But he'd spent most of the first dozen years of his career pinballing around the minor leagues, playing in places such as Nashville, Buffalo, and Tacoma. There were injuries and physical setbacks. Out of desperation, he made a mid-career conversion to throwing the knuckleball, a temperamental pitch that either magically flutters and leaves hitters cleaving the air or that floats like the head of a dandelion and is punished by opposing batters. When Dickey, deep into his 30s, made the major leagues for good, he was full of appreciation. This stands to reason, right? His success was hard-won. You'd expect the journeyman who'd considered quitting to savor his the occasion more than, say, Jose Reyes, a fellow ex-Met who made his major-league debut at age 19.

But it goes way beyond that: Dickey imbues baseball with almost mythical meaning. He's familiar with the history and rituals and the objects that take on a talismanic significance. In his excellent memoir, *Wherever I Wind Up*, he writes about baseball less as a sport than as a religion. We asked him if he thought his struggles, the scenic route he took to get to the majors, heightened his esteem for the sport. "Oh, absolutely," he answered almost reflexively. "It was almost like the worse baseball treated me, the more I wanted it to accept me. And once I was [accepted] I forgave it for all the setbacks along the way." Sounds a lot like the severely initiated fraternity pledge or sweat-soaked IKEA bunk-bed assembler, doesn't he?

WHICH brings us back to the hopelessly and admirably loyal fans who root for the San Diego Padres or Seattle Mariners or Detroit Lions. Or Cincinnati Bengals. Or Minnesota Timberwolves. Or so many teams that play along Lake Erie. Why do we continue to put ourselves through the agony? Especially when players change teams as blithely as they change socks? It was more than 20 years ago that Jerry Seinfeld (a Mets fan, of course) made the much-quoted analogy that rooting for sports teams was akin to cheering for laundry, but it's as apt as ever.

There are all sorts of reasons why we stick with miserable teams. For instance, history and tradition and civic pride. Plus, we find the alternative so distasteful: There's something wrong about front-runners and bandwagons and Justin Bieber wearing Heat apparel as soon as Miami started winning titles. But there's more to rooting for laundry than just civic pride. After all, Mets fans didn't suddenly become Yankees fans when the going got tough; Cubs fans didn't all jump ship to the White Sox. We submit that effort justification plays a vital role here.

The misery of losing often cements our loyalty. In some ways it cements identity. The last time the Cubs won the World Series, construction on the *Titanic* had yet to commence. The team's fans haven't simply taken solace in a century-plus of losing; the ritual losing is an essential part of the experience. Not to mention that when you root for a perennial runner-up and it finally wins, the experience is suffused with joy and importance. When, say, the Mets sweep a series, their fans assign it greater value than Yankees fans do when their team sweeps a few miles away. And if and when the long-suffering team wins big (see Mets *and* Cubs, 2015), all that effort is *really* justified.[6]

In that last case, the irony is that winning can have the perverse effect of eroding loyalty, fraying the feelings of community, changing the essential experience. Consider Red Sox fans, who, after decades of disappointment, now suffer from an embarrassment of riches. Once the American League's pitiable, doomstruck franchise—the bridesmaid of the Yankees—the Sox, improbably, won the World Series *three* times between 2004 and '13.

This, of course, brought great collective joy; but it diminished a little each time, and by 2013 there was a palpable sense that something had changed. Fans were no longer as rabid as they'd once

---

6. Baseball isn't the only sport to have experienced longtime-losers-turned-winners in 2015. Here's *Sports Illustrated*'s Chris Ballard on the psychology of rooting for the finally successful Golden State Warriors: "I wonder, though, if all that losing only strengthened our bond to the team. To grow up with success is to take it for granted. But the Warriors made you earn your fandom. Maybe that's why they possess the most loyal supporters in the Bay Area. To experience the roar and swell of Oracle [Arena] at its best is to breathe in decades of history and misery and hope, to feel the heart of Oakland beating, to know what eternal optimism amid perennial disappointment feel like."

been. A release valve had been toggled, and all that effort and pressure had been expelled. After Boston's first World Series win, the media personality Bill Simmons, one of those long-suffering fans, wrote a book titled *Now I Can Die in Peace*. It's hard to imagine Red Sox fans from the current generation thinking in these existential terms if the team wins yet again.

We exchanged e-mails with Elliot Aronson last year. The former Stanford grad student is now a professor emeritus, retired after decades of research studies and successful academic books. We asked him what he thought of applying the old Aronson-Mills effort-justification study to the plight of the long-suffering sports fan.

Turns out Aronson is a lifelong member of Red Sox Nation. Naturally, he knew *exactly* what we were talking about. The beleaguered Red Sox fan is little different from the doler of favors, the IKEA assembler, or the hazed Greek pledge—the more we suffer, the more we come to love what we have suffered for. Aronson explained that consistent disappointment at the hands of the Yankees not only fueled Boston fans' hatred of pinstripes "but also made us love the Sox more."

"I was 14 years old when the Sox lost to the Cards in seven games in 1946," Aronson told us. "I had a recurring dream in which Johnny Pesky did not freeze prior to throwing home." In this dream Enos Slaughter was thrown out at the plate instead of scoring from first on a long single to win the game—and the Series—in the ninth inning. Aronson said the play haunted his sleep for decades. For 58 years, to be exact.

"After the 2004 season, when the Sox came back against the Yanks in the playoffs and went on to beat the Cards in four straight," Aronson told us, "I stopped having that particular dream."

Why We Need Rivals

Serena Williams was a point away from winning still another Grand Slam tennis title. The problem was that her adversary in the 2015 Australian Open final, Maria Sharapova, was starting to dial in her shots. There they were, deep in a tiebreaker this night in Melbourne, each of their swipes at the ball freighted with significance. One point to Serena, and victory would be hers. One point to Sharapova, and she would have a chance to push the match into a third set—with momentum on her side.

Wearing a yellow-and-pink ensemble that highlighted her muscled physique, Serena bounced the ball on the baseline. She then went into her service motion, uncoiling her body, torquing, and trying to hit the holy hell out of the ball she'd tossed in the air. The serve shot over the net and past Sharapova's racket for an ace. Serena triumphantly dropped her racket, flashed a high-wattage smile, took several paces toward the net, and began to celebr—

"Let," the chair umpire intoned. "First service."

Imperceptibly, Serena's serve had ticked the net, triggering its sensors and necessitating a *let*, tennis locution for a do-over. Some in the crowd groaned and others giggled at the irony. "As if we haven't had enough drama," one of the television commentators intoned, laughing. This was akin to a kicker making a dramatic game-winning field goal only to learn that the play had been whistled dead before the snap, and . . . well, sorry, try again.

Her celebration aborted, Serena returned to the baseline to collect herself. Then she hit *the same serve* as before, to the same spot on the court. Though Sharapova had a dress-rehearsal a moment earlier, she could only wave as the ball whizzed past. This time it didn't touch the net. Game. Set. Matchless. The title went to Serena, who then celebrated for real, shrieking and climbing into the friends' box to embrace her entourage, a *de rigueur* routine in today's tennis.

"That serve, you just don't do that," said Martina Navratilova, watching from a TV booth above the court. "That's some unbelievable mental strength."

The victory gave Serena her 19th major singles championship, vaulting her past Navratilova and Chris Evert. Both the title and the dramatic end to the match solidified Serena's claim to the mythical status of GOAT (Greatest Of All Time) in women's tennis. It also extended her dominance over Sharapova.

On paper (and pixels), anyway, Serena and Sharapova are rivals. They went to Australia ranked No. 1 and No. 2, respectively, and each held up her end of the bargain by making the final. Over the last decade, Serena has won the most major titles among WTA players. Sharapova has won the second most. They are the only two active women to have won each of the four major titles at least once, the so-called Career Slam. The Australian Open final marked their 19th head-to-head match. In many ways, they are a study in striking contrasts. One is Russian; the other, American. One is blond and statuesque; the other, African American and more compactly built. Their games are comparably powerful, but Serena is the better athlete, Sharapova the more consistent ball-striker.

A current of personal animus runs through the rivalry as well. Sharapova's great breakthrough came in the 2004 Wimbledon final, where, as a 17-year-old, she beat defending champion . . . Serena Williams. At the time it was one of the great Wimbledon upsets. It was also the match that launched a thousand endorsements. Soon Sharapova—though still less accomplished—was making more off-court income than Serena ever had. (Even Nike, which sponsors them both, paid Sharapova more, building a campaign titled *I Feel Pretty* around her physical appearance.) It's not hard to see why Serena, accustomed to the meritocracy of tennis, felt this was a great injustice. Her camp knew a surefire way to motivate her. They would point to Sharapova and (half) jokingly say, "Just remember, you *made* her."

In 2013 the rivalry gathered still more heft—and more heat. Serena reportedly had a romantic relationship with Grigor Dimitrov, a young Bulgarian player. When that ended, Dimitrov became the boyfriend of . . . Sharapova. In an interview with *Rolling Stone*, Serena said offhandedly, "If [Maria] wants to be with the guy with a black heart, go for it." Sharapova fired back, suggesting that Serena was "the other woman" in an adulterous relationship. "If [Serena] wants to talk about something personal," Sharapova said, "maybe she should talk about her relationship and her boyfriend that was married and is getting a divorce and has kids." As the young say: Shots fired.

To say that Serena has warmed to this dynamic is to traffic in understatement. She has beaten Sharapova so comprehensively that it raises a Zen-type question: When one side of a rivalry does all the winning, is it still a rivalry? The 2015 Australian Open final marked Serena's 16th straight win over Sharapova, a streak that dated back to 2005. Less a head-to-head than a foot-to-backside, Serena's record against Sharapova swelled to 17-2.[1]

But it's not just that Serena wins; it's that she elevates her game. She plays better tennis against Sharapova—again, often thought of as the second-best player in the world—than she does against anyone else. This happened again in Australia. Serena displayed more power and accuracy against Sharapova than against her previous six opponents. In her first two matches, Serena played opponents ranked outside the top 100. She served 11 and 5 aces, respectively. Against Sharapova? *Eighteen* aces, a record for a women's final and

---

1.   In the 2015 Wimbledon semifinals, Serena would defeat Sharapova yet again to make it 18-2.

as many as Andy Murray and Novak Djokovic would hit *combined* in the four-set men's final the following night.

Here's the funny part, though: Despite Sharapova's ghastly won-loss record against Serena, the rivalry inspires *her* to play better, too. There is no discernible drop in her play when Serena is on the other side of the net. In Sharapova's previous match, a routine win in the semifinals, she hit three aces and seven double faults. Against Serena, Sharapova had more aces (five) and fewer double faults (four). In Sharapova's previous two victories she had more errors than winners. Against Serena she "cleaned up [her] game," as she put it. Despite losing the final, Sharapova summoned her best tennis of the tournament. "Did you ever see Maria play better than tonight?" Serena's coach, Patrick Mouratoglou, asked aloud after the match.

From her perch above the court, Navratilova smiled knowingly. For 15 years, she and Evert had an iconic rivalry that, like, Serena-Sharapova, was replete with contrasts. Evert-Navratilova, though, was as close as Serena-Sharapova has been lopsided. Their 80 matches were split 43–37 in favor of Navratilova. They even retired with the same number of Grand Slam singles titles, 18. But Navratilova knew this about a rivalry: It ennobles both the winner and the loser.

"I became a better player because of Chris Evert, and she became a better player because of me," Navratilova says. "Some of this is [specific to] tennis—you can only be as good as the ball hit to you. You can only hit great if you are pushed to hit great shots. But some of this is just competition. It really does make you better. I look at my main rivals—I would add Steffi Graf and Monica Seles—and those aren't just my most memorable matches, they're my *best* matches, when I raised my level because I felt forced to. Sometimes you say, 'If my rival wasn't there, think of how much more successful I would have been.' But that's the wrong way to look at it. You really should be thankful that someone exists that pushes you."

In other words, even if Serena keeps winning every match they play, she should continue convincing herself that Sharapova is an archrival—Pepsi to her Coke, Tesla to her Edison, Aaron Burr to her Alexander Hamilton—and not just another player she needs to

dispatch en route to winning the trophy. And even if she keeps losing every matchup, Sharapova would do well to continue perceiving
Serena as a nemesis, not some immovable force. They'd both be
foolish to give up on the power bestowed by rivalry.

GAVIN Kilduff's first exposure to rivalry came as a 10-year-old. His
family had recently moved to State College, Pennsylvania, home of
Penn State University. Before that, Gavin hadn't had much exposure to sports. But in that fall of 1990, the Penn State football team
played Notre Dame. This was before Penn State joined the Big Ten
conference, and the two teams—as the top independent schools in
the nation, each with a storied history—were fierce football rivals.

At the time, Notre Dame was a dynastic program that had won
the national championship two years earlier and had beaten Penn
State two years in a row, the first time Notre Dame had done this
since the 1920s. The Irish, ranked No. 1 in the country, were favored
to beat the Nittany Lions in 1990 as well. That day in South Bend,
Notre Dame took a 14-0 lead, but Penn State fought back to tie
the score late in the game. With less than a minute to play, Irish
quarterback Rick Mirer threw an interception. Penn State kicked a
field goal to win, 24-21, denying Notre Dame a chance at another
national title.

Back in Kilduff's new hometown, bedlam ensued. He recalls:
"After Penn State wins this big game, there was this huge crowd of
students that broke into Beaver Stadium—even though the game,
obviously, wasn't played there. They ran onto the field, tore out the
goalposts, took them up to the top of the stadium, threw them over
the edge, and then transported them to Joe Paterno's house, which
was in the neighborhood where [my family] happened to be living.
We saw this crazy crowd. The culture there, as everyone knows,
is all about football. . . . Clearly, beating Notre Dame meant more
than beating another team."

More than a decade later, when Kilduff entered graduate school
in business administration at Berkeley, he still remembered that
scene vividly and thought he might focus his research on the study

of competition. He looked into the literature and was surprised to discover that the predominant viewpoint among psychologists was that competition was *bad* for motivation. *Huh?* This ran counter to Kilduff's intuition and experience. From observing Penn State football to playing Ping-Pong and video games with his friends, Kilduff *knew* that competition could be a galvanizing force.

As he read more, he started to understand why the studies showed that competition dulled motivation: Many of them focused on educational settings, where the participants didn't have any reason (or desire) to compete with one another. Instead, they were coerced into competition by an authority. Imagine a teacher imposing a strict curve so that every additional point one student earns is at the expense of every other student's score.

In Kilduff's description, "Two people are brought into a lab. *You two have to compete for this $10 prize. Go for it!* versus *You two are going to cooperate and work together to achieve $10.* Yeah, under those circumstances, you can see why competition can be a detrimental force." Involuntary competition proved to have a particularly negative impact on *internal* motivation: Participants would get through a competitive task but then express drastically reduced interest in engaging in similar tasks down the line. But Kilduff was not interested in how externally imposed competition influences people's internal drive to compete again. He wanted to study how competition affects performance in the heat of the battle. This was a question researchers *had* examined, but the seminal work in the area was more than 100 years old.

In 1898, Norman Triplett of Indiana University conducted what is often referred to as the first lab experiment in social psychology. Triplett was a cycling aficionado and had noticed that cyclists seemed to turn in better times when racing against one another than during solo rides racing against the clock. He wanted to test this observation in a controlled laboratory setting. This led him to create his *competition machine*.

Triplett's brainchild was a Y-shaped apparatus attached to a heavy table. At the end of each branch of the Y was an old fishing reel. This is where Triplett's competitors would sit, each assigned to a reel, each charged with cranking as quickly as possible to thread a band of twisted silk cord through a pulley at the other end of the machine. The band was circular and four meters in length. Triplett had sewn a small flag to it so that when the flag made its way around the circle and back to its starting point, he knew that a competitor had cranked through four meters.

Triplett asked his study participants to complete a 16-meter circuit as quickly as possible: That's four complete cycles of the four-meter band. Much like the cyclists who inspired his work, participants sometimes competed solo (against no one but the clock) and sometimes in pairs. The participants were children, mostly pre-teens. Triplett found that on average, their times decreased—that is, improved—from the solo trials to the pair races.

In short, not surprisingly, even though the participants were always told to crank as quickly as possible, their performance was better against a direct competitor. Something about having an opponent gets us to dig deeper, into otherwise-untapped reserves.

More than a century later, Gavin Kilduff decided to go further than Triplett. Kilduff, now a professor at NYU's Stern School of Business, didn't merely want to study competition that made sense (in sports or business, as opposed to classrooms). He wanted to study what he calls "turbo-competition." That is, competition selected by both parties: Each knows his opponent, each wants a fight, and each has a major stake in the outcome. He wanted to study, in a word, rivalry.

WHAT makes for a rivalry? To our (and Kilduff's) surprise, researchers paid scant attention to this question until relatively recently. In 2010, Kilduff joined with Hillary Elfenbein and Barry Staw to tackle the question in a study published in the *Academy of Management Journal*. (As we've noted throughout this book, process and terminology often cross seamlessly between the worlds of sports and business.) "We conceptualize *rivalry*," the authors wrote, "as a subjective competitive relationship that an actor has with another actor that entails increased psychological involvement and perceived stakes of competition for the focal actor, independent of the objective characteristics of the situation."

Hmm. Fortunately, they then clarified in plainer English: "In other words, rivalry exists when an actor places greater significance on the outcomes of competition against—or is more 'competitive' toward—certain opponents as compared to others."

Better. But even better yet? The research article opens with parallel quotes from two men whose names have become so synonymous with rivalry that they inspired a Broadway show on the very topic:

> *"When the new schedule would come out each year, I'd grab it and circle the Boston games. To me, it was The Two and the other 80."*
>
> —*Magic Johnson*

> *"The first thing I would do every morning was look at the box scores to see what Magic did. I didn't care about anything else."*
>
> —*Larry Bird*

That's rivalry reduced to its essence.

Of course, Kilduff's article goes beyond mere definitions. Befitting a management publication savvy enough to open with Magic/Bird quotes, the authors decided to collect data via a survey of sports experts: college basketball aficionados. They surveyed more than 400 student sportswriters at 73 universities across major conferences. Student journalists at each school were asked to rate the degree to which their university considered each of the other schools in its conference to be a close rival, with higher scores indicating stronger rivalries.

This method allowed the researchers to draw conclusions regarding the factors that play significant roles in the development (and persistence) of rivalries. Some findings were intuitive. For example, the number of times two teams have played each other predicts rivalry strength. But also important is the competitiveness of these matchups: The closer two teams are to an even head-to-head record, the stronger their rivalry tends to be. Makes sense, right? If, say, Duke almost always beats Clemson, it militates against a rivalry.

Interestingly, it is the *historic* win-loss split that makes the biggest difference; the two teams' more recent series tally proves to be less important. Rivalry, once formed, does not dissipate quickly, even if the circumstances that forged it have long since shifted. As we write this, the Harvard football team has beaten Yale 14 of their last 15 meetings. This has done little to diminish the intensity of the rivalry—one that Yale still leads 65-59-8.[2]

There were other surprising findings. Remember that each university's sportswriters were asked about *their own* school's perception of the rivalry, not how the other school or outsiders viewed the relationship. This left open the possibility of unrequited rivalry—of, say, Washington State fans saying, *Our biggest rival is the University of Washington*, only to be jilted by Huskies fans who cite the Oregon Ducks as their nemesis. There were some of these asymmetries. But for the most part perceptions of rivalry were reciprocal. When School A rated School B as a major rival, School B typically returned the (dis)favor.

The strongest predictor of rivalry to come out of these statistical models? Similarity. Teams within the same state are far more likely to be archrivals; even the distance in miles between two teams' campuses correlates with perceived rivalry. (Would Duke and North Carolina share such passionate dislike if they were not just eight miles apart?) But there's more than simple geography at play here. Other forms of similarity matter, too. The closer two programs are in terms of basketball reputation—i.e., all-time winning percentage and number of conference titles—the stronger their rivalry. The closer two schools are in terms of perceived *academic* reputation? Same finding: more likely to be rivals.

---

2. Yes, eight ties is a lot. But note that the most recent was in 1968, the famed "Harvard Beats Yale 29–29" game that spawned a documentary.

Take Amherst and Williams, which are only 60 or so miles apart in the western half of Massachusetts. The two liberal arts colleges have similarly sized student bodies, comparably photogenic campuses, commensurately lofty *U.S News & World Report* rankings, and even an overlapping history. (Amherst was founded when a traitor defected from Williams[3] to start a new school.) Yet they have a fiercer rivalry than the Clintons and Fox News.

Or consider DePauw and Wabash, two like-sized schools in central Indiana, only 27 miles apart. Their rivalry is such that in 1998, on the eve of their 105th football game, Wabash students stole De-Pauw's 350-pound Monon Bell, a heist that was described in a cover story in the next day's school paper. (Lead sentence: "Gentlemen, we have the bell.") Yet even citizens of Indiana frequently confuse the schools, so similar are their profiles. Likewise, many U.S. citizens might conflate Army and Navy, but the competition between the two service academies is so intense that cadets don't say hello when they pass on the quad; they say, "Beat Navy."[4]

The role of similarity in rivalry may seem to be intuitive: Of course nearby schools with overlapping fan bases and recruitment territories don't like each other; if Auburn and Alabama were not in the same state, fighting over recruits the way Greek city-states once fought over similarly scarce and valuable resources, would they be such polarizing forces? But the finding actually flies in the face of the conventional (and research) wisdom that we're attracted to those who are similar to us, whether in personal values, past experiences, demographics, physical appearance, or even genetics. While we're not as literal about the whole endeavor as Narcissus was, we're usually drawn to those who remind us of ourselves.

Perhaps it shouldn't surprise us, though, that similarity has dif-

---

3. Full disclosure: Sam's alma mater. Note that this disclosure has no bearing on the accuracy of the preceding word *traitor*.

4. For a psychodynamic perspective, Freud's concept of the "narcissism of small differences" makes similar predictions about personal rivals: the conflict between similar individuals with only minor differences between them is often quite heated.

ferent effects on those reviewing a website dating profile than it does on those who meet while in direct competition for scarce resources. We'd propose that the line between love and hate is just as thin as is often suggested. There is something unsatisfying about conceptualizing attraction and rivalry as opposite endpoints of a continuum; both phenomena are fraught with passion, arousal, and the potential for flouting rational thought.

Indeed, there's a closeness, a kinship, that comes with being bracketed together. Sure, Jack Nicklaus deprived Arnold Palmer of a bunch of trophies, just as Magic prevented Bird from winning a few more NBA titles and just as Rafael Nadal undercuts Roger Federer's claim to being the best tennis player ever (and vice versa). But there's a reason why all these sets of nemeses maintain a cordial social relationship today. Most rivals have the good sense to know that each is better off for the existence of the other. Often more rancor passes between the fans than between the combatants. Our most formative rivalries are often with those we love, as in sibling rivalry. Athletes often embody the very notion of frenemies.

THE most pressing question about rivalry, though, isn't how to define it or where it comes from. Rather, it's what effects it has on individual and team performance.

Examining the conventional wisdom that rivalry ennobles and that athletes perform their best against rivals turns out to be a tricky exercise. The elevation of one team ("rising to the occasion") could also be framed as the decline of the other. When teams are rivals, countervailing forces are at play.

When the Seahawks shut down the 49ers, is it because Seattle's defense meets the challenge or because San Francisco's offense fails to execute? Is a low field-goal percentage in basketball a function of tenacious defense or weak offense? Does a shutout in a Red Sox–Yankees game mean that one team pitched well or that the other hit poorly? And should we differentiate between team sports and individual sports, or between strength sports and precision sports?

Kilduff recently took on this thorny set of questions in a study of competitive runners. He returned to his roots, examining a running club in the State College area. First, he asked runners about their perceived rivalries. More than half (57 percent) indicated that they felt a rivalry with at least one other local runner, and the number was even higher (77 percent) among those who had competed in at least five races the year before. When asked how these rivalries affected them, the majority said that having rivals motivated them to work harder and push themselves further.

Self-reported perceptions about rivalry are all well and good, but just as Triplett knew when he created his competition machine, observable performance is where the rubber meets the road. So Kilduff pored through race results. And, consistent with what the runners had claimed, performance was better in races involving at least one rival. Specifically, the presence of a rival predicted a pace close to five seconds faster per kilometer (about 7½ seconds faster per mile). This might not seem like a huge change, but it's close to 25 seconds shaved off a 5K time—hardly insignificant.

Kilduff has also examined the effects of rivalry in team sports. In his 2010 paper, he reported that men's college basketball teams blocked more shots and had higher overall defense-efficiency scores in games against defined rivals. Both outcomes are consistent with increases in effort. (Steals were also higher in rivalry games, though this difference was not statistically significant.) "It made some sense for our theory," says Kilduff, "because the common wisdom is that defense is a little more effort-based than offense."

In another paper, Kilduff analyzed nearly 3,000 matches over an eight-year span in Serie A, the top Italian soccer league, comparing games between rivals located in the same city (Roma vs. Lazio, Genoa vs. Sampdoria[5]) with intercity matches. The analyses revealed a notable increase in both yellow and red cards in rivalry games. This was consistent with the findings of a British research

---

5. A representative quote from a former Genoa CFC coach about the Genoa Derby against Sampdoria: "The only thing that counts in Genoa is the Derby. If you don't win it, it's like robbing a bank and getting out with a suitcase full of rags."

team a few years before. Its primary aim was to study home-field advantage in the English Premier League, but the researchers also found that before playing games against supposedly fierce rivals, players had higher testosterone levels than before other games. Interestingly, while players at all positions exhibited this effect, it was particularly strong among goalkeepers. In short, the effects of rivalry on athletic performance can be seen even at the neuro-chemical level.

This mirrored data gathered by Catapult, an Australian analytics and technology company at the forefront of biometric research in sports. Athletes wear Catapult's device, a sensor no bigger than an iPhone, under their jerseys during training and competition, providing access to 1,000 data points per second. Looking at data from Aussie Rules football games,[6] the Catapult scientists saw that when one club played a nearby club (for instance, Adelaide vs. Port Adelaide), players showed higher-intensity accelerations and work rates early in the matches, a tapering off in quarters two and three, and then a surge of intensity in the fourth quarter. This, said the Catapult scientists, was consistent with the testosterone spike found by the British researchers.

Of course, these effects can show up in the box score as well. According to a *Wall Street Journal* analysis of 15 top betting lines, in the last 25 years double-digit college football underdogs have kept their final margin within single digits 48 percent of the time in rivalry games, compared with only 39 percent in all other games. Teams that were betting-line underdogs also pulled off upsets at a higher rate in rivalry games. As the *Journal* put it: "The added effort may explain why rivalries seem to produce so many unexpected, unforgettable moments."

Still other research has explored the motivational impact of getting feedback from a rival. In one set of studies, researchers in the United Kingdom asked high-achieving university athletes to play

6. Athletes in U.S. pro leagues are prohibited from wearing Catapult devices during games.

multiple rounds of darts blindfolded. Halfway through, the participants (who got to take off the blindfold while they took a break) were told that they weren't performing very well and weren't showing any indication of future improvement.

When this feedback came from a researcher who was wearing a sweatshirt from the athletes' own university, the participants' subsequent performance got even worse. This downward spiral didn't occur, however, when the feedback came from a researcher wearing a rival school's sweatshirt. The dart throwers motivated to prove a rival wrong recovered the most from their earlier poor showing.

Notably, the arousing and motivating power of rivalry is not limited to on-field performance. Kilduff also has unpublished data that suggest that rivalry can lead decision-makers to adopt riskier, more aggressive strategies. NFL coaches, for instance, are more likely to go for it on fourth down or try for two-point conversions in rivalry games than they are in non-rivalry games.

Other than his upbringing in State College, why is Kilduff, a business-school professor, so invested in sports rivalries? (And why are business schools and publications so interested in his work?) Because similar tendencies have been observed in business and financial settings.

One recent study conducted by Israeli researchers focused on auction behaviors. Anyone who has ever gotten into a bidding war on eBay knows full well that the emergence of an identifiable competitor can goad you into spending more money than you intended on that lamp, Burberry bag, or hard-to-find *Star Wars* action figure that your kids need to fill a gap in their newly expanding collection.[7] But you also know from this experience just how easy it is to develop an active distaste for a rival bidder you'll never meet.

The Israeli study demonstrates just how little it takes to work up a healthy sense of rivalry during an auction. Researchers gave participants an auction ID number and the opportunity to bid on

---

7.   That's our story, and we're sticking to it. The collection belongs to them.

consumer items. These were real bids backed by their own real shekels. The auction was of the sealed-bid variety, meaning that unlike in the escalating eBay battle, participants had only one shot to submit the highest bid.

Half of the participants were told that, for each auction, their bid would be randomly paired with that of another person in the study: Another sealed bid would be pulled out of a hat, and the higher of the two bids would win. Other participants were given the ID number of the person they'd be competing against. When the researchers examined the sealed bids, they found that knowing the ID number of their opponent produced bids that were, on average, almost 50 percent higher. That's how primed and ready we are to be motivated by rivalry: Simply learning that we have an identifiable rival is enough to do the trick—even if this "identifiability" comes only in the form of Bidder #0621 or #9963.

In many instances, rivalry has been a critical ingredient in business success. In 2010, one year before he died, Steve Jobs famously sent an e-mail to his top senior executives in which he outlined Apple's strategic plan for the coming year. The top objective listed? "Holy war with Google." Jobs's rivalry with Bill Gates was similarly legendary. Many view rivalries as the fire that fueled technological advances in the personal computing revolution. To paraphrase *Financial Times* reporter John Gapper, these were the feuds that made Silicon Valley fertile.

Jobs was renowned for trying to fire up the troops by referring to hated rivals. "Behind the lurid language and the emotional outbursts lay an entirely rational calculation," writes Gapper. "His company was likely to perform best if it had an enemy to fight. Its senior executives would work harder, its engineers and designers would be more inventive." First, the archenemy was IBM. Then Microsoft. Later Google. "The trick," according to Gapper, "was not to be too fussy about who that enemy was."

Of course, no one, not least Kilduff, is suggesting that rivalry is some sort of panacea when it comes to improving motivation or assuring fair and healthy competition. There is a dark side to rivalry as well. (Recall the red/yellow-card findings from earlier; also see

Tribal Warfare, page 191.) The presence of a rival can lead to spikes in aggressive and even unethical behavior—yet another reason why Kilduff's work has important implications for the business world.

Consider a recent article Kilduff published with collaborators in Chile, the United States, and England. In one study, they instructed MBA students to imagine themselves in a negotiation with one of their company's chief competitors. When asked to ponder the likelihood that their competitor would be willing to use unethical negotiating tactics (for example, misrepresenting facts to gain a negotiating edge), the participants were more likely to report that they, too, would resort to such tactics. Additional studies demonstrated that merely thinking about a past competition with a rival made people more likely to cheat on a laboratory problem-solving task.

As Kilduff suspected from an early age, rivalry has great potential to shape effort and performance. But the science of rivalry emerges as complex and even contradictory. It can lead us to work harder, but it can also sap motivation for future engagement. It can bring out the best in a workforce, but it can also open the door for rule-bending and outright deceit. It can turn similar others into enemies, but it can also grease the skids for lifelong (and legendary) friendships.

Why We Want Gronk at Our Backyard Barbecue—and Why He Wants to Be There

It was sometime between the cocktail hour and the candle-lighting ceremony that the Town Cars started pulling up to the Oceanside Jewish Center on Long Island. Staggered to arrive every half hour, the cars each contained a prodigiously large man. Dressed for the occasion, Ottis Anderson, Stephen Baker, Ahmad Bradshaw, Michael Cox, Walter Thurmond, Henry Hynoski, and Prince Amukamara came ready to party.

Most of their teammates and colleagues spent this 2014 Memorial Day weekend—smack in the middle of the NFL off-season—frolicking in Vegas or South Beach or the Hamptons. But these seven current and former members of the New York Giants had a different event on their social calendar.

They were headed to A. J. Rovner's bar mitzvah party.

Bless Aunt Barbara and Uncle Dennis, who had flown in from Florida. Same for Dad's college baseball teammates, who came from as far away as California. And A.J. was thrilled to spend the day with his siblings and scores of friends from camp and school in the Rockaways section of Long Island. But, unmistakably, the honored guests at this party were the Giants. Scattered among the tables, they were feted like royalty. They were fed generously and approached for autographs and photos. They were asked to show their Super Bowl rings and peppered with questions about the coming season.

It was a situation that called for conviviality, and fortunately the Giants had large reserves from which to draw. It was a situation that called for a suspension of irony, and fortunately the players were happy to oblige. In an air full of shouting and loud music, they danced the hora and helped raise A.J. in his chair. After the meal they played Pop-A-Shot and air hockey and posed with kids in the photo booths. They noshed and kibitzed, comporting themselves like mensches.

Amukamara posted an image and a video from the night on his Instagram feed. He sounded downright rabbinic when he added the tag: *Bar Mitzvahs are no joke!!!* (Can we get an *Amen?*)

When a video of the players dancing inevitably made its way to YouTube, the header read, "Prince Amukamara crashes Bar Mitzvah party." But Amukamara and his teammates didn't crash at all. They were expected guests. Marc Rovner, a New York lawyer, paid handsomely for their attendance. Marc, in fact, cut the friends-and-family guest list by 100 adults to offset the expense of hiring the Giants. He has no regrets. "I wanted to make it special," he says. "We're a family of Giants fans—we go to all the games, the preseason camp, the Super Bowls when they make it—and I figured, you only live once."

For most of the players, their appearance was arranged via Thuzio, a business that, as its press material puts it, "connects the public with professional athletes [to] provide a wide variety of experiences." Which is to say, it enables us commoners to spend time in the company of the contemporary lords who are professional athletes.

Thuzio was founded by Mark Gerson, an amiable Yale Law School grad and New York City tech entrepreneur. The inspiration: In 2003, Gerson was in the market for a 60th birthday gift for his father, a Brooklyn Dodgers fan since childhood. Through a mutual friend, Gerson arranged a dinner at a Westchester restaurant with Ralph Branca, the former Dodgers pitcher best known for being on the mound when Bobby Thomson hit the Shot Heard 'Round the World—the seminal game-winning home run that clinched the 1951 pennant for the Giants. In his 70s, Branca still had cachet; but how could it be accessed? There was no agent involved, no contract. "It wasn't systematized," Gerson says. "I offered him something, and he accepted."

Not knowing what to expect or whether the awkwardness quotient would be insurmountable, the Gersons were pleasantly surprised by what followed. More than a decade later, the younger Gerson can still recall the conversation with a stunning level of precision. "Best gift I ever got him," he says. "Much better than a tie."

Through another mutual friend, Gerson knew Tiki Barber, the former Giants running back. Barber was renowned for his ability to run the ball—he retired as the leading rusher in Giants history—but also renowned for his urbane ways. Unlike his teammates, who preferred suburbia, Barber, a self-styled *bon vivant*, lived in Manhattan. He was a regular on the Gotham benefit circuit and moonlighted on morning television, ending up with a correspondent's position on the *Today* show. He made more than a few appearances at corporate functions, birthday parties, and, yes, bar mitzvahs. Sometimes he was paid; sometimes he was doing a favor for friends.

Over cigars, Gerson and Barber discussed the peculiar dynamic of such appearances. "[Sports] are people's passion, right?" Barber said. "There are these intimate interactions with athletes that people have affinity for. . . . They want the aura, the stories, whatever it is. But there was no market." To change that, the two men created Thuzio.com (playing on the word *enthusiast*) and launched it in 2012.

It's easy to lose yourself for hours on the Thuzio website, scanning the available athletes and the accompanying price guide. Sure, there are the predictable golf outings and dinners and corporate appearances. But there also are more creative offerings. It all has echoes of the MasterCard "priceless" commercials. Except that there are very clear prices:

- Lunching with Pete Rose: $8,125 (which is, curiously, $1,875 less than lunch with Rose's Cincinnati Reds contemporary Johnny Bench).

- Elk hunting with Ryan Klesko, once an Atlanta Braves first baseman and corner outfielder of some distinction: $9,000.

- Playing a pickup basketball game with former NBA All-Star and gifted trash talker Gary Payton: $12,500.

- Attending a gymnastics meet with Olympic hero and gold medalist Kerri Strug: $2,240.

- Playing paintball with retired Red Sox infielder Kevin Youkilis: $3,600.

- Conscripting Ralph Sampson, the former NBA All-Star and top pick in the 1983 draft, to officiate your league's NBA Fantasy Draft: $5,000.

Other play dates are available on demand. In 2014, Roger Clemens was the featured speaker at an intimate Thuzio-arranged corporate dinner in the banquet room of a Manhattan steakhouse. As the night wore on, Clemens departed from script, plugged his iPhone into a karaoke machine, and joined guests in singing various country music hits. Jose Canseco, an art enthusiast, recently joined clients in California for an unlikely day of painting. John Starks made a surprise appearance at a Manhattan bachelor party and smoked cigars with the groom and his bros on a roof deck. And you can arrange for a two-hour appearance from U.S. midfielder and 2015 World Cup hero Carli Lloyd at your next event, though be warned that the price tag did skyrocket 200 percent the week after her title game hat trick.

In some cases these interactions are drenched in nostalgia. Of the 20,000 sports figures under contract to Thuzio—a number likely to have increased by the time you read this—many are retired. This is as good a place as any to note that our introduction to Thuzio (and the inspiration for this chapter) came when Jon's son, the irremediable Mets fan, received a video message from Mookie Wilson as a bar mitzvah gift. Reading off a prompter on Thuzio's app, Wilson offered the following with great cheer:

"Hey Ben, I hear it's your bar mitzvah! Mazel tov, from Mookie Wilson! Your accomplishment is just like the time I beat Buckner to first base in Game Six of the 1986 World Series. Only yours comes with a big ol' party, tons of lox, and Uncle Saul complaining about the chicken. You know, some people are surprised when they learn my real name isn't Mookie Wilson. It's Herbert Morris Bloomfield. Why, I remember my very own bar mitzvah back in Bamberg, South Carolina. We schlepped to the synagogue for brisket and Manische-witz. My mother fell off the chair doing the hora. . . . Well, by now you probably figured out that I'm not Jewish. But you are. So con-grats on your big day."

For this, Wilson was paid $99, less Thuzio's 20 percent commis-sion.

A surprising number of the athletes listed, though, are active, many in the meatiest years of their career. Jrue Holiday might be a starting guard for the New Orleans Pelicans in the middle of a four-year, $41 million contract (an annual average salary of $10,250,000, or roughly $40,000 per weekday), but he is happy to supplement his income with a $2,500 fee for joining you for lunch or dinner.

True to his, er, festive reputation, Rob Gronkowski, the New England Patriots' tight end, will show up at your backyard barbecue for $15,000. As a Knicks shooting guard, J. R. Smith might have been making $6 million annually, but he was still happy to channel his inner Amukamara and show up at New York–area bar mitzvahs; after being traded to the Cavaliers, Smith presumably took his jump shot and his open social calendar with him to northeastern Ohio.

Snicker, if you must, but there is clearly a market here. By the summer of 2014, Thuzio had raised $6 million in Series A fund-ing. Gerson and Barber reached the following conclusion: This is the new iteration of fan-athlete connection. For decades there were autographs. Then there were selfies. In between there were quirks. (In 2002, a baseball fan—or so we hope—paid $250 at an auction for gum chewed by major-league pitcher Tim Hudson; that same year someone paid $23,000 for bone chips from the elbow of Mariners reliever Jeff Nelson.) Now we have Thuzio-brokered interactions. As Barber told us, "We're getting closer to those that we admire. We have services for social networking. But the experience itself—the memory, the story you can tell—that is very powerful."

The question is, *why* is this so powerful?

Why would there be a market to play a pickup game with NBA guard Ramon Sessions ($2,000)? To join San Francisco 49ers linebacker NaVorro Bowman for a round of golf ($4,000)? To play Ping-Pong with Giants linebacker Jonathan Goff ($200)? To share steaks with Lawrence Taylor, as five recently minted MBAs did, each chipping in $2,000 of his hedge-fund signing bonus for a rollicking evening with perhaps the greatest linebacker ever? Why do we want to be in the orbit of the famous?

The Thuzio promotional material calls it a "connection," but really, it's something more fleeting. It's not as though clients are starting or even seeking lifelong friendships; these are simply blind dates, or "one-offs," to use Barber's term. (Realizing that, Thuzio altered its business model to include more corporate outings and a "Thuzio Executive Club," increasing its chance of repeat business.) It's not as though the Thuzio customer *truly* thinks he's matching skills when he—the majority of clients are men—plays Kenny Anderson, the former NBA point guard, in a game of one-on-one, or tries to hit a knuckleball thrown by R. A. Dickey.[1]

BEHAVIORAL science identifies various possible explanations for Thuzio's allure to Joe and Jane Sports Fan. For starters, consider that for more than a century, companies have spent big money on celebrity product endorsements. Why? Because they're betting that the positive feelings consumers have for beloved actors or athletes will transfer to their brands.

We do the same thing on a more personal level with celebrities: We tend to view ourselves in a positive light (see *Inner Mayweather,*

---

1. If you were wondering, clients can't use Thuzio for creative pranks. At the start of the 2014 college football season, a customer attempted to lease the services of Tiki Barber and his twin, Ronde, proud University of Virginia alumni, to make a video message parroting the phrase "Virginia Tech Rules. Go Hokies!" Perceiving this as an act of treason—and, more important, a social media flame accelerant—the Barbers kindly refused.

page 30) and to view success and fame in a positive light; therefore, anything that increases our proximity to famous athletes and other celebrities has the potential to rub off on us in ego-friendly ways. In the 1970s, Arizona State University psychologist Bob Cialdini gave a name to this tendency to publicly associate the self with successful others. *Basking in reflected glory*, Cialdini called it. Or BIRGing, for short.

In the first BIRGing studies, researchers explored the phenomenon at universities that had big-time football teams, such as LSU, Michigan, Notre Dame, and USC. Their initial study was simple: It found a statistically significant tendency for students to wear more apparel emblazoned with their school's name or logo on Mondays after the football team won compared to Mondays after a tie or loss.

Subsequent studies provided empirical evidence for yet another behavior familiar to sports fans: Students were more likely to use first-person language such as *we* in describing wins than they were when talking about losses. So it's "We beat Wisconsin!" But it's "They lost to Indiana."

An interesting aspect of this tendency to BIRG: It's exaggerated when one has been dealt a setback in another walk of life. Poor grade on an exam? Rejected job application? That's when we become *most* likely to append ourselves to the success stories of tangentially related others, seeking an ego boost by association. "People appear to feel that they can share in the glory of a successful other," writes Cialdini. "The more intriguing form of the phenomenon occurs when the one who basks in the glory of another has done nothing to bring about the other's success."

So it is that your co-worker brags about his best friend's brother's roommate's cup of coffee in the major leagues. And though this is something of a cynical take, perhaps it also explains why people shell out a few hundred dollars for the privilege of rubbing shoulders with a former Pro Bowler. (And would pay even more to literally rub those shoulders. Remember the chewing-gum and bone-chip auctions we mentioned earlier? Research indicates that the more physical contact someone famous has had with an object,

the more people will pay for it, as if celebrity is somehow a conta-
gious condition.)

Research also suggests that associating with elite (or once elite)
athletes bestows upon the rest of us peasants an aura of legitimacy
and accomplishment. Hobnobbing with a star permits you to assert that you've finally made it into an exclusive club—never mind
that it's a temporary membership with a booking fee. And the less
secure we are in our own standing, the more we're motivated to put
on such airs, to name-drop, to assure others that we really, truly
belong.

By this line of thinking, then, who are the individuals most likely
to seek out the validation provided by a Thuzio connection? Perhaps
those with one foot just inside the circles of fame or athletic prowess and one foot outside: the ex–college athletes who never hit the
big time, the rabid sports junkies whose sports knowledge far out-
strips their athletic skills, the business leaders who are well known
in certain circles but are not celebrities on a larger stage . . . people
who fancy themselves members of the club, but just barely, which
motivates them to publicly assert legitimacy. Think about the old
joke:

Q: How do you know if a guy went to Harvard?

A: He just told you.

Actually, research demonstrates that it's not the Harvard grad
who is most likely to go out of her way to mention her Ivy League
status but rather the alum of one of the "lesser" Ivies. (Think Ed
Helms's cloying character Andy Bernard in *The Office*, who relent-
lessly brings up his Cornell a cappella bona fides.) This was the
hypothesis recently tested by Paul Rozin and his fellow researchers
at Penn. When they asked a national sample to free-associate to the
phrase *Ivy League*, more than 40 percent of responses were "Harvard" and fewer than 2 percent were "Penn." So perhaps it shouldn't
be surprising that when samples of Harvard and Penn undergrads
were asked to write down how they describe their university to oth-

ers, far more of the Penn students touted their Ivy League affiliation; the Harvard students presumably felt less of a need to.

Rozin and colleagues argue that it's those individuals perceived as just barely over the membership border in a particular social category who are most likely to emphasize or exaggerate their group status. This is why small airports are more likely to use the word *international* to describe themselves than are major airports. It's the Tulsa International Airport—even if its website offers no evidence of direct flights outside the U.S.—but it's simply O'Hare, Logan, or Atlanta.

This is the reason why chiropractors and osteopaths, Rozin argues, may be more likely than MDs to insist on the title *Doctor*. Why the nouveaux riches show their wealth more ostentatiously than the old-money set. And, back to the topic at hand, perhaps why those with merely tangential ties to the world of sports are most drawn to Thuzio.

In all candor, though, we're not totally satisfied with these explanations. Yes, people often bask in reflected glory, especially after a threat to the ego. Yes, those least secure in their own standing most want others to know that they belong. And, sure, some may get a rise out of compelling famous athletes to act (and tweet) at their command.

But these accounts seem too cynical to us. Spend a few minutes on Thuzio.com if you haven't yet: The experience doesn't feel anything like an exercise in narcissism or self-promotion.[2] After all, many purchases on the site are made as gifts for others. We confess: Once we started working on this chapter, Thuzio videos became our go-to present for friends and relatives. When his best friend from high school turned 40, Sam figured who better to relate the milestone birthday wishes than one Elbert (Ickey) Woods, former star of their hometown Cincinnati Bengals:

"Hey, Matt. This is Ickey Woods. Your buddy Sam tells me you're

---

2 Granted, few exercises in self-promotion *do* feel like that, since they often occur outside our conscious awareness. But still . . .

having a birthday party. He also tells me that he's sorry he can't shuffle down to Nashville for it, so he sent me instead. Actually, you and I have a lot in common, Matt. It was in Cincinnati where both of us first hit it big. Also, no one calls either of us by our actual first names. And both of us have starred in car insurance commercials. . . . Okay, well, two out of three ain't bad. Congrats on the big 4-0. Sam and I are sorry we can't join you in person, but next time we're all in the Queen City at the same time, let's grab dinner, just the three of us. You know, like in the old days."

OF course, even a gift can be a way to signal one's own accomplishments and status, but there's clearly more to the fan experience on Thuzio than matters of ego. There's a certain wistful nostalgia born of scrolling through the site's profiles, as in, *Oh, I remember that guy!* and *I had his poster in my bedroom when I was 12.* "Ask someone, 'Remember the time you met an athlete you admired?' and everyone has a story," says Gerson. "You remember everything, the context, what the athlete said. It just creates this lasting impression." People, places, and objects that remind us of our youth usually make us happy, which makes Thuzio a clear emotional draw for those of us whose childhood memories are intertwined with sports events and experiences.

Indeed, nostalgia provokes a powerful and rewarding response, "serving as a repository of positive affect," according to psychologists in a recent review article on the topic. In studies in which people have been asked to conjure up nostalgic events from their lives, one clear result is elation. Others include an increase in positive self-regard, making an unpredictable world seem somehow more orderly and less threatening, and a strengthening of social bonds. "Nostalgia is a social emotion," proposes the same paper. "Close others come to be momentarily part of one's present . . . thus counteracting the effect of loneliness."

Thuzio strikes a chord because it taps into a form of nostalgia specific to the sports fan. For many of us browsing the site, there's a stark contrast between the then and now of our fan experience.

Back in the day, when these star athletes were in their primes, they (and even their less famous teammates) seemed like residents of another universe, inaccessible to mere mortals like us. And, in fact, they were. Short of a chance encounter in the hotel elevator or a friend-of-a-friend who had "connections," sharing a conversation (let alone a meal) with one of our heroes was once thought to be unattainable, a fantasy.

Cue the Internet era. And Gerson and Barber's brainchild. Suddenly what once was impossible is now just a few clicks away. That in itself is intoxicating. It's a pleasure to browse through these athletes' profiles as if on a platonic version of Tinder, to realize that an actual (or at least virtual) connection is there for the asking if you're willing to spend the money. For just $99, Mookie Wilson will not only make the day of your family friend by offering personalized congratulations but also will also throw in his best Yiddish accent. For those of us on the other side of 20, Thuzio opens doors that were always closed back in our formative years as sports fans.

After spending more time than we'd like to admit lost among the profiles on the site, we've come to believe that the Thuzio experience transcends the need for ego satisfaction or basking in reflected glory. There's an underlying emotional draw to the website. It captures the zeitgeist of the modern digital consumer era: a nearly perfect marriage of fanaticism, nostalgia, disposable income, and the irrepressible human desire to make social connections.

THE other side of the Thuzio equation is no less fascinating. What motivates the athletes to take part? Sure, some of it is purely financial—especially in the case of former players and coaches whose earning potential has diminished since their heydays. Who wouldn't want to make $20,000 (or in the case of bigger-name clients such as Mike Ditka and Bob Knight, double that) for playing a round of golf or speaking at a dinner? "You're having fun, telling some stories, and making more money per hour than the top lawyer," says Barber. "It's like, why not?"

But that doesn't explain Mookie Wilson or Ickey Woods netting

$80 after commission for recording a video. And what about the active players? Rob Gronkowski makes roughly $500,000 per NFL game. Given the labor/leisure trade-off, it's puzzling that he would seek an extra $15,000 to show up at a barbecue.[3]

Independently, Barber and Gerson claim that the active athletes have recognized that their earning potential won't last forever, and, says Barber, "You should get it while you can." They assert that athletes are, in effect, creating their own actuarial table. Amortized over their lifetime, that $2,500 breakfast date or $10,000 birthday party makes sense right now, while their earning potential is at its peak. It's an intriguing theory, but it seems awfully charitable, especially given what we know about many athletes' famously imprudent budgeting skills and spending habits.

An additional explanation: The athletes also like being the center of attention, whether overseeing a fantasy draft or being the main attraction at a dinner reception. While most of us (at least under the influence of Sodium Pentathol) would admit to a fondness for attention, this, too, seems an inadequate explanation. These are, after all, professional athletes. What does holding court at a steakhouse do for you that performing in front of 80,000 fans and a national television audience does not?

Once again, we'd propose that there's more than ego and cold calculation involved here. As we found in our analysis of what draws fans to the Thuzio site, emotion and other social processes play an underrated role in the athletes' willingness to get involved. Sure, there are financial motivations—but talk to athletes who have signed with Thuzio and a common theme emerges: These interac-

---

3.   Of course, there's a long history of athletes making curious economic decisions along these lines, perhaps most famously when Chicago Bulls rookie Ron Artest applied for a job at Circuit City, reportedly because he wanted to take advantage of the employee discount on a new stereo. Or consider these 2015 tweets from Miami Dolphins defensive tackle A. J. Francis: "Just applied to be an Uber driver . . . I hope my background check goes well . . . People ask me why would you want to be an Uber driver if you play in the NFL . . . You know what's better than NFL money? More money." Francis needs to check out Thuzio: presumably, he could earn a month's worth of Uber fares by offering to drive a few Miami fans to work just one time.

tions are usually fun. Gronkowski is going to spend his summer weekend wearing Zubaz pants and drinking beer at a barbecue anyway, so why not earn a little cash while he's at it? Why not get paid to have fun?

And it's not just *any* athlete who agrees to be listed on Thuzio. In many cases it's the gregarious type, the fan favorite, the clubhouse glue guy, the reliable "good quote" always up for talking with the media after games. Mookie and Ickey? Yes. *Trick-or-treating with Albert Belle? Hold your own press conference with Bill Belichick?* Not so much.

There's a similar argument to be made about the appeal of Twitter to athletes. We often talk about this in terms of athletes seeking to expand the reach of their "brands" or using social media for product endorsement. But when Marion Hambrick and colleagues at the University of Louisville conducted a content analysis of thousands of tweets from athletes across a wide range of team and individual sports, they found that only 5 percent of tweets fell into the category *promotional*. The most common category? *Interactivity*, or direct contact with fans, at 34 percent.

Thuzio offers its athletes similar prospects: direct interaction with fans, but in an attractive package in a controlled environment—not hordes of angry opposing fans or autograph seekers interrupting dinner, but rather someone fond enough of you to pay for a limited-time engagement on prearranged terms.

So back to our earlier question: What does holding court at a steakhouse do for the athlete that performing on the field in front of thousands of fans does not? Actual social connection. We humans thrive on this stuff, particularly when it makes us feel good about ourselves. We like spending time with those who like spending time with us; we're attracted to those who find us attractive. There's a reciprocity to liking that keeps us coming back for more.

Now, far be it from us to claim to know what it's like to be cheered on in a stadium by tens of thousands of adoring fans—it's not an occupational hazard of our particular lines of work. But one of the basic precepts of social psychology is that one-on-one interaction feels very different from interacting with the nameless, faceless masses. The roar of the crowd doubtless boosts ego, as well as adrenaline. But face-to-face conversation fills other needs; the fawned-on individual feels good in a different way. Why else does the comedian look for an excuse to visit the bar after a successful set? Or the public speaker linger a bit longer than necessary at the end of the talk?

Our conclusion: Thuzio isn't a one-sided exchange of services for money. It's a two-sided experience. Both parties get something out of the transaction, and the fees are often the least of it.

Tribal Warfare

WHY THE AGONY OF THE OTHER TEAM'S DEFEAT FEELS JUST AS GOOD AS THE THRILL OF OUR TEAM'S VICTORY

When the Los Angeles Dodgers opened the 2011 baseball season by hosting San Francisco, they deployed 457 security people at the ballpark to avoid hostilities. That didn't stop a millionaire from chartering a plane to fly over Dodger Stadium displaying the message DODGERS STILL SUCK, FROM SF CHAMP FANS. And it didn't prevent Bryan Stow, a Giants fan and paramedic from Santa Cruz, from being beaten to within an inch of his life in the parking lot after the game. His crime? Allegedly he told a gloating L.A. fan to pipe down, adding, "I'd rather eat my own feces than a Dodger Dog." He ended up in a coma and suffered permanent brain damage.

That same year, after the Philadelphia Flyers lost 3–2 to the New York Rangers in the Winter Classic, a pack of Flyers fans repaired to Geno's, a popular cheesesteak shack in South Philly. Standing in line, a hometown fan wearing a Claude Giroux jersey exchanged trash talk with a Rangers fan wearing Ryan Callahan's jersey. The Rangers fan, Neal Auricchio, an off-duty policeman and an Iraq War veteran from Woodbridge, New Jersey, held up his hands and flashed the universal let's-all-just-calm-down sign. The Flyers fan was having none of that. Dennis Veteri was a 32-year-old Philadelphian with a criminal record so long it could be serialized. This literal Broad Street Bully knocked out Auricchio with a punch to the face. Auricchio suffered a concussion and lacerations that required facial reconstructive surgery. Veteri ended up with a litany of assault charges.

We see this sort of thing before, during, and after games and matches. The strange phenomenon of the bleacher brawl has become as much a part of the sports tableau as the Kiss-Cam and that catchy White Stripes song. There are plenty of reasons why. Fans get a rush watching others compete—and sometimes fight—so they leave the arena "all jacked up," girded for battle of their own (see *Acting on Impulse*, page 90). As always, alcohol clouds judgment, kills inhibition, and fuels conflict. So it's easy to chalk up these worst-case scenarios to toxic combinations of arousal, booze, and miscreant personalities. More sobering (no pun intended), though, is the conclusion that these notorious episodes are only extreme examples of a more universal tendency: Sports fandom begets a tribal mentality.

You probably don't need research studies (or us) to convince you that the allegiance of sports fans runs deep. But *just how deep* is fascinating. The experience of rooting for your favorite team can actually be captured at a neural level. In 2010, Mina Cikara (then a Princeton postdoctoral researcher, now a Harvard professor) joined two other colleagues to scan the brains of Yankees and Red Sox fans as they viewed a series of baseball game updates. Using functional magnetic resonance imaging, or fMRI—in effect, a video of brain activity—the researchers monitored changes in blood flow to different regions of the brain in real time. What they found was extraordinary.

When fans saw highlights of their own team doing well—getting a big out, stealing a base, hitting a homer—activity increased in a region called the ventral striatum, often referred to as the pleasure center of the brain. Self-reports of how much pleasure each fan experienced based on the game results followed a similar pattern. But what happened to fans when their team failed? The researchers found greater activity in the anterior cingulate cortex, the region of the brain associated with emotional responses to pain—whether our own or the witnessed pain of a loved one. Here, though, the spike was triggered by mere news of a batter striking out or a pitcher walking the bases loaded. Even though the baseball fans weren't observing physical pain, each had a neurological experience akin to that of watching his spouse suffer an intense headache or break a bone.

Even more striking was how the fans responded to the performance of their rivals. According to both the fMRI and participants' self-reports, when a Red Sox player committed an error, Yankees fans experienced a surge of joy. When a Yankee was thrown out trying to steal second, Red Sox fans felt pleasure. And they did so to the same degree as when they witnessed the positive plays of their own team: Seeing a rival lose was just as gratifying as seeing their own team win. It was *schadenfreude* (extracting pleasure from someone else's misfortune) distilled to its neural essence.[1]

As a control, the researchers showed the same fans miscues and errors committed by players on non-rival teams, such as the Blue Jays and Orioles. When the participants saw the outcomes of these plays, they were indifferent. In other words, only when the other team was their big rival did watching its slipups create just as powerful an emotion as seeing their favorite team succeed. For that matter, watching a rival succeed proved *even more painful* than their own team's failure, as any fan who has been trapped in enemy territory when an archrival wins a title can attest.

But back to the bleacher brawl. The fMRI study looked at more than just brain activity and fans' perceptions. After presenting the series of highlights, researchers also asked respondents to assess the level of aggression they felt toward their archrival. Most troubling to Cikara and her colleagues: Data indicated that those fans whose brains showed the greatest pleasure response to a rival player's failure were also the ones who reported harboring the most aggressive tendencies. If we can take them at their word, these are

---

1. Ever heard of the word *mitgefül*? We hadn't either. It's the opposite of schadenfreude, defined as sadness derived from the sadness of others. If you needed further evidence of just how widespread our tendency is to enjoy seeing our enemies lose, just ponder that one of these words has become commonplace among non–German speakers and the other remains unfamiliar.

the fans most likely to pour beer on or curse at an opposing fan. "The failures . . . of a rival out-group member may give . . . a feeling that may motivate harming rivals," the researchers suggest. Applying this idea beyond the world of sports fandom to more global conflicts, the researchers draw grim conclusions about rival tribes' abilities to resolve tension and refrain from violence. "A potent predictor of *schadenfreude*," they explain in a follow-up study, "is envy."

Who among us can't relate? When the perfectly pleasant classmate next to us in class fails the exam, we're unaffected. But when the straight-A student, whom we may view as an annoyance and a rival, fails the same test, we're much more likely to get that private jolt of glee. Which gives us more guilty pleasure, seeing a common thief arrested or a multimillionaire charged with insider trading? When people seem to "deserve" their misfortune, or when we feel resentment or envy, empathy falls by the wayside and a dark side of human nature rears its head.

There are unsettling truths underlying the whimsical scarlet-and-gray T-shirt that reads, *My two favorite teams are Ohio State and whoever is playing Michigan* (or, for that matter, the maize-and-blue *Ohowihateohiostate* bumper sticker):

- Many of us watch sports to root *against* as much as to root *for*.

- The failures of our enemies can be just as enjoyable as our own successes.

- The more we take pleasure in the missteps of our rivals, the more susceptible we may be to the type of harassment and violence detailed earlier.

Think back to Dennis Veteri, the fan at the Philly cheesesteak joint who fancied himself an amateur hockey goon. Research suggests that setbacks for the Flyers in the game earlier that afternoon—taking a bad penalty; giving up a goal—would have triggered activity in regions of his brain that are normally activated by personal pain. Such pain would only be exacerbated by the fact that it was inflicted by particularly hated rivals, the Rangers, in a tight 3–2 game with the outcome in the balance until the final horn. And, unfortunately, one "effective" way of replacing this distress with pleasure would have been to see misfortune inflicted upon the hated rivals—or at least someone who roots for them.

Just a couple miles from where Veteri's brutal encounter with Neal Auricchio occurred, law enforcement once opened what it called Eagles Court in the intestines of Veterans Stadium. It was such a foregone conclusion that Eagles fans would turn unruly and violent during NFL games that it made sense for the city to build a court—complete with judge and holding cell—inside the venue. Given the violence that persists in the stands during games (and afterward in parking lots), some municipalities might be wise to resurrect the idea. And add extra staff when the home team plays a heated rival.

Why We Are All Comeback Kids

Pinpointing Brett Favre's best NFL game is a fool's errand, on the order of picking Usain Bolt's best race or LeBron James's most fearsome dunk. Favre, who redefined football's concept of durable, holds virtually every league passing record. His Hall of Fame career encompassed 186 wins—including a Super Bowl—over two full decades, not to mention 6,300 completions, 508 of them for touchdowns.

But say this about the game Favre played in Week 16 of the 2003 season: It occupies a prominent spot in his Greatest Hits compendium. Favre's team, the Green Bay Packers, entered the game with an 8-6 record, angling for a spot in the postseason. Though the opposition, the Raiders, were in the throes of still another misbegotten season, the game was played in Oakland, home to famously inhospitable fans. That it was on *Monday Night Football* added to the intrigue.

The game marked Favre's 205th consecutive start, an NFL record for a quarterback. On the Packers' fourth play from scrimmage, he threw a 47-yard completion to receiver Robert Ferguson. On the sixth play, Favre guided an impeccably timed spiral toward Wesley Walls, who leaped and caught the ball in the back of the end zone for a touchdown. The quarterback looked up and pointed to the sky.

It was the *amuse-bouche* on the tasting menu that Favre was to serve that evening. With pass after pass, he shredded the Raiders' defense. There were darts and missiles and thunderbolts whose accuracy matched their force. There were lofted, arcing passes garnished with touch. Favre threw from the pocket and threw on the run. He threw into single coverage and lasered the ball into double coverage. He succeeded with savvy play calls, delivering the ball to his first-option receiver, and with typical Favre improvisation, throwing off his back foot to second and third options.

Favre started the game with nine straight completions. With his second touchdown he passed Fran Tarkenton on the NFL's all-time list with 343, trailing only Dan Marino. By the end of the first half he had thrown for 311 yards and four touchdowns, statistically the best half of his career. He continued in much the same manner until the Packers' coach, Mike Sherman, pulled him from the game in an act that was equal parts sportsmanship and, for the Raiders, mercy.

Favre's final stats for the game: 399 yards passing (three shy of his career high at the time), four touchdowns, and an astronomical passer rating of 155. More important, the Packers won 41–7, positioning themselves for the playoffs. After the game, observers exhausted their superlatives in praising Favre's performance. "I was just speechless, which is fun if you're just watching at home, but not real good if you're an analyst," recalls John Madden, who'd been working (or trying to, anyway) in the *Monday Night Football* booth that night. "It was just a spectacular, spectacular performance."

What made Favre's performance more spectacular still: The day before the game his father had died unexpectedly. In the late afternoon of December 21, barely 24 hours before the Packers-Raiders kickoff, Irv Favre had been driving on back roads in Mississippi and suffered a heart attack behind the wheel. His car flew off of Route 603 and landed in a ditch. According to the Mississippi State Highway Patrol, he was pronounced dead at 6:15 p.m. Irv Favre was 58.

Brett and Irv had shared an exceptionally close, if complex, relationship. Nicknamed Big Irv, Favre père was a high school football coach who conformed to stereotype. He was tough. Once, when he fell off a roof and blood spewed from his head, he refused to go to a hospital, settling for an ice pack instead. He was plainspoken as well as soft-spoken, one of those men who talked only when he felt that he had something worth saying. He could be stingy in his praise, even toward his highly decorated son. "Get your ass up" was a favorite response when Brett complained of injury. When Brett had a bad game, Irv would tell him, "You couldn't hit a bull in the ass with a bass fiddle."

Irv expressed affection through deeds, not words. "I don't think I ever remember my father telling me he loved me, and in no way is that an indication of a complaint," Brett once told journalist Les Carpenter. "If my father had told me he loved me I would have had to go take a shower." But Irv Favre was his son's best coach and his best friend.

Brett was at the Packers' team hotel in the Berkeley Hills when he learned of his father's passing. He told Sherman, who then gave his quarterback the option of sitting out the game. "For about five minutes there was some indecision about whether I would play," Favre would recall. "It didn't take long for me to say, 'You gotta play in this game.' What better way to honor your father?"

So "under tremendous emotional duress," as Al Michaels put it during the broadcast, Favre started in Oakland. And he played to the outer limits of his abilities. Early in the game Madden marveled on air, "How he does it, I have no idea. There's no road map for this."

Well, actually, there's . . . an entire atlas. An athlete returning to play—and play well—in the aftermath of tragedy is one of the most familiar tropes in sports.

A few years after Favre's game in Oakland, Baltimore Ravens wide receiver Torrey Smith turned in a virtuoso performance the day he found out that his brother had died in a motorcycle accident. ("Just to come out and show up and play is one thing," Ravens quarterback Joe Flacco said that night. "To come and play the way he did . . . it was really unbelievable.")

On a Saturday in 2012, Jovan Belcher, a linebacker for the Kansas City Chiefs, killed the mother of his child and then drove to the team's practice facility, where, in front of his coach and general manager, he turned the gun on himself and committed suicide. The next day the Chiefs blocked out "the mother of all distractions," as one columnist put it, to defeat the Carolina Panthers for Kansas City's only home win of the season. "It was a miraculous display of mental toughness," Chris Berman gushed on ESPN.

And such displays aren't limited to football. Days after his mother died in 1990, heavyweight boxer Buster Douglas flew to Japan and knocked out the supposedly indestructible Mike Tyson in perhaps the greatest boxing upset of all time. That same spring, in the weeks after Loyola Marymount's star basketball player, Hank Gathers, collapsed and died on the court during a game, the Lions played on in the NCAA Tournament, reaching the Elite Eight in a Cinderella story that captivated the country.

The legend of Chris Paul, the surpassing NBA point guard, dates back to 2002, when he was a high schooler in Winston-Salem, North Carolina. Grieving over the murder of his 61-year-old grandfather, Paul scored 61 points, purposely missing a free throw at the end of the game so he would have one point for each year of PaPa Chili's life.

During the 2014 NHL playoffs, the mother of Martin St. Louis, the quicksilver right wing of the New York Rangers, died of a heart attack. A day later he was in uniform, playing with no discernible drop-off as the Rangers staved off elimination and beat the Pittsburgh Penguins. ("Grieving Star Inspires a Rout by the Rangers" was the *New York Times* headline.) St. Louis played the following game as well, scoring a goal as the Rangers won again to push the series to a seventh game. It was Mother's Day.

During the 2015 World Series, Kansas City Royals pitcher Edinson Volquez lost his father, Daniel. Mid-series, Volquez went home to the Dominican Republic for the funeral. He returned to start the decisive Game Five, giving up just two hits over six innings. It was "unbelievable what Volquez achieved against incalculable odds," wrote the *Kansas City Star*.

In the face of profound tragedy, returning to work—never mind having a productive day at the office—strikes most of us as unthinkable. But doing so in sports has hardened into convention. The game must go on. In fact, when it *doesn't*—say, when Westfield-Brocton

(N.Y.) High canceled its 2013 football season after a teammate died following a helmet-to-helmet hit during a game—it's newsworthy.

The lore of the bounce-back athlete isn't limited to recovery from bereavement, either—it includes returning from many other kinds of turmoil. Witness Kobe Bryant scoring 42 points in the playoffs against San Antonio in 2004, just hours after his arraignment for sexual assault. Or the 2014 Los Angeles Clippers fending off Golden State in a playoff series marred by the disclosure that their owner, Donald Sterling, had been recorded making racially inflammatory statements.

Apart from his status during his playing days as a top-shelf NHL goaltender, Martin Brodeur of the New Jersey Devils might have been the King of Compartmentalization. During the 2003 playoffs, Brodeur's wife, Melanie, the mother of his four children, filed for divorce. Worse, she alleged that her husband "committed adultery on numerous occasions at a variety of locations." Worse still: One of Martin's alleged mistresses was Melanie's sister, Genevieve.

Although unmentioned in the court filings, this twist became public and triggered a predictable onslaught of taunting from opponents and fans. "Uncle Daddy" was among the few chants clean enough to print here. One sign among many: "Tickets to a Stanley Cup playoff game: $95. Alimony demanded from your wife: $9 million. Sex with your sister-in-law: priceless."

Even Melanie allegedly taunted Martin, calling him two hours before a game to announce that she was going on a date with a man he knew well. But there was no indication that any of this affected Brodeur's play. He was brilliant, an impermeable wall in front of the net. His goals against average during the postseason, a stingy 1.65 per game, was more than 20 percent better than during the regular season. The Devils won the Stanley Cup. (Several years later Martin married Genevieve. They must have had the most awkward receiving line in wedding history.)

THIS familiar story line in sports, the *comeback from adversity*, is usually framed in terms of the players' exceptionalism. Athletes are these aristocrats of nature, these outliers, these freaks. They don't just jump higher and run faster than we do; they are also mentally stronger, imbued with superhuman powers of compartmentalization, able to cycle through stages of grief or distraction that would incapacitate the rest of us. Not only do athletes come back from in-game deficits that would deflate mere mortals, but they also bounce back from the type of personal loss that would leave the rest of us barely functioning for weeks. They are, in the pop sports-psychology locution, "wired differently."

Except . . . they're not.

Most of us operate under the assumption that grief is a long process that needs to be negotiated patiently. It was Freud who used the German word *Trauerarbeit* to characterize the "work of grieving." It was Elisabeth Kübler-Ross who gave us the five stages of grief— denial, anger, bargaining, depression, and acceptance. In Judaism the relatives of the deceased spend a weeklong shiva period receiving visitors before even thinking of resuming their routines.

Other religions have similar mourning periods, and popular culture reinforces the notion that bad things happen when we resume a normal life too soon after a loss. In AMC's *Breaking Bad* (for our non-laundered money, the greatest show in the history of television), Jesse Pinkman's girlfriend, Jane, died after a drug overdose. That sent Jesse, a junkie who was already a lost soul, reeling.

But Jane's father, Donald—a buttoned-down, straitlaced type— returned to work as an air traffic controller after a brief hiatus and, still distraught from his daughter's death, made an error that caused a 737 to collide with another plane, killing scores of passengers. While newscasters questioned whether Donald had been allowed to return to work too soon, the poor guy attempted suicide. The moral was clear: He should have been more patient, let "nature run its course," let "time heal his wounds."

BUT here's the reality: Confronted with tragic or painful events, we humans often cope well. *Really well*. Within days, even hours, of trauma, we can regain our equilibrium and baseline function. Grief is not always the paralyzing force it's built up to be.

When we encounter an emotionally turbulent event such as a death in the family, a primitive set of brain and hormonal responses is activated. We get a surge of cortisol, the stress hormone. This can be disorienting; after a rush of cortisol, people describe a feeling akin to an altered state of consciousness, as the brain/body system kicks into emergency mode. This feeling subsides after a few hours, however, allowing us to continue with life as we know it fairly quickly. "There's that emergency response state, and then it's kind of done and we can think clearly again," explains George Bonanno, a Columbia University professor who specializes in trauma and grief. "Durability is the norm, not the exception."

How so? Bonanno has proposed and found evidence of four distinct trajectories of response in the wake of a potentially traumatic event (chart, below). There's *chronic* distress, an immediately high level of dysfunction that never really goes away. There's *delayed* reaction, whereby an individual initially experiences only a moderate level of grief and disruption but then gets worse rather than better

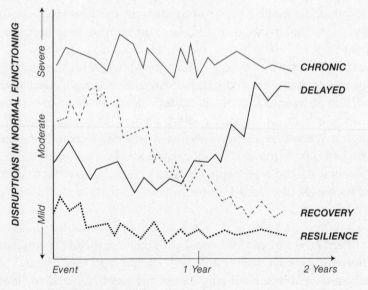

Adapted from Bonanno, 2004.

as time goes by. There's *recovery*, the gradual process of working through acute distress, in the "let nature run its course" manner. And, finally, there's *resilience*, the absence of major symptoms or dysfunction.

For many years, clinicians and researchers saw the bottom line on this graph, *resilience*, as an anomaly. Worse than that: Responding to bereavement without outward distress was viewed as a sign that something else was probably wrong with you. Some psychiatrists even argued that the ability to carry on normally in the face of loss indicated hidden psychopathology in need of treatment (and that a variety of other psychological symptoms that people struggled with could be traced back to earlier grief they had never completely "worked through").

Now we know better. Those first three types of response— *chronic*, *delayed*, and *recovery*? None is as common as *resilience*. In fact, resilience is more common than the other three types combined. In the typical bereavement case, research indicates that no more than 15 percent of people experience chronically elevated states of grief that disrupt regular functioning.

None of this is meant to minimize the profound impact of death or trauma, nor to marginalize those whose lives are sidetracked by grief. No one is implying that dealing with death is a piece of cake, that we can always Favre our way through life's losses, figuratively applying ice packs and rubbing dirt on wounds, even though more substantive treatment may be called for. For that matter, chronic distress rates do rise above the 15 percent range under particularly jarring circumstances—such as losing someone suddenly to an act of violence, or losing a child.

Still, it's surprising to most of us (including, apparently, some mental health professionals) to learn just how common resilience is—even in dealing with the worst of the worst, such as military combat or a terrorist strike. Take, for example, September 11, 2001. As Bonanno writes in his book *The Other Side of Sadness*, the vast majority of New York City residents showed no symptoms of trauma in the months after the attacks. Even among those who lost loved ones, rates of resilience were high. Of course, some people did experience chronic disruption to their ability to function. The prevalence of post-traumatic stress disorder (PTSD) among New Yorkers was estimated at 6 percent, a number that climbed closer to 30 percent for those injured and for those who lost a loved one *and* witnessed part of the attacks. As Bonanno notes, this is as emotionally wrenching as an experience can get: looking on helplessly while a loved one is trapped inside a burning building. "That is about the highest proportion of PTSD that any event will produce," Bonanno writes. "And yet just as many people who had experienced this same horror—one in three—had no trauma reaction at all."

Another common misconception about grief, beyond the assumption that it's usually incapacitating? That it's linear. That when we suffer a loss, our distress surges dramatically before beginning a slow but steady return to normality. That we progress through stages of grief in predictable order, from denial to anger to bargaining and so forth. But look again at the lines on that graph on page 202. Sometimes the effects of grief aren't immediately evident. And it's often not a smooth, ski-slope-like decline; instead, you see the rocky ups and downs of a hospital EKG.

Grief doesn't move in a straight line or arc. It comes and goes. It oscillates. During bereavement it's actually quite normal for people to smile or laugh as they talk about their loved one. In fact, this is one of the main reasons for the high rate of resilience: Grief usually isn't static or relentless. If it were, it wouldn't be as tolerable. Here's Bonanno again: "Fluctuation is adaptive because it allows us to engage in contrasting activities. We can't inhale and exhale at the same time, so we breathe in cycles." So it is with grief. "We can't reflect on the reality of a loss and engage with the world around us at the same time," he writes. "So we do that in cycles too."

Much of what we assume about grief turns out to be wrong. Maybe this shouldn't be surprising. Because when it comes to predicting the impact of various life events on our emotions—*affective forecasting* is what behavioral scientists, most famously Harvard's Dan Gilbert, call it—our success record is something akin to that of a Cleveland sports team. (We stink, but often in an endearing way.)

Ask us whether a particular event—the end of a romantic relationship; failing to get a promotion at work—will have positive or negative effect on us, and we get it right. That's easy. But what we get wrong is the intensity and duration of that emotional response, which we typically overestimate.

In one study, college students in dating relationships were asked to imagine how they would feel two months after the relationship ended. Their predictions overshot the mark dramatically: They thought they'd be far more miserable than they really would be. Which we know because the researchers compared their emotional forecasts to the reported happiness levels of other college students whose relationships *had* ended months earlier.

On a scale of 1–7, students still in relationships predicted a post-breakup happiness rating of 3.9. But students who had just gone through a breakup rated their happiness at 5.5. They weren't miserable at all. In fact, the newly single students were just as happy as the students still in couples, if not a tiny bit happier. Other studies yield similar findings: In one, college professors drastically overestimated how terrible they would feel after being denied tenure and having to look for another job. Forget about our intuitions regarding the effects of grief and our ability to bounce back from loss— we're pretty poor at predicting even how smaller bumps on the road of life will affect us.

The same goes for positive life events. That old yarn about people who win the lottery being no happier than the rest of us? It's usually tied to a 1978 study of 22 lottery winners, who reported happiness levels that were no greater than those of a control group (and who rated a variety of ordinary daily activities as less pleasurable than did the comparison group). Recent research tells a more complicated story: Lottery winners are at least a bit happier than the rest of us, and people with higher incomes typically report better mood than those who make less, but the differences are much smaller than you'd expect. Even with a positive event such as winning money, we return to emotional equilibrium much sooner than conventional wisdom suggests. "Winning the lottery is a happy event," writes Daniel Kahneman, author and Nobel Prize–winning behavioral economist. "But the elation does not last."

That even our intuitions about what makes us happy are flawed is a sobering realization. After all, so many of the choices we make—what neighborhood to live in, whom to marry—are largely based on such assumptions. Similarly disconcerting is the idea that even the greatest of life's spikes in happiness can be short-lived. After an immediate uptick in mood, we grow accustomed to our new situation, allowing the regular ups and downs of daily existence to resume. But this is the price we pay for our Pro Bowl–caliber ability to bounce back from the other side of the coin, the lousy hands life deals us.

The end of a college fling, a scratch-off ticket . . . we concede that these experiences are far removed from losing a loved one. But the underlying message is consistent: We're more emotionally resourceful and resilient than we think we are. And one thing that seems to help recovery is a return to the routine. "Paraplegics are often unhappy, but they are not unhappy all the time," writes Kahneman. Why? "Because they spend most of the time experiencing and thinking about other things than their disability."

Consider yet another type of trauma. Researchers have catalogued the various coping strategies employed by rape victims to get through the trying times after their attacks. Alas, some of these responses—withdrawing from friends or just staying home—predict an *increase* in negative symptoms. What predicts the desirable decrease in distress? Keeping busy. Getting back to a routine. If we're oscillating between negative emotional responses and engagement with the world around us, then more time devoted to the latter leaves less time to wrestle with the former.

On November 24, 1963, the NFL played a full slate of games. This, of course, was the weekend of John F. Kennedy's assassination. Though the entire nation was in mourning, Kennedy's press secretary, Pierre Salinger, thought that this bit of familiarity and routine—the pro football schedule—might help lift the collective mood. Implied: Only people as exceptional as athletes could pull off something like this. Pete Rozelle, then the NFL commissioner, would later refer to going ahead with the games as the biggest mistake of his career. But the games were played—and on Monday everyone else went back to work, too.

• • •

GIVEN conclusions like these, you might ask why more of us don't emulate Favre. If returning to normal rhythms accelerates recovery—and many of us get through some of the worst circumstances in life relatively unscathed—why aren't more of us back at work pulling off the performance of our careers the day after losing a parent or burying a childhood friend?

Socialization explains a lot. A pilot who returns to the cockpit the day after her husband's death or a salesman who goes back on his route immediately after losing a child would likely be regarded as cold and soulless (the very reaction Rozelle was worried about after Kennedy's assassination). And few of us are in the position of Favre or Chris Paul or Buster Douglas; that is, many of us have jobs that discourage returning to work so soon after trauma. We are urged to take bereavement leaves. We can swap shifts, postpone appointments, and adjust schedules in ways that don't apply to the sports world. Game 7, on the other hand, happens when the schedule says it happens; the Chicago Bears don't lend a spare quarterback to Green Bay in a gesture of goodwill. The games must go on. And so they do.

That Monday night in Oakland in 2003? After Favre's first touchdown pass, the Packers' kicker, Ryan Longwell, felt self-conscious as he lined up for the extra point. He realized he was crying, moved by sympathy for Favre. Any embarrassment abated when he looked at his holder, Doug Pederson, and saw that Pederson was crying, too. Green Bay receiver Donald Driver says that as the game unfolded, the entire team was "literally in awe" over what was happening. The television audience was as well. As Al Michaels put it after Favre's fourth touchdown, "Bring this script to a studio, and they throw it out. I mean, this is like fantasy." Even Raider Nation, so notoriously hostile, was moved to give Favre a standing ovation.

When the game ended and Favre's performance was the obvious story line, Lisa Guerrero, *Monday Night Football*'s sideline reporter, found the quarterback, who said, "I knew my dad would want me to play. I love him so much. I love this game so much. . . . I didn't ex-

pect this kind of performance, but I know he was watching tonight."
With that, Favre departed for the locker room and broke down, his
grief now oscillating back into the picture, the seemingly invincible
superhero a mere mortal after all.

The next time we encounter athletes performing—and performing well—so soon after a horrific event, we shouldn't be quite so
awed. We can take comfort (the cold variety, to be sure) in knowing
this: If we had to, we could probably pull it off, too. There are a lot
of things Brett Favre and other pro athletes can do that the rest of
us can't. But this isn't one of them.

Why Running on a Treadmill Is Like Running a Business

First, full disclosure: Before working on this book, Jon co-wrote a memoir with Al Michaels, the prominent television play-by-play announcer. The current voice of NBC's *Sunday Night Football*, Michaels has covered Super Bowls, World Series, NBA Finals, prize fights, Triple Crown horse races, and the Olympics, including, of course, the iconic "Miracle on Ice" hockey game at the 1980 Winter Games in Lake Placid. Yet ask him to list some of the most memorable sporting events he's ever called, and he's quick to mention an athlete and a race you're less likely to have seen: Gabriela Andersen-Schiess's agonizing finish in the 1984 Olympic Marathon. Who? What? Over to you, Al. . . .

Joan Benoit of the United States, then 27, wins the race and the gold medal. Grete Waitz of Norway wins the silver. Okay, no real surprise there. Then, around 20 minutes later, a Swiss long distance runner, Gabriela Andersen-Schiess, comes into the L.A. Coliseum, where the event ends, and she is clearly in distress. I mean, she is beyond exhausted. Teetering. Weaving. A baseball cap is pulled down over her face. The fans are all cheering like crazy for her to finish. I grew up in L.A. and went to the first Super Bowl at this venue. Been there a million times. And I've never heard it this loud. People see what's going on—a few times she looks as though she's going to topple over and completely collapse—and they're going absolutely nuts.

Andersen-Schiess was 39, but she was a legitimate medal contender. A dual citizen of Switzerland and the United States, she ran for Switzerland but worked as a ski instructor in Idaho when she wasn't training. Her past times were impressive. She'd won a marathon eight months earlier in Sacramento. There was nothing about the weather to explain her condition: It was warm but not hot, 66 degrees at the race's start in Santa Monica and 76 degrees by the end. It was humid, but the sky was clear, free of the smog that had plagued other events. Still, as Andersen-Schiess would later put it, "Something went haywire." In the second half of the race, she felt woozy. With a few miles to go, she was in visible distress.

By the last mile she was barely able to stay on her feet. As she entered the Coliseum tunnel, her head hung limply to one side. Orbiting the inside track of the arena, she weaved in and out of lanes like a drunk driver, at one point nearly hitting traffic cones. Her left arm dangled to the side. She was clearly suffering from heat exhaustion. (Feel free to spark up YouTube.)

As Michaels puts it: "I had recently covered the Indy 500 when one of the drivers died in a time trial. I had covered a football game when an official had a heart attack and died, and now I'm thinking *here we go again*. I thought she was going to die."

He wasn't alone. Race officials ran out to attend to Andersen-Schiess. She had the wherewithal to wave them off, aware that if they made physical contact with her, she would be disqualified. (That rule has since been changed.) When officials saw that she was still sweating, they deduced that she was not completely dehydrated and permitted her to continue.

It was now more than 20 minutes after Benoit had taken her victory lap. The gold medalist had recovered and was mingling with the crowd, signing autographs. With 75,000 fans standing and cheering an anguished woman few of them could identify by name, Andersen-Schiess staggered and lurched toward the finish line, hell-bent on completing the race. Never mind that the final 400 meters had taken her nearly five minutes to run.

Finally she staggered over the line. Before she could take another step she fell into the arms of three officials. As applause eddied around the stadium, she was whisked away for immediate medical attention. She finished in 37th place, but it didn't much matter. Her agonizing run to the finish line—this courageous/reckless quest to finish 42,195 meters—would siphon attention from everything else that day, including Benoit's gold-medal race.

Andersen-Schiess would come to embody what is cloyingly called "the Olympic spirit," her feat popping up periodically on Greatest Olympic Moments lists and compilations. The *Los Angeles Times* gushed that her effort "transformed the Swiss runner into an international symbol of courage and determination." But she would also come to embody something else: *the power of the finish line*.

Athletes, it seems, have a remarkable capacity for (sports cliché alert) wringing every last drop of effort and energy out of themselves during a competition. One way they do this is by anchoring their expenditure of energy to the end of a game or race or fight—treating the finish line or final buzzer as an all-encompassing motivator, like the artificial rabbit chased by greyhounds or the water source eyed by the weary desert traveler.

Examples of this are abundant and familiar to fans in all sports. We've seen boxers and UFC fighters punch and kick and grab and gouge ferociously until the final bell (or, in UFC, the cacophonous air horn)—at which point they collapse from exhaustion, sometimes unable even to raise an arm in triumph without assistance. At the 2012 Olympic Games in London, Jon watched the triathlon while stationed near the finish line. How was it that the same athletes who were running sub-five-minute miles on one side of the tape were suddenly in agony on the other, cramped or curled into a fetal position as soon as they crossed the line?

In the thick compendium of Michael Jordan Moments, his performance against the Utah Jazz in Game 5 of the 1997 NBA Finals ranks prominently. Early in the morning of the game, Jordan summoned

Chicago Bulls medical personnel to his hotel in Park City, Utah. Severely dehydrated, he was sweating profusely and shaking uncontrollably. He was told that there was no way he would play that night. He tried to get some sleep and slogged into the arena at 4:30 p.m., long after the rest of the team. "The way he looked, there's no way I thought he could even put on his uniform," Scottie Pippen, Jordan's teammate, later told reporters. "I'd never seen him like that. He looked bad—I mean, really bad."

Jordan's trainer, Tim Grover, would later reveal in his book *Relentless* that Jordan had food poisoning, and Grover strongly implied that the "poisoning" was intentional. (Marooned in Park City, where room service closed early, Jordan had ordered a late-night pizza. "Everybody knew where we were staying," Grover recalled. "I take the pizza and I said, 'I got a bad feeling about this.'") At the time, though, Jordan was diagnosed with the flu, and when he did more than simply put on his uniform—when he took the floor and played—a shorthand was created: This would forever be known as the Flu Game.

You likely know the rest. Visibly weak and unsteady, Jordan struggled through the first several minutes. But then he began to do a convincing impersonation of . . . Michael Jordan. He scored 38 points, grabbed seven rebounds, handed out five assists, and hit the critical three-pointer that enabled the Bulls to beat the Jazz in this fulcrum game and close out the series two nights later. "Somehow I found the energy to stay strong," Jordan said, shrugging. Phil Jackson, the Bulls' coach, was more effusive: "Because of the circumstances, I'd have to say this is the greatest game I've seen Michael play."

The enduring image of the Flu Game, though, came immediately after the final horn. With the scoreboard clock at 0:00, Jordan collapsed, unable to leave the court under his own power. One moment he was running 94 feet and elevating above the rim; the next he was entirely spent, slackly clutching Pippen for support simply so he could get to the locker room.

• • •

MORE metaphorical finish lines—existential final buzzers—also hold great motivating powers. Who among us hasn't heard stories like that of Lydia Angiyou, the Quebec mother who, in 2006, wrestled a polar bear long enough for her son, who was playing hockey nearby, to escape? Or Nick Harris, the 5'7" Kansas man who, in 2009, lifted a Mercury sedan off a pinned six-year-old neighbor?

We humans possess the ability to perform extraordinary feats—to exhibit what is called hysterical strength—when the only alternative is death. These superhero exploits, scientists have concluded, result from the fact that the brain forces the body to keep much of its muscle power in reserve except when it is required to preserve life.

Consider the tremendous strength that is contained in a human body when all of its muscle fibers are fired—or "recruited"—at once. When a man who is electrocuted is flung across the room, it is not by any electrical explosion but rather by the force of his own muscles contracting in unison. *He is jumping.* Given the risk of injury or exhaustion, the brain, it seems, usually does not allow all or even nearly all of the body's power or endurance to be marshaled.

Remarkable as feats of hysterical athleticism are, they have this in common: Under duress, people summon powers that allow them to pull off deeds that, attempted in any other context, would end in failure (as well as embarrassment). Nick Harris, the Kansan strong man, tried to replicate his feat of newfound strength several times later the same day. What happened? He couldn't come close to lifting a car. But that one time, with a life on the line, "somehow—adrenaline, hand of God, whatever you want to call it—I don't know how I did it," he said.

A particularly poignant example: Several years ago Jon and his colleague David Epstein wrote a feature story on Rhiannon Hull for *Sports Illustrated.* Rhiannon, a star high school runner in Eugene, Oregon (d/b/a Track Town, USA), had been a member of the dynastic University of Oregon distance team and had considered a professional career as a runner. In her early 30s, after becoming a wife and mother, she moved to Costa Rica seeking what locals call *la pura vida,* the pure life.

On a gloomy autumn day in 2011—"The sky looked angry," one resident recalled—Rhiannon took her six-year-old son, Julian, to the beach. It was low tide, but at one point the mother and son stepped off a sandy ledge and were swept by the current into open water. Suddenly a day at the beach had turned into the ultimate endurance race. Hull would fight not just for her life but for Julian's as well. Her physique, 5'2" and 100 pounds of sinewy muscle, was usually an asset, but it wouldn't help her stay buoyant now. Nor would her instincts to overpower a challenge. The way to beat a riptide is to float passively until it drags you far enough out that you can swim around it back to safety. While Rhiannon was plenty strong, she was now holding up a boy with nearly half her body weight, and likely in a state of panic. (Julian would later describe what he was doing as "standing on Mommy.")

Rhiannon and Julian were about 130 feet from shore when a pair of teenage surfers spotted them and began paddling furiously toward them. By the time the surfers arrived, they later estimated, Rhiannon and Julian had been in the water for nearly half an hour. That is, half an hour in a battle against a foe of boundless energy and power, while Rhiannon carried 45 pounds of the most precious cargo imaginable.

Caleb and Johan, the surfers, said that as they closed in they could see that Rhiannon was exhausted. She was pushing Julian up to keep him above the water. She would sink under him and then reappear. She seemed to shove him toward the surfers. Caleb reached out and snatched Julian. He turned and placed him on the surfboard. The rescuers were less than 10 feet away, but in the time it took Caleb to turn back around, Rhiannon took her last breath and vanished into the sea.

This was, at once, a heroic story and a searing tragedy. As Rhiannon's friends and family struggled to make sense of it, they articulated an irony: After handing off Julian, didn't she have one last surge of energy to save her own life? Instead, it seems that delivering Julian to safety was Rhiannon's mental finish line. Once she crossed that threshold, her brain and body were done. She had no physical reserves left.

• • •

THE power of the finish line is not mere legend. The phenomenon has been documented and quantified. In a 2009 study at the University of Cape Town, in South Africa, researchers tested the hypothesis that during exercise, "the brain generates an appropriate and acceptable perceived exertion strategy based . . . on the expected duration of exercise that remains." In plainer terms: The brain works backward from the finish line, calculating—and recalibrating on the fly—how hard to let the body work, depending on how much more work remains to be done.

The Cape Town researchers recruited competitive cyclists to complete a series of time trials under controlled conditions. Once a week for four weeks, the cyclists completed a simulated 40-kilometer time trial on their own bikes rigged up to an electronic ergometer (which essentially turned them into computerized stationary bikes), under instructions to produce the fastest time possible. Not only did this produce computerized data on their power output, but the cyclists were also asked to provide an RPE—a self-reported Rating of Perceived Exertion—every five kilometers.

In terms of both actual power output and RPE, the cyclists exerted themselves more on each successive trial. At first they rode conservatively. Like any of us trying out a new running route or exercise routine, they weren't sure what to expect the first time. So their brains held back, forcing their bodies to keep more in reserve given the uncertainty ahead. By the fourth time trial, the cyclists were quite familiar with the (simulated) terrain and what it would take to conquer it, and their performance continued its upward trajectory.

Then the researchers pulled the rug out from under the riders. On the fifth and final time trial, everything remained the same: same 40-kilometer distance; same bike. The only difference? This time, information about completed distance was withheld. Now the cyclists had no idea how much ground they had covered. And, more important, they were in the dark about how much distance remained. To further confuse them, the researchers asked them for

RPEs not every five kilometers, as before, but at random intervals: after 18, 27, 33, and 38 kilometers.

The cyclists' power output plummeted. RPE dropped, too. Stripped of its ability to focus on an end point for the body's work, the brain reverted to a conservative strategy, holding more energy in reserve for the uncharted territory ahead. Until, that is, the finish line came into focus. At 39 kilometers, the researchers ended the suspense and informed the cyclists that there was only one kilometer to go. At that point the bikes (and brains) kicked into high gear. Like the starting pitcher told to empty the tank because the next batter is his last one, the cyclists ramped it back up, depleting their energy reserves with the finish line within reach.

Studies like this force many of us to change the way we think about exertion. Our basic assumption is that fatigue is located in the body. Why does a runner's pace slow? Because she's tired, we assume. Because something in the muscles, lungs, heart, or elsewhere is starting to fail. But fatigue is more than just a breakdown in the complex physiological machinery of the body, according to Ross Tucker, a researcher and senior lecturer in exercise physiology in Cape Town. According to Tucker, when it comes to elite athletes, "it's not failure; it's regulation."

In other words, the body and brain have an amazing collaboration when it comes to pacing. Through a complicated internal network of monitoring, regulating, and making continuous adjustments, racers regularly finish competitive endurance events without mishap. Remarkably, they're able to keep in reserve enough energy to get to the finish line, that most tempting of desert oases. Indeed, in every event between the mile and 10,000 meters, world-record-beating athletes do not slow down steadily over the race as toxic metabolites build up and their muscles tire. Rather, they typically pick up the pace in the final stretch.

"There's this tug-of-war," suggests Tucker. "I could possibly go faster, but I'm risking bodily harm to do so." So the brain steps in, protecting the body, preventing catastrophic failure in any single organ or system—much like the conscientious homeowner who stashes an emergency cash reserve for unexpected repairs. The brain typically wins the tug-of-war, at least until the finish line appears. Then it slacks off on the rope. Then, and only then, does the brain allow a competitor to move the body's needle dangerously close to empty.

This notion that fatigue is mental as much as physical is further illustrated when researchers set out to dupe the brain. Another study in Cape Town examined exertion among runners. Male and female members of local running clubs were asked to complete three treadmill sessions. In the first, the runners were told to jog for 20 minutes at 75 percent of peak speed. In the second trial, they were told to run for just 10 minutes, but nine minutes in they were informed that they'd actually need to continue on the treadmill for a full 20 minutes. In the third trial they were not told how far they would have to run but were stopped after 20 minutes.

To recap, all the runners completed three 20-minute treadmill sessions, but their expectations for each run were different. While the body was faced with the same task each time, the brain was given different parameters.

In the first trial, the runners paced themselves for a 20-minute run. In the third trial (when they didn't know how long the run would last), they held back, just like the cyclists described earlier. But what about the second trial—the one when the runners *thought* it was going to be a 10-minute run but then were surprised with a bonus 10 minutes? What happens when the finish line appears . . . and then, cruelly, gets moved on us? Well, in short, it sucks.

Over the second half of that second session (again: a session that they had expected to end 10 minutes earlier), runners reported greater fatigue and exertion; their RPEs skyrocketed. They also reported a much lower rate of happiness. All of this despite the fact that there was no change in their actual exercise intensity and no significant difference in their heart rate or oxygen consumption or stride frequency. Which is to say there was no physiological basis for their increase in perceived exertion (or decrease in contentment).

So why, then, did the runners say they were tired? Why did they feel lousy? Because the finish line they had counted on had come and gone, yet there they were, still running. Because it's frustrating to budget for one physical task only to be surprised with a more daunting one. The researchers concluded that the runners expressed feelings of fatigue because that's what they *expected* to feel once the initial finish line had been conquered. Mind over matter goes out the window when the mind gets tricked (not to mention pissed off).

THE power of the finish line has implications that go beyond the realm of athletic performance. Tucker offers, "If you don't know the finish line, you can't allocate the physical resources to do the job effectively." True. But the same conclusion applies to allocating other resources, whether you're a CEO trying to work with a budget or a student wrestling with time management. It's tough to pack a suitcase when you don't know how long the trip will last.

Storied feats of finish-line-fueled heroism aren't limited to the Olympic track. We talked with Dan Pink, author of *Drive: The Surprising Truth About What Motivates Us,* and regaled him with the saga of Gabriela Andersen-Schiess. He suggested that corporate lore is filled with similar tales of seemingly otherworldly perseverance. "The first analogy I think of is shipping software," he told us. "You hear about these teams of programmers . . . who end up pulling, say, five all-nighters in a row in order to get a new piece of software to ship on time. It's knowing that the software has to ship on a certain date that allows them to draw on these previously unimagined reservoirs of effort, capacity, and talent." On a regular basis, seemingly ordinary people pull off feats like these—it's just that Al Michaels isn't there to do the play-by-play.

Indeed, *motivation* is a buzzword these days—in education, industry, entrepreneurship. How can we increase students' persistence on academic tasks? How can we intensify employee engagement? Go to any business website about how to boost productivity, and one of the tips you're likely to find is to break down large objectives into smaller, more concrete goals. In other words, to create clear finish lines (with mileposts along the way).

There's science behind this idea, too. One of the biggest obstacles to productivity and innovation is simply not knowing where to start. Major projects are daunting, sometimes paralyzingly so. Research demonstrates that turning them into more immediate and attainable goals can jump-start motivation, leaving us less likely to procrastinate and more willing to persevere even when the going gets tough.

As an example, in 2014 researchers from business schools in Singapore and the United States conducted a study of more than 100 early-stage entrepreneurs. Off and on for three months the entrepreneurs were texted a daily survey about their efforts to create viable business ventures. The questions concerned progress made toward their ultimate goals, and perceptions of their effort intensity—more or less the same type of RPE data the Cape Town researchers collected from athletes.

What predicted the entrepreneurs' effort intensity? Perceived progress. The budding businessmen and -women who believed they were making steady progress reported working harder. And what facilitated a sense of making progress? Setting smaller, attainable goals. "Entrepreneurs can increase perceptions of progress by establishing multiple milestones along their lengthy entrepreneurial goal pursuit," the researchers wrote, "reducing ambitious goals into bite-sized progress markers."

Goals are reference points. Clear evidence of progress allows entrepreneurs to exert more effort, much like passing five-kilometer milestones en route to a known finish line allows cyclists to pedal harder. When goals are achievable, we will spend the energy to pursue them. "Bite-sized progress markers" are more motivating than ill-defined big-picture objectives.

Sometimes we create these interim finish lines ourselves. But sometimes others set them for us. Research on charitable giving finds that as an initiative nears its stated fund-raising goals, contributions increase dramatically. One study monitored online donations to kiva.org, a microloan website through which individuals around the globe request small-scale loans to help alleviate poverty or kick-start modest business endeavors. Each potential loan recipient posts a specific target amount needed to, say, replace their family's refrigerator or buy cattle for a fledgling dairy.

The researchers found that when a potential recipient's request was still far from reaching its goal—less than a third of the way there—average donations were modest. When the request was between one- and two-thirds of the way to full funding, the donation rate doubled. And donors were most generous of all down the homestretch, when the target amount was within reach. Why? As the researchers determined through follow-up analyses, people prefer contributing to a cause that's likely to succeed. It's more satisfying to donate when we sense that our efforts make a difference. We derive more satisfaction when our help allows others to hit a target.

These examples seem to generate a clear take-home message: If you're looking to boost motivation—in yourself or others—create attainable goals. What entrepreneur, manager, teacher, or parent couldn't make use of such a lesson?[1]

Alas, the story isn't quite that simple. When it comes to effort and exertion, the finish line can be a bane as well as a boon. Yes, it can help people achieve a goal. In the short term, that's great. But hitting a target can also undermine effort. "A finish line marks a stopping point," explains Gretchen Rubin, author of *Better Than Before: Mastering the Habits of Our Everyday Lives*. "Once we stop, we must start over, and starting over is harder than starting." Especially when the effort required to get to that point has been depleting.

Sure, a clear view of the finish line prompts the cyclist to pedal harder and complete the time trial. But it doesn't necessarily persuade him to get back on the bike the next day to start training again. That requires intrinsic drive. Which is why over time, self-generated finish lines are more motivating than those that others impose upon us. The sales manager eager to rally her troops by creating concrete

---

1. Indeed, both of us currently coach daughters in Little League softball. It only seemed natural to try to capitalize on the power of the finish line in that pursuit as well. Sam's effort? Try to turn a nebulous, big-picture objective of getting the girls more engaged while in the outfield into a "bite-sized progress marker." Specifically: If the team records 10 outfield putouts during the season, Coach treats everyone to ice cream. Outfield motivation has shown a clear uptick. So has confusion on the opposing bench as our girls celebrate a harmless fly-out to right with an exuberance unbefitting the double-digit deficit on the scoreboard.

milestones might wish to tread lightly; goals, deadlines, and targets imposed by others—especially unilaterally or without buy-in—have a way of *undermining* motivation in the long run.

In fact, some research even equates goal-setting with antibiotics use, suggesting that goals are powerful in small doses but have been dangerously overprescribed. In a paper titled "Goals Gone Wild" (that's right, even academics have a sense of humor), researchers identify a litany of problematic side effects when organizations become too goal-happy. For example, goals narrow your focus and can promote risk-taking and even unethical behavior. The auto executive concerned about hitting a release date might overlook safety-test results in the rush to get a car to market.

Researchers suggest that managers inclined to set new goals for their organization first ask themselves questions such as: Are the goals too narrow? Are they too challenging? Is the time horizon reasonable? In what ways might these goals encourage unethical behavior or unacceptable levels of risk? How can these goals be tailored to individual abilities and circumstances while preserving fairness?

As Dan Pink explained to us, "The skillful manager has to figure out when to deploy finish lines and when not, and not to think that they're universally helpful or universally harmful." And the worst thing that a manager can do? Changing the finish line mid-course. "I've seen it so many times in business settings . . . *that* is absolutely destructive and completely demoralizes people." And, once more, the corporate lingo for this problem is borrowed from the sports pages: *moving the goalposts*.

Finish lines are, indeed, powerful. But without a responsible brain calling the shots, their pursuit can turn dangerous.

AS this chapter approaches its own finish line, let's return to Gabriela Andersen-Schiess, our 1984 Olympic marathoner. Al Michaels and others who watched her persevere were amazed for obvious reasons. It was (and remains) an awe-inspiring sight. Perhaps even more amazing, though? As close to collapse—or even death—as she appeared to be upon completing the race, the science suggests that she could have run yet a bit longer if she had to. It just depended on where the final tape was.

Research allows us to predict that Andersen-Schiess's collapse that day could have happened anywhere on the course—it was a simple matter of where her brain would allow it to take place. Had the finish line been closer to where she entered the Coliseum, she likely would have depleted her reserves to cross it and collapsed there instead. Had she needed to run 800 meters on the track rather than 400, she might have been able to drag her exhausted body the extra distance, willing herself to make it as her brain/body calculations adjusted and re-rationed accordingly.

But all this resilience depended on her knowing where the finish line was. Imagine, instead, if she had entered the homestretch, seen the final tape, and *then* watched as the race organizers, in some sort of cruel joke, moved it farther away. Her pacing thrown off and her eleventh-hour energy reserves depleted—not to mention, her psyche demoralized—that would've been too much for even her Olympic spirit to overcome.[2] So it goes for goals in the non-sporting world as well. While there remains debate about the best way to implement business goals, there seems little question that moving the finish line after the proverbial race has begun is a recipe for disaster.

Because in reality, it isn't the finish line alone that is so powerful. It's the interaction between the finish line and the brain. This is what allows elite athletes to walk the exhilarating tightrope between extraordinary performance and catastrophic breakdown yet also compels frustrated entrepreneurs to give up because progress is coming at too slow a pace. *In order to go our hardest, we need to know*

---

2. Consider the story of Englishman Jim Peters, then the marathon world-record holder, trying to complete the event at the 1954 Empire Games in Vancouver. Peters entered the stadium for the final leg with a huge lead, but suffering from serious heat exhaustion. Weaving on the track, it took him 11 minutes to slowly drag himself past what the English contingent believed to be the finish line, at which point he promptly collapsed. Alas, the actual finish was on the other side of the track, a few hundred yards away. Peters never made it there. And when he woke up in the hospital, he still believed that he had won the race.

when we can finally stop. In the absence of a clear finish line, the brain will hold the body back.

We'll give the final words on this topic to an expert we haven't heard from yet. Someone who knows a great deal about the ebb and flow of athletic performance, who's well versed in the yin and yang of goal achievement but also of starting over: Andre Agassi, a latter-day guru when it comes to the double-edged effects of the finish line on motivation.[3]

Here's what Agassi writes in his autobiography, *Open*: "The objective is to get within reach of that finish line, because then it gives off a magnetic force. When you're close, you can feel that force pulling you, and you can use that force to get across. But just before you come within range, or just after, you feel another force, equally strong, pushing you away. It's inexplicable, mystical, these twin forces, these contradictory energies, but they both exist."

---

3.   Tip of the cap here to Gretchen Rubin, who has previously cited Agassi in writing about motivation.

Why the World Cup Doesn't Lead to World Peace

(EVEN IF J. LO AND PITBULL CLAIM OTHERWISE)

> Put your flags up in the sky (put them in the sky)
> And wave them side to side (side to side) . . .
> Show the world we are one (one love, life)

Take a bow—or better yet, hike up your jersey and zigzag mania-cally toward the corner flag in self-congratulation—if you identified the above lyrics as the opening lines to "We Are One," the official anthem of the 2014 World Cup, performed by Jennifer Lopez, Pitbull, and Claudia Leitte. Predictably, it goes heavy on themes of unity and international amity. As Pitbull explained in anticipation of the song's release, "I truly believe that this great game and the power of music will help unify us, because we are best when we are one."

This, of course, is a common trope at international competi-tions: the admirable sentiment that sports transcend differences and borders, that sports ease conflict. For example, according to its website, the International Olympic Committee "actively pursues the goals of protecting the interests of the athletes and sport in general, and contributing to the search for peaceful and diplomatic solutions to the conflicts around the world." Indeed, Baron Pierre de Coubertin, founder of the IOC, championed the effort to revive the modern Games in large part because of his belief that such in-ternational competition provided a safe release valve for energies that would otherwise be directed toward nationalistic agitation and violence.

But claims such as these provoke the question, Do global events—the World Cup in particular—truly lead to world peace?

In a word: No.

In four words (plus a comma): Actually, just the opposite.

Andrew Bertoli is a Ph.D. candidate in political science at Berkeley. In the summer of 2014, while most of us were busy being dazzled by the sorcery of Lionel Messi, Neymar, and James Rodríguez, Bertoli's version of watching soccer involved running a series of multiple regression analyses. He crunched numbers for every FIFA World Cup qualifying run in the years 1958–2010. In particular, he was interested in pairs of teams in which one country barely qualified for the tournament and the other just missed qualifying.

Take, for example, the qualifying matches played by African nations in 2010. Five teams from the Confederation of African Football qualified for the World Cup finals through the play-in process that year. (As the World Cup host nation, South Africa received an automatic bid.) Two of the successful teams, Nigeria and Algeria, qualified narrowly. Nigeria won its qualification group with a total of 12 points earned across six matches, only one point ahead of Tunisia, which failed to make the cut. Algeria and Egypt tied atop their qualifying group with 13 points, but when Algeria won the tie-breaking playoff game, it advanced to South Africa and Egypt stayed home.

Bertoli's idea was to compare pairs of nations like these in terms of how peaceful they were after the run-up to qualification. If participating in the World Cup helps bring about global harmony, then, he hypothesized, countries that just made it into the final tournament (such as Nigeria and Algeria) might be expected to initiate less international aggression than countries that just missed (such as Tunisia and Egypt).

To test this theory, Bertoli used a variable often employed in international relations and security research, something called militarized interstate disputes, or MIDs. Wars occur too infrequently to be a useful measure for statistical analysis (bad news for statisticians, good news for the rest of humanity). The MID measure, though, is broader; it includes any dispute in which one nation explicitly threatens, displays, or initiates force against another. Bertoli's strategy was to examine these pairs of countries with similar-caliber soccer teams and see whether competing in an event like the World Cup led to greater international peace.

It didn't. In the six months prior to a qualification run, the countries represented by the qualifying and non-qualifying teams showed *no difference* in their baseline levels of interstate aggression. And in fact, after qualification had ended, the qualifying nations became significantly *more* aggressive, and they remained so for three years!

During this period, nations whose teams narrowly qualified for the World Cup were four times as likely as non-qualifiers to attack a traditional rival country. And the military actions taken by qualifying nations were more violent than the (fewer) actions taken by non-qualifiers. In fact, in a follow-up analysis of actual World Cup matches, Bertoli found that international aggression was even more likely to occur between countries whose teams had competed against each other in the same round-robin group, giving a macabre twist to popular Group of Death nomenclature.

Specific examples: the Soviet Union was no stranger to international disputes in the decade or two after World War II. But its military seemed to be in a particularly feisty mood in the aftermath of making a World Cup. The Soviets tallied six MIDs in the three years leading up to qualifying for the 1958 Cup, a number that jumped to 12 in the three years after the tournament, and then up to 15 in the years after the 1962 Cup.

The United States, too. From zero conflicts to one after 1950. From five before the 2002 Cup to eight in the years right after.

Even France got in on the action. No MIDs leading up to the 1934 Cup but one in the years right after. A jump from one to four conflicts after the 1958 Cup. From zero to three after 1978.

So if you were thinking it was incongruous that anything run by an organization that has elected Sepp Blatter as its leader five times could be the cure for many of the world's ills, well, you were right.

Though in this case, for once, FIFA isn't to blame for the lapse in morality.[1]

Perhaps these research findings shouldn't surprise us for other reasons as well. Forget about international diplomacy—or lack thereof. There's hardly a shortage of stories about violent conflict among international soccer players and spectators. The 2006 World Cup match between host country Germany and neighboring Poland was something other than an exercise in togetherness. Rather, this game between two old geopolitical rivals resulted in more than 300 arrests and a police effort to stave off a full-fledged riot.

The contentious rivalry (understatement alert) between Algeria and Egypt took a dramatic turn for the worse in 1989, when the two teams met in a winner-take-all World Cup qualifying match for Italia '90. A controversial goal led to a 1–0 Egypt victory, which was followed by riots that cost the Egyptian team doctor his eye and spurred an Interpol arrest warrant for assault for Algerian star Lahkdar Belloumi that wasn't rescinded until 2009.

More recently, a Euro 2016 qualifier between Serbia and Albania was abandoned mid-game after a drone flying an Albanian protest flag flew over the pitch, a Serbian defender pulled down the flag, and an all-out brawl ensued. That the drone was allegedly controlled from a VIP luxury box by the brother of the Albanian prime minister only added fuel to the international conflagration. Or at least that's what Serbian state television would have us believe.

And in perhaps the most extreme example, international soccer has even served as the namesake for war. That would be *La guerra*

---

1.   To be clear: We're not diminishing the positive role that sports can play in international relations and peace-related initiatives, from Ping-Pong diplomacy to the aforementioned IOC/United Nations Peace Through Sport initiative. What we are suggesting is that pitting nations against each other in competition is no panacea for global conflict. And the Olympics, too, have provided support for this conclusion, whether in the form of boycott-related politics or the tensions that followed the accidental display of South Korean flags next to scoreboard photos of North Korea's women's soccer players on the opening day of London 2012—a glitch that caused the North Koreans to retreat angrily to their locker room for an hour before negotiations and an official apology finally lured them back onto the pitch.

del fútbol (the Soccer War), a four-day conflict between El Salvador and Honduras in 1969, when lingering geopolitical tensions were inflamed by a home-and-home World Cup qualifying series.

Bertoli offers several possible explanations for the link between World Cup participation and an increase in MIDs. For one, as the examples above illustrate, international sporting events are often marred by spectator violence. In some instances, the military is called upon to restore order, further heightening international tensions. And these skirmishes are reported by the respective national media, which can further color the attitudes of each country's citizens and leaders toward the other's.

Bertoli also suggests that there is a long and inglorious history of leaders using sports to fan the flames of nationalism—particularly when doing so allows them to distract the citizenry from domestic woes. In the qualifying run to the 2010 World Cup, tensions between Algeria and Egypt once again flared up with lethal consequences in the form of fan violence and rioting. Many accused then-president Hosni Mubarak of taking advantage of the turmoil to distract Egyptians from various problems back home. And the recent showcase of Russian nationalism that was the 2014 Sochi Winter Olympics has hardly ushered in an era of peace that "transcends differences and borders" for Russia's neighbors.

Even without such efforts to manipulate populations and inflame passions, international competition is just that—a competition. Consider the insight of novelist George Orwell, regarding an ill-fated series of not-so "friendlies" between Moscow Dynamo and British clubs in 1945 right after the end of World War II:

> Even if one didn't know from concrete examples (the 1936 Olympic Games, for instance) that international sporting contests lead to orgies of hatred, one could deduce it from general principles. . . . On the village green, where you pick up sides and no feeling of local patriotism is involved, it is possible to play simply for the fun and exercise: but as soon as the question of prestige arises, as soon as you feel that you and some large unit will be disgraced if you lose, the most savage combative instincts are aroused. . . . If you wanted to add to the vast fund

of ill-will existing in the world at this moment, you could hardly do it better than by a series of football matches between Jews and Arabs, Germans and Czechs, Indians and British, Russians and Poles.

Competing against others tends to highlight those aspects of our identities that differentiate us from opponents.[2] And it's just a 20-meter free kick from nationalism to jingoism—which is more dangerous in some cultures than in others. Bertoli found that while the link between playing in the World Cup and international aggression was evident in both democracies and non-democracies, it was especially strong among the latter, suggesting that sports-related nationalism may be particularly problematic in authoritarian states. And interestingly, the difference in interstate disputes between qualifiers and non-qualifiers was significant only in countries where soccer is the most popular sport and, therefore, a likely outlet for nationalist sentiment. No statistically reliable difference emerged in less soccer-mad locales.

For the 2010 World Cup, it was Shakira who was summoned to perform the theme song. While asking your forgiveness for the evitable earworm we're about to insert, you'll recall the militaristic opening lyrics to "Waka, Waka (This Time for Africa)":

You're a good soldier
Choosing your battles . . .

No, not quite the kumbaya overtones of "We Are One." But, insofar as capturing the World Cup's impact on international relations, it strikes more honest chords.

---

2. For example, a recent research finding indicates that in UEFA Champions League matches, a referee is 8 to 10 percent more forgiving in his calls—regarding offsides calls, fouls, and yellow and red cards—when the player in question is from his home country. This own-nationality bias is even stronger among more experienced refs and is particularly pronounced when the player in question is also a member of his country's national team.

Why Our Moral Compass Is More Flexible Than an Olympic Gymnast

Fenway Park was just starting to fill up on a flawless spring Saturday afternoon in 2015 when the boos began to echo and cascade. They gathered in volume as Alex Rodriguez made his way to the cage for pregame batting practice. If Rodriguez thought that having hit his 660th home run the previous night—tying Willie Mays's career total—would mute his critics, he was deeply mistaken.

Booo!!!

The jeering was guttural and angry, untinged by irony. And the chorus was broken only by shouts of "A-Fraud!" and the old Fenway favorite, "You suck!" Most of the hecklers were outfitted in Red Sox attire. A few wore customized shirts reading A-ROID with the number 13 below it and the *I* and *1* in the shapes of syringes.

BOOOO!!!!

It didn't help that Rodriguez was a member of the Yankees, the Red Sox' historic and bitter rival. But in recent years (and with Boston's recent World Series titles) the rivalry has retreated a bit from its hot-blooded peak, and Red Sox fans have graciously, if grudgingly, cheered for Mariano Rivera and Derek Jeter as they closed out their careers. And on this afternoon the crowd was more indifferent than insolent when Yankees such as, say, Chris Young and Brett Gardner took their cuts.

But in Boston, as elsewhere, Rodriguez is perceived as something much worse than a hated Yankee: He's a liar and a cheater who undermined honest competition and disgraced baseball. Rodriguez was suspended for the entire 2014 season based on overwhelming evidence that he not only obtained illegal performance-enhancing substances from a shady Biogenesis anti-aging clinic in South Florida but also hindered baseball's investigation when the allegations came to light. This after he'd been forced to admit to more-limited PED use earlier in his career.

¡¡¡¡¡BOOOOO!!!!!

Rob Pressman, a 44-year-old pharmaceutical sales rep and real estate agent from Rhode Island, was among those leading the Fenway jeers. Pressman had already taken a photo of Rodriguez and texted it to friends who were Yankees fans with an "A-Fraud" caption. His young daughters at his side, he tried to explain why Rodriguez was so loathsome. "You want to emphasize the fact that drugs aren't good for you," he said. "And it's just not right, and that's why they pay penalties for that."

A reasonable argument. Except that Pressman made his case while wearing a Red Sox No. 24 jersey. That is, the jersey of Manny Ramirez, the former Boston slugger who . . . twice tested positive for performance-enhancing drugs and retired in disgrace in 2011 after still another positive test.

To his credit, Pressman, when pressed, recognized a certain, well, inconsistency. He condemned Ramirez: "It's wrong what he did." But, he added, "the one thing I think I could give Manny respect for is he just enjoyed life as a big goofball. Where most of us live a stressed life and you can't just relax and enjoy things, he had that uncanny ability." There was even a phrase for this endearing insouciance: *Manny being Manny*.

Not far from Pressman, Russell Bellisle, a security worker, also from Rhode Island, entered the park through a turnstile on Yawkey Way near Gate D. He proudly announced that he planned to boo Rodriguez at every at-bat. Why was A-Rod so intensely dislikable? "Probably the steroids," he said.

But wait, Bellisle was wearing a David Ortiz jersey, in homage to the beloved Red Sox star who has also been linked to PEDs—

although not nearly to the extent of A-Rod. Ortiz ended up on base-ball's naughty list during the widespread survey testing of 2003. Bellisle's defense of Big Papi? "I think if he did it, if he really did it, I think he would have admitted to it. He seems a little more honest than A-Rod."

It's much the same everywhere. A-Rod is perceived similarly in Milwaukee. But the very Brewers fans who vilify him wear the jersey of Ryan Braun, who was not only suspended for multiple PED offenses—and used the same South Florida clinic as Rodriguez—but also, with Armstrongian disregard for others, blamed an initial positive result on the incompetence of the professional whose job it was to collect and transport the test sample. You would be within your rights to argue that Braun was guilty of a deeper ethical breach than A-Rod.

Rodriguez began his career in Seattle, on Mariners teams that reached the American League Championship Series in 1995 and 2000, high points in the organization's history. But these days he is treated just as inhospitably in the Pacific Northwest as in Boston and Milwaukee. When he comes to bat at Safeco Field, he isn't showered with Monopoly money the way he was when he first left as a free agent. Instead he is showered with a serenade of "Sterrrr-roids, sterrrr-roids." It's hard not to notice, though, how many of these fans wear the jerseys of the Seattle Seahawks, residents of the stadium just across the street and the NFL's leaders in PED-related suspensions: five bans since 2011 and a sixth overturned on procedural grounds.

The same weekend that Rodriguez hit his 660th home run, Floyd Mayweather Jr. fought Manny Pacquiao in Las Vegas in the (nearly annual) Fight of the Century. Mayweather earned the GNP of a small nation for his 36 minutes of work. But that was the problem. The fight went the 12-round distance, and Mayweather won by decision. Disrespected as ever (see page 30), he was booed so loudly that one could barely hear the official announcement of the decision. Mayweather is a fairly offensive human being who seems to relish the role of Darth Vader, Keyser Söze, and Clubber Lang rolled into one. But criticism this night was less about his history of (unapologetic) domestic violence or (unapologetic) mercenary impulses than about his ring performance. He was merely evasive and technically excellent. He didn't attempt to knock out Pacquiao. ("Mayweather Wins, Preens, Is Booed" read a *New York Times* headline.)

Wait—as fans, aren't we deeply concerned about head injuries in sports and uncomfortable with the barbarity of the NFL? Aren't we worried about concussions at every level of sports, even youth soccer, in which kids are being taught not to use their heads? Now we're disappointed because two men didn't attempt to divorce each other from consciousness? There weren't enough head shots? The winner was insufficiently violent?

Teams, too, exhibit these inconsistent standards. During that same busy sports weekend in May 2015, the NFL wrapped up its annual draft. The first player chosen was Jameis Winston, whose list of alleged crimes and misdemeanors is sufficiently long to be broken into a chapter book.[1] Using a vocabulary that has now hardened like poured cement, teams invoked the same phrases to describe Winston: *Character issues. Potential for distraction. Red flags.*

Unless, that is, they were those teams at the top of the draft and in need of a quarterback. In that case they reached a different conclusion. Here's Tampa Bay Buccaneers general manager Jason Licht in February 2015, before the draft, talking about the importance of character in the organization's evaluation of prospects: "Our head coach [Lovie Smith] is one of the finest human beings I have ever met, inside or outside football. Character is very important to him,

---

1. Winston's "incident list" while at Florida State included, most seriously, an allegation of sexual assault. Multiple investigations—deeply flawed investigations, critics contend—concluded that there was not enough evidence to file criminal charges. (A civil suit is pending as we write this.) But Winston's list also included a pellet-gun exchange that resulted in $4,000 in damage to campus property; accusations that he helped himself to soda from the dispenser of a Tallahassee Burger King without paying; famously "forgetting" to pay for $32.72 worth of crab legs at a local grocery store; and jumping on a table and screaming a sexually charged Internet meme. Taken cumulatively, as they were, these acts had the perverse impact of diminishing—not heightening—the severity of the rape allegation. Once the acts were conflated, the composite portrait of Winston was that of a knuckleheaded prankster lacking in maturity and good judgment rather than a sexual predator who had possibly committed a felony.

it's very important to me, so we will make sure that the decision we make is best for the Tampa Bay Buccaneers."

An understandable (and commendable) stance, especially given that in 2014 Licht inherited a team that had weathered more than its share of off-field problems. According to one analysis, Tampa Bay's roster boasted the fifth-largest number of players arrested in the NFL since 2000.

But just a few months after Licht made his declaration, the Bucs made Jameis Winston the first overall pick of the draft and the new face of their franchise. Licht claimed that the organization had spoken about Winston with "upwards of 75 people" and found no good reason not to draft him. "We were not going to mistake charisma for character," Licht told *SI*'s Peter King. "He kept checking every box."

The Manny Ramirez apologist who boos Alex Rodriguez . . . the general manager who touts character while drafting Jameis Winston . . . the university athletic director who extols the virtues of amateurism from the plush confines of an arena funded by boosters and TV contracts . . . All are examples of moral hypocrisy, sprinkled with selective outrage, in the sports ecosystem. And all are completely in keeping with normal human behavior.

IT takes very little to goad people into an us-versus-them mindset. The sweatshirt revealing a stranger's alma mater, the political bumper sticker on another driver's car, the ethnic origin implied by someone's last name . . . all are cues upon which we pounce in forming impressions of and sensing connections to others around us. Sports, of course, provide countless examples, some in the extreme, such as the European soccer stadiums that mandate segregated (and sometimes fenced-in) seating by which team you're rooting for. But behavioral scientists have long recognized that even far more trivial group identities shape how we see the world.

Perhaps most famously, Henri Tajfel, a Polish-born psychologist, conducted a series of studies in which he randomly assigned schoolboys in England to different groups based on the most insignificant criteria. In one study, the teenagers were shown pairs of abstract paintings. Their task was simple: Just report which in each set they liked more. Then, at random, some were informed that they preferred the art of Wassily Kandinsky. Others were told that they were, apparently, fans of Paul Klee. In another similar study, a series of slides depicting dot clusters was shown to teenagers at the same school. Each image was projected for less than a half second, and the respondents' job was to estimate how many dots were in each cluster. Once again, the boys were subsequently assigned to one of two groups, supposedly on the basis of their responses. In reality, half of the boys were chosen at random to learn that that they were chronic dot overestimators. The other half were told that they were, supposedly, dot underestimators.

Tajfel referred to studies like these as using *minimal groups*. That is, group membership was assigned based on the most trivial considerations. The critical outcome measures in this research weren't which paintings the boys really liked or how many dots they really counted. (Again, they were separated into groups at random.) Rather, what the researchers cared about was the way that minimal group membership affected individuals' reactions to the other people in the study.

Once divided into groups, the boys were informed that they'd be moving on to a new, unrelated task in which they would use various numerical charts to assign financial rewards and penalties to classmates. In one task, they were given options for allocating a certain number of pennies between two classmates (we'll call them Student 1 and Student 2). Another task required them to choose an amount of money for one student to receive and an amount for another student to pay.

Each of these decisions translated into actual financial gains and losses for other students. But each decision was also anonymous: A participant did not know the identity of Students 1 and 2—only which one was, say, a fellow Kandinsky lover and which one wasn't. Or which was a fellow dot overestimator and which wasn't.

Across these different experiments, participants were far more generous with their fellow Kandinsky (or Klee) fans or with their fellow dot over- or underestimators. To be precise: 72 percent of boys in the painting study demonstrated regular economic favoritism toward their own group; 81 percent in the dot study did so.

If being assigned to groups at random like this—on the flimsiest criteria—can foster a tribal mentality, then imagine what happens when competition is added to the mix (see *Tribal Warfare*, page 191). In yet another famous study of schoolboys, Muzafer Sherif, a Turkish American psychologist, observed a Boy Scouts of America summer camp in Robbers Cave State Park, Oklahoma. The campers were 12-year-olds from middle-class families with no history of behavioral problems or domestic unrest. You never would have guessed this from watching them at camp, though.

According to Sherif, a visitor would've sworn that these were "wicked, disturbed and vicious bunches of youngsters." This was a landlocked version of *Lord of the Flies*. The kids taunted each other vulgarly, ransacked cabins, and stole personal property. Why? Simply because, once they had been assigned to one of two competing tribes, they worked up an antipathy toward the other group.

Upon arrival, half of the boys had been assigned to a group that came to call itself the Rattlers; the other half became the Eagles. In their first days at camp, each group had been assigned to its own cabin, and the two residences were located far enough apart to prevent intergroup contact. Building cohesion within each unit was easy: The boys worked on collaborative projects, they hiked and swam together, they prepared group meals.

Fostering hostility and dislike toward the other group proved just as easy. All it took was a period of competition that was introduced several days into the camp. After a few rounds of football and tug-of-war, the two groups were at each other's throats.

It proved far more difficult to bridge the gulf between the Rattlers and Eagles than it had been to create it. Various strategies failed. Simply telling the groups positive things about each other had little effect. Bringing them together in neutral, noncompetitive situations actually backfired, as the boys found something to squabble over even during a joint movie screening. Eventually the researchers had to create scenarios that required the two groups to depend on each other; for instance, they arranged for the camp truck to break down on a camping trip, forcing the boys to work together to pull it back up a hill with a rope.

In short, even when determined at random, team affiliation can have powerful consequences that are difficult to prevent or undo. Throw in competition over a scarce resource—whether a camp trophy, the American League East division title, or disputed international boundaries—and the psychological stakes grow exponentially.

WHICH brings us back to questions about moral hypocrisy—about people who fail to "practice what they preach" and the tendency of their supporters to turn a blind eye when they do so. It turns out that we don't just give more money to fellow group members when afforded the opportunity. We more often give them the benefit of the doubt for morally questionable behavior as well.

Our general sense of morality is, in a word, flexible. One of the clearest examples is that we cut ourselves a great deal of slack when evaluating our own morally ambiguous behavior. Consider a study conducted just a few years ago by Carlo Valdesolo and Dave DeSteno at Northeastern University in Boston. They informed participants—none of whom, to our knowledge at least, was also present across town in the Fenway bleachers to boo A-Rod on the weekend he hit No. 660—that there were two potential tasks to complete in the experiment. And also that the research participants could choose which task to keep for themselves and which to delegate to other, unknown people they would never meet.

It wasn't much of a choice, really. One of the tasks was much less onerous than the other. The "green task," as it was called, took about 10 minutes. It involved a brief survey and a photo-based scavenger hunt. It was like a puzzle you might find in an airline magazine to pass the time on a flight—mildly stimulating but hardly demanding.

The "red task," however, was more like being sent back to SAT prep class: A series of logic problems. Tedious mental rotation questions in which you'd have to think about what various 3-D shapes would look like if turned *n* degrees to the left or right. And the clincher: Getting through it all would take close to an hour.

To decide between the tasks, the participants were allowed to use a computerized randomizer that would, in essence, flip a coin. Or they could just pick based on personal preference. In the entire study, only two brave (altruistic?) souls (suckers?) opted for the randomizer; all the others simply assigned themselves the preferable green task. But when asked to rate how fair they had been in this process, the participants who chose the green task gave themselves a rating of close to 4 on a 5-point scale. As in, *pretty fair—even though I did stick the other guy with the hard task just because I felt like it.* Perhaps not surprisingly, we're usually generous when it comes to evaluating our own morality.

In fact, studies from across the behavioral sciences have identified a veritable bias blind spot, a failure to recognize in ourselves the prejudices and ethical violations we so easily spot in others. In one study, researchers asked respondents to evaluate a series of common biases, several of which we've cited in other chapters of this book, from self-serving false narratives to the halo effect. Participants rated these biases as prevalent among Americans on average but much less so in themselves.

The same goes for perceptions of (im)morality. In their book *Blind Spots*, business school professors Max Bazerman (Harvard) and Ann Tenbrunsel (Notre Dame) chronicle case after case of individuals—politicians, bankers, corporate executives, and Joe/Jane Public—engaging in ethical spinning to convince themselves that their own problematic actions really aren't so bad. For example: "the more tempted we are to behave unethically, the more common—and thus acceptable—we perceive the unethical action to be. That is, the bigger the deduction you'll get for cheating on your taxes, the more likely you will be to believe that others are cheating as well." Again, our sense of morality is remarkably flexible.

But back to the study from Northeastern. Yes, participants saw themselves as "fair" even when they took the preferable green task and stuck another with the less palatable red task. Even more interesting, though, is what happened when they were allowed to watch on a monitor as *other* people made the same decision. When others took the green task and left the red task for someone else? *That* wasn't reasonable. Those other people's disregard for fairness was rated as less acceptable.

With one notable exception. There was one type of "other" who wasn't docked on the fairness ratings, who was given the same benefit of the doubt that we usually reserve for ourselves: a fellow team member. Someone in the "ingroup." Someone who before the green task/red task choice had been assigned by researchers to the same group as the participant because, allegedly, she had a similar cognitive style (minimal groups strike again). In fact, this so-called teammate was given the highest fairness rating of all, on average greater than 4 on the 5-point scale.

For that matter, we're even less likely to *remember* the negative behaviors of members of our own groups and teams. In another study, U.S. researchers used Tajfel's dot task to assign respondents to either of two groups. Then the participants received a series of cards to browse through, each one listing a behavior that had supposedly been disclosed by a previous participant. Some of these behaviors were positive: describing a proud accomplishment, a memorable vacation, or a charitable endeavor. Others were negative: detailing instances of dishonesty or other immoral actions.

Participants believed that one pile of cards, listing both positive and negative behaviors, had been written by members of their own dot group (their fellow over- or underestimators). The other pile of cards was, in theory, written by the group to which the respondents had no affiliation. Both piles, though, included the same number of positive and negative cards. Despite this, when later given a surprise memory test, participants were far more likely to remember the negative behaviors associated with the other group than those associated with their own group. In other words, our memory gets selectively and conveniently sharper when it comes to the bad things that *other* groups do.

So it would seem that the one exception to our tendency to call out—and even remember—the moral transgressions of others comes when the others in question are part of "us" as opposed to "them." We're willing to excuse moral failures so long as they belong to members of our team. So it goes for the arbitrarily assigned research teammate. So it goes for Red Sox fans and Manny Ramirez. And Brewers fans and Ryan Braun. Not to mention Yankees fans and Andy Pettitte, Giants fans and Barry Bonds, Ravens fans and Ray Lewis/Rice, Seahawks fans and various suspended players . . .

OF course, this type of moral hypocrisy transcends sports. In fact, the conveniently malleable sense of morality demonstrated by sports fans may be among the *least* problematic examples of this general human tendency. Sports fans, after all, often recognize and even embrace the irrationality of their calling. They admit that the third baseman or shooting guard they root for one season will be jeered the next year, when he's wearing a different team's jersey. They may even realize that their lifelong attachments are too deeply ingrained to be undermined by inconvenient truths or the reality of test results.

But moral hypocrisy is all too prevalent in other domains as well. From the "family values" governor embroiled in a salacious extramarital affair to the jingoistic fat cat who made a fortune through foreign outsourcing, examples abound. As we write this chapter, Jon Stewart is nearing the end of his seminal 17-year run hosting *The Daily Show*. Pick the opening segment of any of the show's 2,600+ episodes, and odds are good that you'll see an example of hypocrisy writ large: the juxtaposition of a politician or pundit saying one thing in one clip but doing something to the contrary in a second clip. Or an activist who, without a trace of self-awareness or irony, tolerates in one constituency behavior that he'd never abide in another group.

Even the noblest professions are not exempt from such hypocrisy. For instance, most physicians would insist that the meals, gifts, and financial incentives offered by pharmaceutical reps have no effect on their medical decisions. According to one survey, 61 percent of medical residents claimed that such promotions had no effect on their practice, while only 16 percent believed that their fellow physicians were similarly unswayed. But studies tracking actual pharmacy inventories tell a different story: a physician who attends seminars sponsored by drug companies is then more likely to prescribe that company's drugs to her patients.

And think of the myriad ways in which we, as observers of others' behavior—even the life-and-death variety—often view the same actions and outcomes in very different ways depending on our connections (or lack thereof) to those responsible: The pro-police stalwart becomes, understandably, grief-stricken over an officer's death in the line of duty yet dismisses the death of an unarmed citizen in custody as the victim's own fault. Those skeptical of the police do the opposite. Or one nation mourns the loss of soldiers' lives abroad while justifying civilian casualties as collateral damage, while the other nation does the reverse.

So sports fans may be a lost cause, cognizant that they're rooting for laundry at the expense of a steady moral compass. But there remains an impetus for considering what can be done to address such biases elsewhere, bridging the gulf between how different groups/teams/tribes view the same set of circumstances. Because research tells us that we are *not* helplessly at the mercy of a hypocritical brain—under the right circumstances we *can* be equally sensitive to our own and to others' moral transgressions.

In a follow-up to the Northeastern study, the researchers added a wrinkle to their green task/red task experiment. In this version, some participants were also charged with memorizing a series of seven-digit numbers at the same time as they rated the fairness of their own (and others') decisions. The memorization was intended to increase the respondents' cognitive load—to occupy their mental resources and distract them.

The researchers found that in the baseline condition—i.e., without the digit-memorization task—participants once again viewed their own selection of the easier green task to be fair but the same selfishness on the part of others to be unfair. Under cognitive load, however, this hypocrisy vanished. Distracted by the simultaneous number memorization, respondents didn't have the cognitive wherewithal to engage in their usual rationalization and ethical spin. Their minds too busy trying to remember the numbers, they resorted to a more intuitive understanding of fairness, giving the same ratings to their own performance and that of others.

The finding is cause for optimism regarding our potential to combat hypocrisy. We do indeed have the ability to see the world fairly; we just have to choose to do so (or to be so distracted that we just can't help it). "Hypocrisy is driven by mental processes over which we have volitional control," Valdesolo once explained to the *The New York Times*. "Our gut seems to be equally sensitive to our own and others' transgressions . . . we just need to find ways to better translate our moral feelings into moral actions."

Another way to combat the bias blind spot is simply to learn about it. Did any of the examples in this chapter strike a (dissonant) chord for you, whether due to your own A-ROID shirt, affinity for lunches paid for by pharmaceutical companies, or tendency to overlook the foibles of candidates from your chosen political party? Reading about research on the unconscious processes of bias has been found to make people less sure of their own objectivity and more accurate in assessing the factors that truly color their judgments.

Remember: No one wants to be a hypocrite. So there are ways in which we can capitalize on this aversion to effect positive change in our behavior. Consider one effort to promote condom use in a college population. The researchers tried to *induce* a feeling of hypocrisy by asking the students to (1) help record a safe-sex public-service video intended for a high school audience, and (2) answer questions during a separate interview regarding how often in the past they had failed to use condoms themselves.

Being confronted with their own inconsistencies was uncomfortable for the students in the short run but had positive effects in the long run: Those who felt this hypocrisy reported a greater likelihood of using condoms in the future and also purchased more condoms when given the opportunity to do so.

Similar interventions have been effective in combating prejudice. In one study, college students were asked to write a persuasive essay on the importance of treating all members of their student body fairly, regardless of racial or ethnic background. Some of these students were next asked to write a private essay detailing two times when they might have reacted to or treated a member of another group unfairly. Reminded of their moral inconsistency, these students were less likely to recommend cuts to the budget of minority student groups in a subsequent survey.

Yet as illustrated by our journey into the Fenway bleachers on A-Rod's milestone weekend, most of us still find it easier to see the biases of others than to recognize them in ourselves. There are ways to hold up a figurative mirror and compel people to recognize temporarily the inconsistencies that they ordinarily rationalize away. But for most of us, more consistent self-awareness remains an admirable yet unattainable goal.

A notable exception: the recently retired but still astute observer of the human condition, Jon Stewart, to whom we give the last word here. (Here it is, his Moment of Zen.) Back to May 2015 once more, this time to the immediate aftermath of the release of the Wells Report, the NFL's investigation into "Deflategate," the New England Patriots' alleged underinflation of footballs in the 2014 AFC title game.

Stewart, by his own admission no Boston sports enthusiast, railed against the Patriots, Tom Brady in particular: "Tommy, you cheating fuck. Why? You got four Super Bowl rings. You're married to the biggest supermodel in the world. Your face—your beautiful face—is a wonder of symmetry, a Platonic ideal of beauty that can survive even the stupidest of haircuts. But you, my friend, stood up there in one of America's most sacred places—the podium room before Super Bowl week—and you lied to us."

Stewart dedicated seven full minutes to this skewering of Brady, approaching a crescendo of feigned indignation as he neared the finish line. "And by the way, if you think I wouldn't chastise you if you had committed these acts while in my team's—a New York Giants—uniform," barked Stewart, as the photo behind him morphed from Brady in Patriots white to Brady in Giants blue, "if you think that I wouldn't chastise you for that?" A wry smile crept across Stewart's face. "That would be correct."

Why Unlocking the Mystery of Human Consciousness Is—Like So Much Else in Life—All About Sports

We have asked, and tried to answer, many questions in this book. We've saved the toughest for last.

"Gillian" was only 23 years old. She lay motionless in a British hospital bed in 2005, having suffered severe brain injuries after being struck by two cars while crossing the street. Days became weeks, which became months. Still, she remained unresponsive. Her physicians determined that she met the clinical criteria for a diagnosis of persistent vegetative state (or *unresponsive wakefulness*, the gentler diagnostic name more common today).

Gillian's neurologists continued to be interested, though, in the possibility that she had residual cognitive function—that despite the lack of outward signs of consciousness, her brain might still, in less perceptible ways, be responsive to stimuli. Eager for some sort of resolution, her family agreed to allow neuroscientist Adrian Owen to place Gillian in an MRI scanner. Changes in blood flow throughout her brain would be recorded, and their interpretation would allow Owen to draw conclusions about activity in her different brain regions.

These remain some of humanity's knottiest mysteries: What gives rise to consciousness? Where is it situated in the brain? How do we measure it or even tell whether it's there in the first place? Physicians, philosophers, lawmakers, and others have long looked into such matters, each through their own occupational lenses, each guided by different stakes and stakeholders. But the existential question persists: What does it really mean to have consciousness?

The challenges inherent in assessing consciousness are only amplified under the most tragic circumstances, such as Gillian's. These cases have been known to escalate into hornets' nests of lawsuits, political posturing, and indignant punditry, but the questions they raise are complex even at a scientific level. Differentiating unresponsive wakefulness from a minimally conscious state can be one of the hardest tasks a physician faces; research indicates misdiagnosis rates north of 40 percent.

From a neurological perspective, consciousness has two components: wakefulness and awareness. Wakefulness is straightforward: Can a person open his or her eyes? But awareness—therein lies the rub. Awareness requires evidence of cognitive activity tied to interaction with the surrounding environment. What counts as *sufficient* cognitive activity is often a point of contention.

So consciousness is anything but an either/or diagnosis. In fact, researchers and clinicians have developed an entire continuum of terminology to refer to levels of decreased consciousness, starting with *confusion, drowsiness,* and *stupor* and running through *minimal consciousness, unresponsive wakefulness,* and *coma.* There is a clear appeal, then, to current research that uses cutting-edge technology to identify anything approaching a "brain signature" of what consciousness looks like at a neural level. As with other difficult questions about human nature—*How can we tell if someone is lying? How do we really know if someone harbors particular prejudices?*—the hope is that measuring the brain directly will provide clearer, less subjective answers.

Back to Gillian. For weeks she had been in the same hospital rooms with family members, within earshot of their familiar voices, but this appeared to have had little effect on her consciousness. When her doctors asked her questions that might have emotional resonance, again, there was no visible response.

But now Gillian lay in an MRI tube, giving Owen and his colleagues a direct channel to any brain response. All they needed to do was figure out what type of stimulus her brain might respond to. First they read aloud a series of sentences, some including ambiguous words (for example, *creek* versus *creak*). The neural scan indicated increased response from the left inferior frontal region of Gillian's brain—same as would typically be observed in healthy subjects.

Still, the researchers cautioned, "neural response to the meaning of spoken sentences, although suggestive, is not unequivocal evidence that a person is consciously aware." Apparently, studies of people who are sleeping or under anesthesia demonstrate that evidence of speech perception can be found even in the brains of those lacking in conscious awareness.

So for an even more rigorous effort to assess consciousness, the researchers required a more emotionally resonant stimulus. In their collective scientific wisdom, what they ultimately settled on was . . .

Tennis.

That's right, *tennis*. Owen's research team gave Gillian spoken instructions to imagine herself playing tennis, the ball floating from one side of the court to the other. In response, her brain showed signs of significant activity in the supplementary motor area—the part of the primate brain that contributes to the control of movement. What's more, her neural responses were indistinguishable from those observed in the brains of healthy volunteers used for comparison.

There would be no miraculous recovery for Gillian. But her case inspired a set of procedures, now known collectively as the "tennis test," which have played a major role in recent reconceptualizations of how to assess consciousness. Heated debate continues: Describing responses from colleagues after he published his first tennis-test paper, Owen says, "I received two types of e-mail. . . . 'This is amazing—well done!' and 'How could you possibly say this woman is conscious?'" Without question, though, the work has had an impact, such as inspiring the formation of an international consortium of researchers seeking to generate inexpensive, relatively portable ways of assessing borderline states of consciousness. One possibility is to combine an assessment such as the tennis test with old-fashioned electroencephalography (EEG, in which electrodes are attached to the scalp to measure brain activity).

Amazing, when you think about it: a means by which individuals in a vegetative or unresponsive state, who are minimally conscious or who have locked-in syndrome—unable to move or speak but able to think—may be able to communicate with those around them via modulation of neural activity. Ask the patient a series of questions, tell her to think about tennis only if the answer is *yes*, and then look for activity in the supplementary motor area of the brain.

Nearly as amazing? That when it came to answering an age-old question about consciousness, one with life-and-death implications that cuts to the very core of what it means to be human, this team of neurologists and cognitive scientists turned to athletic competition. There it was in Gillian's MRI scans: *the brain on sports*.

NOW, it's not that we—or the researchers who devised the tennis test—are proposing that sports leave a unique imprint on the brain. Quite the contrary: We've spent the preceding chapters trying to make the case that there are rational underpinnings for all the supposed craziness and unusual behavior that sports seem to trigger. That is, that "your brain on sports" is really just your regular brain acting as it does in other contexts.

After all, *that's* why researchers investigating consciousness and traumatic brain injury came upon the idea that thinking about tennis would be an ideal stimulus. It's because sports = everyday life: the rivalries, the rationalizations, the striving for finish lines. Sports are familiar, they are ubiquitous, they are eminently human. Remember what Errol Morris said about the *It's Not Crazy, It's Sports* short films? "Sports, as we all know, touches on everything." Even for poor Gillian.

As you now know, sports and athletic competition are fertile ground for scientists across disciplines to test their hypotheses about basic aspects of human nature. From economists studying appearance, leadership, and compensation among NFL quarterbacks, to the political scientist investigating international relations via the

World Cup draw, to psychologists exploring praise and performance as they play out on the college ice hockey rink.

All of which is to say that, while it's our hope that you've found this book entertaining, we're also willing to sign off on your petition to get course credit for completing it. Remember this the next time you catch flak for prioritizing a sporting event over a work meeting or family obligation: You didn't have your priorities out of alignment; you were doing background research. You weren't a couch potato passively absorbing the big game; you were simply brushing up on the latest behavioral science. That big-screen TV you just bought, along with the latest sports-channel package? Educational tax write-off, if you ask us.[1]

As many a graduation ceremony speaker has intoned over the years, *a true education never ends*. We concur. But we'll also note: Final exams prove a lot more fun when they come with instant replay, a halftime show, and nachos.

---

1. Note to Legal: Jon and Sam are not certified tax advisers.

ACKNOWLEDGMENTS

FROM JON

When I hear authors describe the process of book writing as an exercise in solitude, I sometimes worry that I am doing it all wrong. This project was predicated on teamwork, partnership, discussion, interaction, and the kindness of strangers. Put simply, it would not have been started—much less completed—without the varied and various contributions of so many. (And the collaborative godsend that is Google Docs.)

I am in arrears: To my longtime agent, Scott Waxman, for "getting" the concept and then getting a proposal in the hands of the right editor and publisher. To Roger Scholl and the good folks at Crown Archetype, who again proved to be the ideal partner. To Jeff Spielberger, Tomago Collins, and Gabe Miller, for their careful readings. To my friend and former colleague David Epstein, for specific suggestions that improved the text immensely and, more generally, for setting the standard for these types of books with *The Sports Gene*. To Chris Hunt, a first-ballot enshrinee in the editor's Hall of Fame.

While too numerous to name individually, I am filled with gratitude for the subjects and experts who were exceedingly generous with their time and candor. (From star athletes and pro coaches to academic researchers, I am ceaselessly amazed how readily people are willing to share their expertise with others.) Thanks to Ellie, Ben, and Allegra, as ever, for excusing me to go write and for indulging the impromptu psychology lectures and experiments.

Above all, thanks to my co-conspirator, Sam Sommers. Never mind his impressive body of work, his sterling academic reputation, his thoroughly enjoyable previous book, *Situations Matter*. When I learned we shared both a Midwest provenance and a fondness for coaching our daughters' softball teams, I knew I had found an ideal doubles partner.

FROM SAM

First and foremost, to Jon Wertheim. For enabling me to transition from an academic who *thinks* he knows a lot about sports to . . . well, an academic who *thinks* he knows a lot about sports and also has a willing publisher. What seemed like it would be great fun from the very first phone call has been that and then some.

Second author has it easy: Ditto to everything Jon wrote. But in particular, thanks to Roger and everyone at Crown Archetype for making this book a reality. And to my indispensable agent, Dan Lazar, for helping me navigate that reality.

Special thanks to our research assistants. In the early going, Scott Blumenthal. For the duration, Ari Panzer, as optimistic a Mets/Jets fan as you'll ever meet. And jack-of-all-trades Olivia Wyatt, who never ran low on patience (a trait perhaps born of being a Twins fan), regardless of the number of times we asked for "one last" analysis or fact-check. Also, my colleagues who offered expert feedback on specific content, namely Mike Norton, Marty Samuels, Lisa Shin, and Heather Urry.

I may not have realized it at the time, but I've enjoyed four decades of prep work for a book filled with sports analyses and arguments, whether in the backseat of long family road trips, in late-night college dorm rooms, or in the stands at youth sports games. Family members and friends alike, you know who you are (and when you were wrong). But in particular: Mom & Dad, Ben, Zach, Matt, Mike (again), and Keith. More recently, Abby & Sophie. And Marilyn, for putting up with it all with a smile.

To Mr. Black, for teaching us that there is serious intellectual discussion to be had about pop culture and life's guiltier pleasures. It's a short walk from critical analysis of Disney World and cult television shows to this book.

And finally, to my own Little League coaches back in the day, who used to say things in team huddles like: *Watch Sam—he may not have the best bat. Or throwing arm. He certainly isn't the fastest guy on the team. Doesn't always make the catch, for that matter. But he's always paying attention and knows the game situation.* Thanks. I think. Hopefully, this book has helped make your case.

REFERENCE NOTES

WHY THE T-SHIRT CANNON HAS SOMETHING TO TEACH US ABOUT HUMAN NATURE

On scarcity and other tricks of the trade for social influence: Cialdini, R. B. (2006). *Influence: The psychology of persuasion*. New York: HarperBusiness.

Hershey's Kiss experiments and more on the allure of free: Ariely, D. (2008). *Predictably irrational: The hidden forces that shape our decisions*. New York: Harper.

Free samples and consumer tendencies: Heilman, C., Lakishyk, K., and Radas, S. (2011). An empirical investigation of in-store sampling promotions. *British Food Journal, 113*, 1252–1266.

On consumer entitlement: Boyd, III, H. C., and Helms, J. E. (2005). Consumer entitlement theory and measurement. *Psychology and Marketing, 22*, 271–286. And on the science of spending money more generally: Dunn, E., and Norton, M. (2013). *Happy money: The science of smarter spending*. New York: Simon & Schuster.

WHY TOM BRADY AND ALL THOSE OTHER QUARTERBACKS ARE SO DAMNED GOOD-LOOKING (OR ARE THEY?)

Economics of attractive QBs: Berri, D. J., Simmons, R., Van Gilder, J., and O'Neill, L. (2011). What does it mean to find the face of the franchise? Physical attractiveness and the evaluation of athletic performance. *Economics Letters, 111*, 200–202.

On facial symmetry and attractiveness: Grammer, K., and Thornhill, R. (1994). Human (*homo sapiens*) facial attractiveness and sexual selection: The role of symmetry and averageness. *Journal of Comparative Psychology, 108,* 233–242.

On attractiveness and labor force earning potential: Mobius, M., and Rosenblatt, T. (2006). Why beauty matters. *American Economic Review, 96,* 225–235.

Nisbett and Wilson halo effect study: Nisbett, R. E., and Wilson, T. D. (1977). The halo effect: Evidence for unconscious alteration of judgments. *Journal of Personality and Social Psychology, 35,* 250–256.

On stereotypes and preferential treatment regarding beauty: Dion, K. K., Berscheid, E., and Walster, E. (1972). What is beautiful is good. *Journal of Personality and Social Psychology, 24,* 285–290. Eagly, A. H., Ashmore, R. D., Makhijani, M. G., and Longo, L. C. (1991). What is beautiful is good, but . . . : A meta-analytic review of research on the physical attractiveness stereotype. *Psychological Bulletin, 110,* 109–128.

Good-looking defendants: Sigall, H., and Ostrove, N. (1975). Beautiful but dangerous: Effects of offender attractiveness and nature of the crime on juridic judgment. *Journal of Personality and Social Psychology, 31,* 410–414.

Science of "gaydar": Rule, N. O., Ambady, N., Adams, R. B., Jr., and Macrae, C. N. (2008). Accuracy and awareness in the perception and categorization of male sexual orientation. *Journal of Personality and Social Psychology, 95,* 1019–1028. Rule, N. O., Rosen, K. S., Slepian, M. L., and Ambady, N. (2011). Mating interest improves women's accuracy in judging male sexual orientation. *Psychological Science, 22,* 881–886.

Princeton study of political candidate impressions based on faces: Todorov, A., Mandisodza, A. N., Goren, A., and Hall, C. (2005). Inferences of competence from faces predict election outcomes. *Science, 308,* 1623–1626.

On perceptions of CEO faces: Rule, N. O., and Ambady, N. (2008). The face of success: Inferences from chief executive officers' appearance predict company profits. *Psychological Science, 19,* 109–111.

WHY WE CHANNEL OUR INNER MAYWEATHER AND SECRETLY CRAVE DISRESPECT

Greenwald, A. G. (1980). The totalitarian ego: Fabrication and revision of personal history. *American Psychologist, 35,* 603–618. Direct quote from p. 603.

On the spotlight effect: Gilovich, T., and Savitsky, K. (1999). The spotlight effect and the illusion of transparency: Egocentric assessments of how we're seen by others. *Current Directions in Psychological Science, 8,* 165–168. Barry Manilow study: Gilovich, T., Medvec, V. H., and Savitsky, K. (2000). The spotlight effect in social judgment: An egocentric bias in estimates of the salience of one's own actions and appearance. *Journal of Personality and Social Psychology, 78,* 211–222. Direct quote from p. 211.

Illusions of control and lottery drawings: Langer, E. J. (1975). The illusion of control. *Journal of Personality and Social Psychology, 32,* 311–328.

Positive illusions as essential for mental health: Taylor, S. E., and Brown, J. D. (1988). Illusion and well-being: A social psychological perspective on mental health. *Psychological Bulletin, 103,* 193–210.

How being an underdog can motivate you: Nurmohamed, S. (2013). Expected to win or lose? The positive effects of an underdog identity on performance. Presented at the annual meeting of the Society for Personality and Social Psychology, New Orleans, LA.

Basketball trailing at halftime study: Berger, J., and Pope, D. (2011). Can losing lead to winning? *Management Science, 57,* 817–827.

The psychology of sandbagging (and Tim Belcher example): Gibson, B., Sachau, D., Doll, B., and Shumate, R. (2002). Sandbagging in competition: Responding to the pressure of being the favorite. *Personality and Social Psychology Bulletin, 28,* 1119–1130.

On perceptions of the underdog. Vandello, J. A., Goldschmied, N. P., and Richards, D. A. R. (2007). The appeal of the underdog. *Personality and Social Psychology Bulletin, 33,* 1603–1616. Michniewicz, K. S., and Vandello, J. A. (2013). The attractive underdog: When disadvantage bolsters attractiveness. *Journal of Social and Personal Relationships, 30,* 942–952.

Study of tennis favorites and underdogs retiring in matches due to injury: Tuckfield, B., Diervorst, B., Milkman, K. L., and Schweitzer, M. E. (November 2013). Ranking systems turn winners into quitters. Poster presented at the annual meeting of the Society for Judgment and Decision Making, Toronto, ON.

Customer-service tricks for manipulating expectation: Sheppard, J. A., Sweeny, K., and Cherry, L. C. (2007). Influencing audience satisfaction by manipulating expectations. *Social Influence, 2,* 98–111.

WHY WE ARE ALL DOG LOVERS AT HEART (BUT NOT DEEP IN OUR HEARTS)

Richmond shapes study: Kim, J., Allison, S. T., Eylon, D., Goethals, G. R., Markus, M. J., Hindle, S. M., and McGuire, H. A. (2008). Rooting for (and then abandoning) the underdog. *Journal of Applied Social Psychology, 38,* 2550–2573. Direct quotes from pp. 2564, 2559.

South Florida Maccabi/CSKA study: Vandello, J. A., Goldschmied, N. P., and Richards, D. A. R. (2007). The appeal of the underdog. *Personality and Social Psychology Bulletin, 33,* 1603–1616.

Bowling Green study: Frazier, J. A., and Snyder, E. E. (1991). The underdog concept in sport. *Sociology of Sport Journal, 8,* 380–388.

Rooting for winners and self-esteem boosts: Cialdini, R. B., Borden, R. J., Thorne, A., Walker, M. R., Freeman, S., and Sloan, L. R. (1976). Basking in reflected glory: Three (football) field studies. *Journal of Personality and Social Psychology, 34,* 366–375. Hirt, E. R., Zillman, D., Erickson, G. A., and Kennedy, C. (1992). Costs and benefits of allegiance: Changes in fans' self-ascribed competencies after team victory versus defeat. *Journal of Personality and Social Psychology, 63,* 724–738.

Underdogs in presidential elections: Goldschmied, N., and Vandello, J. A. (2009). The advantage of disadvantage: Underdogs in the political arena. *Basic and Applied Social Psychology, 31,* 24–31.

Underdog brand biography: Paharia, N., Keinan, A., Avery, J., and Schor, J. B. (2011). The underdog effect: The marketing of disadvantage and determination through brand biography. *Journal of Consumer Research, 37,* 775–790. Direct quote from p. 776.

Coffee-spill likability study: Aronson, E., Willerman, B., and Floyd, J. (1966). The effect of a pratfall on increasing interpersonal attractiveness. *Psychonomic Science, 4,* 227–228.

Gladwell, M. (2003). *David and Goliath: Underdogs, misfits, and the art of battling giants.* New York: Little, Brown. Direct quote from p. 6.

On underdogs and optimism: Goldschmied, N. P., and Vandello, J. A. (2012). The future is bright: The underdog label, availability, and optimism. *Basic and Applied Social Psychology, 34,* 34–43.

Betting on NFL underdogs: Levitt, S. D. (2004). Why are gambling markets organised so differently from financial markets? *The Economic Journal,*

114, 223–246. Simmons, J. P., Nelson, L. D., Galak, J., and Frederick, S. (2011). Intuitive biases in choice versus estimation: Implications for the wisdom of crowds. *Journal of Consumer Research, 38*, 1–15.

WHY HOCKEY GOONS WOULD RATHER FIGHT AT HOME

For review of research on social influence and conformity: Cialdini, R. B., and Goldstein, N. J. (2004). Social influence: Compliance and conformity. *Annual Review of Psychology, 55*, 591–621.

Territorial mice study: Fuxjager, M. J., Forbes-Lorman, R. M., Coss, D. J., Auger, C. J., Auger, A. P., and Marler, C. A. (2010). Winning territorial disputes selectively enhances androgen sensitivity in neural pathways related to motivation and social aggression. *Proceedings of the National Academy of Sciences, 107*, 12393–12398.

THE CURSE OF THE EXPERT: WHY THE BEST PLAYERS MAKE THE WORST COACHES

On experts and their mental representations of tasks: Hinds, P. J., and Pfeffer, J. (2003). Why organizations don't "know what they know": Cognitive and motivational factors affecting the transfer of expertise. In M. Ackerman, V. Pipek, and V. Wulf (eds.), *Beyond knowledge management: Sharing expertise* (pp. 3–26). Cambridge, MA: MIT Press.

Italian neuroscience and basketball perception study: Aglioti, S. M., Cesari, P., Romani, M., and Urgesi, C. (2008). Action anticipation and motor resonance in elite basketball players. *Nature Neuroscience, 11*, 1109–1116. Direct quote from p. 1109.

On brain activation and expert motor anticipation: Wright, M. J., Bishop, D. T., Jackson, R. C., and Abernethy, B. (2010). Functional MRI reveals expert-novice differences during sport-related anticipation. *NeuroReport, 21*, 94–98. Soccer penalty-kick study: Makris, S., and Urgesi, C. (2014). Neural underpinnings of superior action prediction abilities in soccer players. *Social Cognitive and Affective Neuroscience*. DOI: 10.1093/scan/nsu052.

Experts skipping steps: Blessing, S. B., and Anderson, J. R. (1996). How people learn to skip steps. *Journal of Experimental Psychology: Learning, Memory, and Cognition, 22*, 576–598.

Expert electricians: Gitomer, D. H. (1988). Individual differences in technical troubleshooting. *Human Performance, 1*, 111–131. Direct quote regarding the way experts store and process information: Hinds and Pfeffer (2003), p. 4.

Expert LEGO builders study: Hinds, P. J. (1999). The curse of expertise: The effects of expertise and debiasing methods on predictions of novice performance. *Journal of Experimental Psychology: Applied, 5,* 205–221.

Talking about golf and putting study: Flegal, K. E., and Anderson, M. C. (2008). Overthinking skilled motor performance: Or why those who teach can't do. *Psychonomic Bulletin and Review, 15,* 927–932. Direct quote: Beilock, S. (2011). *Choke: Use the secrets of your brain to succeed when it matters most.* New York: Simon & Schuster, p. 225.

On overcoming the curse of expertise: Hinds and Pfeffer (2003); Hinds (1999).

ACTING ON IMPULSE: WHY WE AREN'T SO DIFFERENT FROM THE SPORTS HOTHEAD (L-O-B, CRABTREE!)

For more on hot-state, cold-state, and the disconnect between them: Loewenstein, G. (2005). Hot-cold empathy gaps and medical decision-making. *Health Psychology, 24,* 549–556. Van Boven, L., and Loewenstein, G. (2003). Social projection of transient drive states. *Personality and Social Psychology Bulletin, 29,* 1159–168.

Sexual-arousal study: Ariely, D., and Loewenstein, G. (2006). The heat of the moment: The effect of arousal on sexual decision making. *Journal of Behavioral Decision Making, 19,* 87–98. Direct quotes from p. 89.

Arousal and sexual risk-taking in men and women: Skakoon-Sparling, S., and Cramer, K. (2014). Paretelic/telic state, sexual arousal, and sexual risk-taking in university students. *Journal of Motivation, Emotion, and Personality, 2,* 32–37.

Mass General PET study: Rauch, S. L., Shin, L. M., Doughtery, D. D., Alpert, N. M., Orr, S. P., Lasko, M., Macklin, M. L., Fischman, A. J., and Pitman, R. K. (1999). Neural activation during sexual and competitive arousal in healthy men. *Psychiatry Research: Neuroimaging, 91,* 1–10.

The "high" and "low" roads on the thalamo-cortico-amygdala connection: Ledoux, J. (1996). *The emotional brain: The mysterious underpinnings of emotional life.* New York: Simon & Schuster.

On similar physiological and behavioral patterns—and neural pathways—in competitive and sexual arousal: Lang, P. J., and Bradley, M. M. (2010). Emotion and the motivational brain. *Biological Psychology, 84,* 437–450.

On misattribution of arousal, emotions, and not always knowing how various states affect us: Cotton, J. L. (1981). A review of research on Schachter's theory of emotion and the misattribution of arousal. *European Journal of Social Psychology, 11,* 365–397. Schwarz, N. (2012). Feeling-as-information theory. In P. Van Lange, A. Kruglanski, and E. T. Higgins (eds.), *Handbook of theories of social psychology* (pp. 289–308). Thousand Oaks, CA: Sage. Wilson, T. D., and Gilbert, D. T. (2005). Affective forecasting: Knowing what to want. *Current Directions in Psychological Science, 14,* 131–134.

Iowa State risk-perception study: Blanton, H., and Gerrard, M. (1997). Effect of sexual motivation on men's risk perception for sexually transmitted disease: There must be 50 ways to justify a lover. *Health Psychology, 16,* 374–379. On arousal and the neuroscience of financial decisions: Platt, M. L., and Huetter, S. A. (2008). Risky business: The neuroeconomics of decision making under uncertainty. *Nature Neuroscience, 11,* 398–403.

Arousal and negotiation: Brown, A. D., and Curhan, J. R. (2013). The polarizing effect of arousal on negotiation. *Psychological Science, 24,* 1928–1935.

Arousal and consumers of advertising: Sanbonmatsu, D. M., and Kardes, F. R. (1998). The effects of physiological arousal on information processing and persuasion. *Journal of Consumer Research, 15,* 379–385.

Ariely quote: Ariely, D. (2009). *Predictably irrational: The hidden forces that shape our decisions.* New York: Harper, p. 128.

Review of studies examining links between sports participation and more general aggressiveness: Sønderlund, A. L., O'Brien, K., Kremer, P., Rowland, B., De Groot, P. S., Zinkiewicz, L., and Miller, P. G. (2014). The association between sports participation, alcohol use and aggression and violence: A systematic review. *Journal of Science and Medicine in Sport, 17,* 2–7.

WHY ATHLETES DON'T NEED AN EMPTY BED BEFORE COMPETITION

Treadmill study: Boone, T., and Gilmore, S. (1995). Effects of sexual intercourse on maximal aerobic power, oxygen pulse, and double product in male sedentary subjects. *Journal of Sports Medicine and Physical Fitness, 35,* 214–217.

Bicycle ergometer and mental concentration test study: Sztajzel, J., Périat, M., Marti, V., Krall, P., and Rutishauser, W. (2000). Effect of sexual activity on cycle ergometer stress test parameters, on plasmatic testosterone levels and on concentration capacity. *Journal of Sports Medicine and Physical Fitness*, *40*, 233–239. Direct quote from p. 239.

Rutgers study of female orgasms and pain threshold: Whipple, B., and Komisaruk, B. R. (1985). Elevation of pain threshold by vaginal stimulation in women. *Pain*, *21*, 357–367.

Jannini study: Jannini, E. A., Screponi, E., Carosa, E., Pepe, M., Lo Diudice, F., Trimarchi, F., and Benvenga, S. (2001). Lack of sexual activity from erectile dysfunction is associated with a reversible reduction in serum testosterone. *International Journal of Andrology*, *22*, 385–392.

McGlone, S., and Schrier, I. (2000). Does sex the night before competition decrease performance? *Clinical Journal of Sport Medicine*, *10*, 233–234.

Survey of athletes' beliefs: Pupiš, M., Raković, A., Stanković, D., Kocić, M., and Savanović, V. (2010). Sex and endurance performance. *International Journal of Kinesiology*, *7*, 21–25.

WHY THE COACH'S SEAT IS *ALWAYS* HOT

NFL coaching-change study: Roach, M. A. (2013). Mean reversion or a breath of fresh air? The effect of NFL coaching changes on team performance in the salary cap era. *Applied Economics Letters*, *20*, 1553–1556. Direct quotation: p. 1556.

College football coaching changes: Adler, E. S., Berry, M. J., and Doherty, D. (2013). Pushing 'reset': The conditional effects of coaching replacements on college football performance. *Social Science Quarterly*, *94*, 1–28. Direct quotations: p. 1.

Hockey coaching changes: http://fivethirtyeight.com/features/what-predicts-if-an-nhl-coach-will-be-fired-and-whether-it-matters/.

Baseball coaching changes: Allen, M. P., Panian, S. K., and Lotz, R. E. (1979). Managerial succession and organizational performance: A recalcitrant problem revisited. *Administrative Science Quarterly*, *24*, 167–180.

English soccer study: Audas, R., Dobson, S., and Goddard, J. (2002). The impact of managerial change on team performance in professional sports.

Journal of Economics and Business, 54, 644–650. Serie A study: De Paola, M., and Scoppa, V. (2012). The effects of managerial turnover: Evidence from coach dismissals in Italian soccer teams. *Journal of Sports Economics, 13,* 152–168.

NBA coaching changes: Pfeffer, J., and Davis-Blake, A. (1986). Administrative succession and organizational performance: How administrator experience mediates the succession effect. *Academy of Management Journal, 29,* 72–83. College basketball: Eitzen, D. S., and Yetman, N. R. (1972). Managerial change, longevity, and organizational effectiveness. *Administrative Science Quarterly, 17,* 110–116.

CEO firings: Wiersema, M. (2002). Holes at the top: Why CEO firings backfire. *Harvard Business Review, 80,* 70–77. Direct quotations: pp. 2, 4.

Investing study: Barber, B. M., and Odean, T. (2000): Trading is hazardous to your wealth: The common stock investment performance of individual investors. *Journal of Finance, 55,* 773–806.

Soccer penalty-kick study: Bar-Eli, M., Azar, O. H., Ritov, I., Keidar-Levin, Y., and Schein, G. (2007). Action bias among elite soccer goalkeepers: The case of penalty kicks. *Journal of Economic Psychology, 28,* 606–621.

Kahneman quotation: Kahneman, D. (2011). *Thinking, fast and slow.* New York: Macmillan, p. 284.

WHY SO MANY SUCCESSFUL ULTRA-ENDURANCE ATHLETES ARE ALSO SUCCESSFUL RECOVERING ADDICTS

On the endocannabinoid system and exercise: Heyman, E., et al. (2012). Intense exercise increases circulating endocannabinoid and BDNF levels in humans: Possible implications for reward and depression. *Psychoneuroendocrinology, 37,* 844–851. Sparling, P. B., Giuffrida, A., Piomelli, D., Rosskopf, L., and Dietrich, A. (2003). Exercise activates the endocannabinoid system. *Neuroreport, 14,* 2209–2211.

On exercise and dependence: Hausenblas, H. A., and Downs, D. S. (2002). Exercise dependence: A systematic review. *Psychology of Sport and Exercise, 3,* 89–123.

Zuckerman scale: Zuckerman, M., Kolin, E. A., Price, L., and Zoob, I. (1964). Development of a sensation-seeking scale. *Journal of Consulting Psychology, 28,* 477–482.

Sensation-seeking, personality, drug use, and sports: Zuckerman, M., Bone, R. N., Neary, R., Mangelsdorff, D., and Brustman, B. (1972). What is the sensation seeker? Personality trait and experience correlates of the Sensation-Seeking Scales. *Journal of Consulting and Clinical Psychology*, *39*, 308–321. Jack, S. J., and Ronan, K. R. (1998). Sensation seeking among high- and low-risk sports participants. *Personality and Individual Differences*, *25*, 1063–1083.

Family history of alcoholism study: Corlett, P. R. (May 2015). Pavlovian to instrumental transfer: Tracking the transition from goal-directed to habitual behaviour. Paper presented at the annual meeting of the Society of Biological Psychiatry, Toronto, ON.

WHY GIVING EVERY LITTLE LEAGUE KID A TROPHY IS SUCH A LOUSY IDEA

Trophy expenditures: http://www.nytimes.com/2013/09/25/opinion/losing-is-good-for-you.html.

Youth sports trophy poll: http://reason.com/poll/2014/08/19/57-percent-of-americans-say-only-kids-wh.

Notre Dame hockey study: Anderson, D. C., Crowell, C. R., Doman, M., and Howard, G. S. (1988). Performance posting, goal setting, and activity-contingent praise as applied to a university hockey team. *Journal of Applied Psychology*, *73*, 87–95.

On praise and mindset: Dweck, C. S. (2006). *Mindset: The new psychology of success*. New York: Random House. Mueller, C. M., and Dweck, C. S. (1998). Intelligence praise can undermine motivation and performance. *Journal of Personality and Social Psychology*, *75*, 33–52.

On grit and perseverance: Duckworth, A. (2016). *Grit: Passion, perseverance, and the science of success*. New York: Scribner.

WHY ROOTING FOR THE METS IS LIKE BUILDING THAT IKEA DESK

Franklin, B. (1906 copyright). *The autobiography of Benjamin Franklin*. Boston and New York: Houghton Mifflin. Quotes from pp. 106–107.

Aronson, E., and Mills, J. (1959). The effect of severity of initiation on liking for a group. *Journal of Abnormal and Social Psychology*, *59*, 177–181. Quotes from p. 178. More details from Aronson, E. (2010). *Not by chance alone: My life as a social psychologist*. New York: Basic Books. Direct quote from p. 112.

The IKEA effect: Norton, M. I., Mochon, D., and Ariely, D. (2012). The IKEA effect: When labor leads to love. *Journal of Consumer Psychology*, 22, 453–560.

On assumptions related to effort, both in terms of effort justification and the notion that effort is an indicator of quality (e.g., the more effort it takes to create a work of art, the higher quality people assume it to be): Kruger, J., Wirtz, D., Van Boven, L., and Altermatt, T. W. (2004). The effort heuristic. *Journal of Experimental Social Psychology*, 40, 91–98.

The appeal of membership fees: Dick, A. S., and Lord, K. R. (1998). The impact of membership fees on consumer attitude and choice. *Psychology and Marketing*, 15, 41–58.

The value of self-designed products: Franke, N., and Schreier, M. (2010). Why customers value self-designed products: The importance of process effort and enjoyment. *Journal of Product Innovation Management*, 27, 1020–1031.

Travel-website study: Buell, R. W., and Norton, M. I. (2011). The labor illusion: How operational transparency increases perceived value. *Management Science*, 57, 1564–1579.

On hazing and group affiliation on college campuses: Keating, C. F., Pomerantz, J., Pommer, S. D., Ritt, S. J. H., Miller, L. M., and McCormick, J. (2005). Going to college and unpacking hazing: A functional approach to decrypting initiation practices among undergraduates. *Group Dynamics: Theory, Research, and Practice*, 9, 104–126.

WHY WE NEED RIVALS

Forced competition undermining intrinsic motivation: Deci, E. L., Betley, G., Kahle, J., Abrams, L., and Porac, J. (1981). When trying to win: Competition and intrinsic motivation. *Personality and Social Psychology Bulletin*, 7, 79–83.

Triplett, N. (1898). The dynamogenic factors in pacemaking and competition. *American Journal of Psychology*, 9, 507–533. For more on the social, physiological, and genetic underpinnings of competition: Bronson, P., and Merryman, A. (2013). *Top dog: The science of winning and losing*. New York: Twelve.

On the psychology of rivalry: Kilduff, G. J., Elfenbein, H. A., and Staw, B. M. (2010). The psychology of rivalry: A relationally dependent analysis of competition. *Academy of Management Journal*, 53, 943–969. Direct quotes from pp. 943, 945.

On the many links between similarity and attraction: Tidwell, N. D., East-wick, P. W., and Finkel, E. J. (2013). Perceived, not actual, similarity predicts initial attraction in a live romantic context: Evidence from the speed dating paradigm. *Personal Relationships*, *20*, 199–215. Pinel, E. C., and Long, A. E. (2012). When I's meet: Sharing subjective experience with someone from the outgroup. *Personality and Social Psychology Bulletin*, *38*, 296–307. Mackinnon, S. P., Jordan, C. H., and Wilson, A. E. (2011). Birds of a feather sit together: Physical similarity predicts seating choice. *Personality and Social Psychology Bulletin*, *37*, 879–892. Christakis, N. A., and Fowler, J. H. (2014). Friendship and natural selection. *Proceedings of the National Academy of Sciences*. DOI: 10.1073/pnas.1400825111.

Rivalry and running: Kilduff, G. J. (2014). Driven to win: Rivalry, motivation, and performance. *Social Psychological and Personality Science*, *5*, 944–952.

Italian Serie A study: Kilduff, G. J., Galinsky, A. D., Gallo, E., and Reade, J. J. (2012). Whatever it takes: Rivalry and unethical behavior. Paper presented at the 25th Annual International Association of Conflict Management Conference, Spier, South Africa. Premiership testosterone study: Neave, N., and Wolfson, S. (2003). Testosterone, territoriality, and the 'home advantage.' *Physiology and Behavior*, *78*, 269–275.

Dart study: Rees, T., Salvatore, J., Coffee, P., Haslam, S. A., Sargent, A., and Dobson, T. (2013). Reversing downward performance spirals. *Journal of Experimental Social Psychology*, *49*, 400–403.

Israeli auction study: Haran, U., and Ritov, I. (2014). Know who you're up against: Counterpart identifiability enhances competitive behavior. *Journal of Experimental Social Psychology*, *54*, 115–121.

Rivalry, perspective-taking, and unethical behavior. Pierce, J. R., Kilduff, G. J., Galinsky, A. D., and Sivanathan, N. (2013). From glue to gasoline: How competition turns perspective takers unethical. *Psychological Science*, *24*, 1986–1994.

WHY WE WANT GRONK AT OUR BACKYARD BARBECUE—AND WHY HE WANTS TO BE THERE

For a review on the pros and cons of celebrity endorsements: Erdogan, B. Z. (1999). Celebrity endorsement: A literature review. *Journal of Marketing Management*, *15*, 291–314.

BIRGing: Cialdini, R. B., Borden, R. J., Thorne, A., Walker, M. R., Freeman, S., and Sloan, L. R. (1976). Basking in reflected glory: Three (football) field studies. *Journal of Personality and Social Psychology, 34,* 366–375. Direct quote from p. 366.

Beware the social costs of name-dropping: Lebherz, C., Jonas, K., and Tomljenovic, B. (2009). Are we known by the company we keep? Effects of name-dropping on first impressions. *Social Influence, 4,* 62–79.

Celebrity contagion: Newman, G. E., Diesendruck, G., and Bloom, P. (2011). Celebrity contagion and the value of objects: *Journal of Consumer Research, 38,* 215–228.

Penn "Ivy League" study: Rozin, P., Scott, S. E., Zickgraf, H. F., Ahn, F., and Jiang, H. (2014). Asymmetrical social mach bands: Exaggeration of social identities on the more esteemed side of group borders. *Psychological Science.* DOI: 10.1177/0956797614545131.

On the psychology of nostalgia: Sedikides, C., Wildschut, T., Arendt, J., and Routledge, C. (2008). Nostalgia: Past, present, and future. *Current Directions in Psychological Science, 17,* 304–307. Direct quotes from p. 306.

Study of athletes on Twitter: Hambrick, M. E., Simmons, J. M., Greenhalgh, G. P., and Greenwell, T. C. (2010). Understanding professional athletes' use of Twitter: A content analysis of athlete tweets. *International Journal of Sport Communication, 3,* 454–471. Also: Fredrick, C. H. L., Clavio, G., Pedersen, P. M., and Burch, L. M. (2014). Choosing between the one-way or two-way street: An exploration of relationship promotion by professional athletes on Twitter. *Communication and Sport, 2,* 80–99.

On the reciprocity of liking: Montoya, R. M., and Insko, C. A. (2008). Toward a more complete understanding of the reciprocity of liking effect. *European Journal of Social Psychology, 38,* 477–498.

For more on the psychology of interacting with crowds: Sommers, S. (2011). *Situations matter: Understanding how context transforms your world.* New York: Riverhead.

TRIBAL WARFARE: WHY THE AGONY OF THE OTHER TEAM'S DEFEAT FEELS JUST AS GOOD AS THE THRILL OF OUR TEAM'S VICTORY

fMRI study with Yankees and Red Sox fans: Cikara, M., Botvinick, M. M., and Fiske, S. T. (2011). Us versus them: Social identity shapes neural responses to intergroup competition and harm. *Psychological Science, 22*, 306–313. Direct quote from p. 306.

Follow-up study: Cikara, M., and Fiske, S. T. (2012). Stereotypes and schadenfreude: Affective and physiological markers of pleasure at outgroup misfortunes. *Social Psychological and Personality Science, 3*, 63–71. Direct quote from p. 63.

WHY WE ARE ALL COMEBACK KIDS

On response trajectories to potentially traumatic events: Bonanno, G. A. (2004). Loss, trauma and human resilience: Have we underestimated the human capacity to thrive after extremely aversive events? *American Psychologist, 59*, 20–28; Bonanno, G. A., Westphal, M., and Mancini, A. D. (2011). Resilience to loss and potential trauma. *Annual Review of Clinical Psychology, 7*, 511–535; Bonanno, G. A., and Diminich, E. D. (2013). Positive adjustment to adversity: Trajectories of minimal-impact resilience and emergent resilience. *Journal of Child Psychology and Psychiatry: Annual Research Review, 54*, 378–401.

September 11, PTSD, and the oscillation of grief: Bonanno, G. A. (2009). *The other side of sadness: What the new science of bereavement tells us about life after loss.* New York: Basic Books. Direct quotes from p. 62, p. 40.

Affective forecasting: Wilson, T. D., and Gilbert, D. T. (2005). Affective forecasting: Knowing what to want. *Current Directions in Psychological Science, 14*, 131–134. Gilbert, D. T., et al. (1998). Immune neglect: A source of durability bias in affective forecasting. *Journal of Personality and Social Psychology, 75*, 617–638.

On lottery winners: Brickman, P., Coates, D., and Janoff-Bulman, R. (1978). Winners and accident victims: Is happiness relative? *Journal of Personality and Social Psychology, 36*, 917–927. Gardner, J., and Oswald, A. J. (2007). Money and mental wellbeing: A longitudinal study of medium-sized lottery wins. *Journal of Health Economics, 26*, 49–60.

Coping and rape victims: Frazier, P. A., and Burnett, J. W. (1994). Coping strategies among rape victims. *Journal of Counseling and Development, 72*, 633–639.

WHY RUNNING ON A TREADMILL IS LIKE RUNNING A BUSINESS

Michaels, A., and Wertheim, L. J. (2014). *You can't make this up: Miracles, memories, and the perfect marriage of sports and television.* New York: HarperCollins.

South African cycling and finish line study: Swart, J., Lamberts, R. P., Lambert, M. I., Lambert, E. V., Woolrich, R. W., Johnston, S., and Noakes, T. D. (2009). Exercising with reserve: Exercise regulation by perceived exertion in relation to duration of exercise and knowledge of endpoint. *British Journal of Sports Medicine, 43,* 775–781. Direct quote from p. 775.

World-record running paces: Tucker, R., Dugas, J., and Fitzgerald, M. (2011). *Runner's world, the runner's body: How the latest exercise science can help you run stronger, longer, and faster.* Emmaus, PA: Rodale.

South African running and finish line study: Baden, D. A., McLean, T. L., Tucker, R., Noakes, T. D., and Gibson, A. S. (2005). Effect of anticipation during unknown or unexpected exercise duration on rating of perceived exertion, affect, and physiological function. *British Journal of Sports Medicine, 39,* 742–746.

Pink, D. H. (2009). *Drive: The surprising truth about what motivates us.* New York: Riverhead.

On turning big-picture objectives into smaller, attainable goals, and on goals as reference points: Heath, C., Larrick, L., and Wu, G. (1999). Goals as reference points. *Cognitive Psychology, 38,* 79–109. Entrepreneurs and effort study: Uy, M. A., Foo, M., and Ilies, R. (2014). Perceived progress variability and entrepreneurial effort intensity: The moderating role of venture goal commitment. *Journal of Business Venturing.* DOI: 10.1016/j.jbusvent.2014.02.001.

Microloan donation study: Cryder, C. E., Loewenstein, G., and Seltman, H. (2013). Goal gradient in helping behavior. *Journal of Experimental Social Psychology, 49,* 1078–1083.

Rubin, G. (2015). *Better than before: Mastering the habits of our everyday lives.* New York: Crown.

"Goals Gone Wild": Ordóñez, L. D., Schweitzer, M. E., Galinsky, A. D., and Bazerman, M. H. (2009). Goals gone wild: The systematic side effects of overprescribing goal setting. *Academic of Management Perspectives, 23,* 6–16.

Agassi, A. (2009). *Open: An autobiography.* New York: Knopf. Direct quote from p. 7.

WHY THE WORLD CUP DOESN'T LEAD TO WORLD PEACE

Coubertin, P. (1913). *Essais de psychologie sportive*. Lausanne: Payot.

Analysis of World Cup qualifiers and non-qualifiers from 1958 to 2010: Bertoli, A. (June 17, 2014). The World Cup and interstate conflict: Evidence from a natural experiment. Working paper available here: http://www.andrewbertoli.org/papers/ (retrieved October 14, 2014).

Follow-up study looking at teams assigned to the same World Cup Finals group: Bertoli, A. (September 19, 2014). Countries that played each other at the World Cup were surprisingly likely to have military conflicts afterward. Working paper available here: http://www.andrewbertoli.org/papers/ (retrieved October 14, 2014).

On competition, conflict, and identity: Ashmore, R. D., Jussim, L. J., and Wilder, D. (2001). *Social identity, intergroup conflict, and conflict reduction*. Oxford, UK: Oxford University Press.

Orwell, G. (1945). The sporting spirit. *The London Tribune*. Available here: http://www.orwell.ru/library/articles/spirit/english/e_spirit (retrieved April 19, 2015).

Own-nationality bias among soccer referees: Pope, B. R., and Pope, N. G. (2014). Own-nationality bias: Evidence from UEFA Champions League football referees. *Economic Inquiry*, doi:10.1111/ecin.12180.

WHY OUR MORAL COMPASS IS MORE FLEXIBLE THAN AN OLYMPIC GYMNAST

For more on Tajfel's minimal-group paradigm: Tajfel, H., Billig, M. G., Bundy, R. P., and Flament, C. (1971). Social categorization and intergroup behavior. *European Journal of Social Psychology, 1*, 149–178.

Robbers Cave study: Sherif, M., Harvey, O. J., White, B. J., Hood, W. R., and Sherif, C. W. (1954/1961). *Intergroup conflict and cooperation: The Robbers Cave experiment*. Norman, OK: University of Oklahoma Book Exchange. Sherif, M. (1966). *In common predicament*. Boston: Houghton-Mifflin. Quote from p. 58.

Green/red task Northeastern study: Valdesolo, P., and DeSteno, D. (2007). Moral hypocrisy: Social groups and the flexibility of virtue. *Psychological Science, 18*, 689–690. See also: Batson, C. D., Kobrynowicz, D., Dinnerstein, J. J., Kampf, H., and Wilson, A. D. (1997). In a very different voice: Unmasking moral hypocrisy. *Journal of Personality and Social Psychology, 72*, 1335–1348.

Bias blind spot: Pronin, E., Lin, D. Y., and Ross, L. (2002). The bias blind spot: Perceptions of bias in self versus others. *Personality and Social Psychology Bulletin, 28,* 369–391.

Bazerman, M. H., and Tenbrunsel, A. E. (2011). *Blind spots: Why we fail to do what's right and what to do about it.* Princeton, NJ: Princeton University Press. Direct quote from p. 75.

Social categorization and memory bias: Howard, J. W., and Rothbart, M. (1980). Social categorization and memory for in-group and out-group behavior. *Journal of Personality and Social Psychology, 38,* 301–310.

On physicians, conflict of interest, and bias: Dana, J., and Lowenstein, G. (2003). A social science perspective on gifts to physicians from industry. *Journal of the American Medical Association, 290,* 252–255.

Cognitive load study: Valdesolo, P., and DeSteno, D. (2008). The duality of virtue: Deconstructing the moral hypocrite. *Journal of Experimental Social Psychology, 44,* 1334–1338.

On the effects of learning about unconscious bias: Pronin, E., and Kugler, M. B. (2007). Valuing thoughts, ignoring behavior: The introspection illusion as a source of the bias blind spot. *Journal of Experimental Social Psychology, 43,* 565–578.

Hypocrisy and condom promotion: Stone, J., Aronson, E., Crain, A. L., Winslow, M. P., and Fried, C. B. (1994). Inducing hypocrisy as a means of encouraging young adults to use condoms. *Personality and Social Psychology Bulletin, 20,* 116–128.

Hypocrisy and racism reduction: Hing, L. S. S., Li, W., and Zanna, M. P. (2002). Inducing hypocrisy to reduce prejudicial responses among aversive racists. *Journal of Experimental Social Psychology, 38,* 71–78.

WHY UNLOCKING THE MYSTERY OF HUMAN CONSCIOUSNESS IS—LIKE SO MUCH ELSE IN LIFE—ALL ABOUT SPORTS

On diagnosis accuracy and the vegetative state: Schnakers, C. et al. (2009). Diagnostic accuracy of the vegetative and minimally conscious state: Clinical consensus versus standardized neurobehavioral assessment. *BMC Neurology, 9.* doi:10.1186/1471-2377-9-35.

Tennis test: Owen, A. M., et al. (2006). Detecting awareness in the vegetative state. *Science, 313*, 1402. Subsequent research: Chennu, S., et al. (2014). Spectral signatures of reorganized brain networks in disorders of consciousness. *PLoS Computational Biology, 10*. doi: 10.1371/journal.pcbi.1003887.

On current efforts and EEG: Underwood, E. (2014). An easy consciousness test? *Science, 346*, 531–532.

INDEX

ABOUT THE AUTHORS

L. JON WERTHEIM is the executive editor of *Sports Illustrated*. A sports journalist with a passion for psychology and economics, he is the author of such *New York Times* bestsellers as *Scorecasting* (written with Toby Moskowitz) and *You Can't Make This Up* (written with Al Michaels). A huge sports fan, SAM SOMMERS is an experimental psychologist at Tufts University who studies the psychology of everyday life. He is the author of the critically acclaimed book *Situations Matter*.

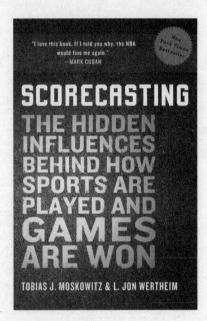